THE INTERNATIONAL CONTAINMENT OF DISPLACED PERSONS

To my parents

The International Containment of Displaced Persons

Humanitarian spaces without exit

CÉCILE DUBERNET

Ashgate

Aldershot • Burlington USA • Singapore • Sydney

Published by
Ashgate Publishing Limited
Gower House
Croft Road
Aldershot
Hampshire GU11 3HR
England

Ashgate Publishing Company
131 Main Street
Burlington, VT 05401-5600 USA

Ashgate website: http://www.ashgate.com

British Library Cataloguing in Publication Data
Dubernet, Cécile
    The international containment of displaced persons :
    humanitarian spaces without exit
    1.United Nations Protection Force 2.Humanitarian
    intervention 3.Refugees - International cooperation
    I.Title
    341.5'84'09049

Library of Congress Control Number: 2001090208

ISBN 0 7546 1772 6

Printed and bound in Great Britain by Antony Rowe Ltd.,
Chippenham, Wiltshire.

Contents

Acknowledgments

As the reader will see, I am indebted to several writers on humanitarian interventions and displaced persons. I wish to thank particularly Gil Loescher, Francis Deng, Roberta Cohen, Michael Barutciski, David Keen and Jon Bennett for their thought provoking analyses. I also want to thank the field workers who took the time to write and process the reports used in the course of this research, as well as John Fawcett and Louis Gentile for answering endless questions.

I further want to thank Eric Herring for his stimulating comments and Frank Hülsemann for his patience and support. My gratitude also goes to Cyril Hershon and to fellow students and friends for their time spent on numerous ill-crafted drafts of this work. Last but not least, I thank Christ who set me free and never despaired of us.

All mistakes remain my entire responsibility.

List of Abbreviations

AFP	Agence France Presse [French News Agency]
BiH	Bosnia i Herzegovina [Bosnia and Herzegovina]
BSA	Bosnian Serb Army
CANBAT	Canadian Battalion
CNN	Cable News Network
DPA	Dayton Peace Agreement
DPKO	Department of Peace Keeping Operations
EC	European Community
ECOMOG	Economic Community of West Africa Monitoring Group
EU	European Union
FAR	Forces Armées Rwandaises [Rwandese Armed Forces]
FIDH	Fédération Internationale des Droits de l'Homme [International Federation for Human Rights]
ICG	International Crisis Group
ICRC	International Committee of the Red Cross
IDPs	Internally Displaced Persons
IFOR	Implementation Force
IOC	Integrated Operation Centre
IOM	International Organisation for Migration
IPTF	International Police Task Force
IRC	International Rescue Committee
JNA	Yugoslav National Army
KLA	Kosovo Liberation Army
MOU	Memorandum of Understanding
MSF	Médecins Sans Frontières [Doctors Without Borders]
NATO	North Atlantic Treaty Organisation
NGO	Non Governmental Organisation
ODA	Overseas Development Administration
ORC	Open Relief Centre
OSCE	Organisation for Security and Cooperation in Europe
RPA	Rwandese Patriotic Army
RPF	Rwanda Patriotic Front
RPG	Refugee Policy Group
SCF	Save the Children Fund
SFOR	Stabilisation Force
SOAS	School of Oriental and African Studies
UNAMIR	United Nations Mission for Rwanda

UNDHA	United Nations Department for Humanitarian Affairs
UNDP	United Nations Development Programme
UNDPI	United Nations Department of Public Information
UNITAF	United Nations International Task Force
UNHCR	United Nations High Commissioner for Refugees
UNOSOM	United Nations Operation for Somalia
UNPAs	United Nations Protected Areas
UNPROFOR	United Nations Protection Force
UNREO	United Nations Rwanda Emergency Office
UNSC	United Nations Security Council
UNSG	United Nations Secretary-General
USCR	United States Committee for Refugees
USAID	United States Agency for International Development
WFP	World Food Programme

Introduction: Presence *does not* Equal Protection

> UN soldiers had special night vision equipment allowing them to spot escapees as soon as they began their dash from the perimeter and when this happened, an armored personnel carrier would hunt the escapees, shining a spotlight on them to ease the chase. The problem was that Serb snipers opened fire as soon as someone was caught in the spotlight.[1]

The above quotation illustrates the situation faced by Sarajevans trying to escape their besieged town in the winter of 1992-1993. That UNPROFOR, the United Nations Protection Force, failed to protect Bosnian civilians is known. That they occasionally transformed themselves into the watchdogs of the assailants begs questions regarding the nature of the UN mission, especially with regards to civilians seeking to flee the conflict. At the end of the 1990s, the issue remains topical. In 1998, the Yugoslav province of Kosovo imploded. Serb security forces stepped up their attacks on the Kosovo Albanian population in late February 1998. By June, the assaults had turned into a fully fledged war against civilians witnessed by an international community very reluctant to interfere.[2] Despite a cease-fire agreed to in October of the same year, Serb police forces and the army responded to the provocation of the Kosovo Liberation Army, the KLA, in disproportionate ways, slaughtering civilians in villages.[3] Observers from the Organisation for the Security and Cooperation in Europe - the so-called "OSCE verifiers" - dispatched to Kosovo to monitor the cease-fire, stood by powerless. Verifiers were well named. Like UNPROFOR six years before, they were deployed to observe, negotiate and ring the alarm bell, but not directly to protect civilians. International presence was also intended to encourage scores of displaced persons to return to their burnt-down farms. Until March 1999, that is one year into the conflict, the Bosnian war seemed to repeat itself. As in Bosnia, but also northern Iraq or Rwanda, the assumption underlying the deployment of lightly armed troops in Kosovo in 1998 had remained that presence equals protection: in other words, that Western governments react with might and anger to barbaric acts that come to their attention. Therefore assailants restrain themselves in front of observers. Nevertheless, time and time again, widely broadcast

1

deliberate violence against civilians brought about little more than rhetoric. Numerous aid workers found themselves powerless and frustrated. Many lives were ruined before any substantial military protection of civilians was attempted. What *was* attempted is still a matter of controversy. Key questions regarding the 1990s' interventions into complex emergencies, including early responses to the crises in Kosovo and in East Timor remain open. Why did the international community stand by forced migration and ethnic cleasing for so long? Why does it still ignore the devastation and suffering of displaced persons in Congo? What does it try to achieve during humanitarian operations?

This work examines four important post Cold-War interventions launched on behalf of people on the move: international action in Iraq, Bosnia, Somalia and Rwanda. Because these crises accompanied the emergence of the concept of Internally Displaced Persons (henceforth IDPs) in international relations, they have shaped current understandings of forced displacement issues, such as ethnic cleansing, need and humanitarian action. As reforms of humanitarian action are underway at the time of writing, it is essential to grasp what international actors sought to achieve with regard to IDPs, and what they achieved in fact.

Looking at attitudes towards IDPs, this research concluded that UN-backed interventions regarding displaced civilians were primarily about deterring, sometimes preventing them from escaping places of conflict. Protection in this context became a device by which international protagonists sought to contain people on the move within the confines of their collapsed states. As a result, levels of safety effectively granted by the international community depended less on the vulnerability of populations than on Western fears of mass border crossings. These findings help one to grasp why the international community not only participated in the "incarceration of the victims"[4] as illustrated above in Sarajevo, but also why it stood by watching massacres in Srebrenica, Kibeho or Recak in Kosovo. To sum up, this book suggests an alternative understanding of the nature of international protection. As far as IDPs were concerned, protection was a means to an end, a tool of containment policies. It is the author's hope that more research expands the use and highlights the limits of this concept. This work may also contribute to a long overdue reflection on both recent experiences and current reforms of international action towards displaced persons. Indeed, it is time to clarify what has been hidden by the myth that international presence enhanced civilian protection.

Notes

1   Maass, Peter, *Love Thy Neighbour, A Story of War* (London: Papermac, 1996), 170.

2   See *Bosnia Report, Special Issue with Kosova Supplement*, New Series No. 3, March-May 1998, The Bosnian Institute, 5-16.

3   "L'Europe face à la barbarie," *Le Monde*, 19 January 1999, 1-3.

4   Chimni, B., "The Incarceration of Victims: Deconstructing Safety Zones," in Al-Nauimi, Najeeb and Meese, Richard, eds., *International Legal Issues Arising under the United Nation Decade of International Law, Proceedings of the Qatar International Law Conference' 94* (The Hague: Martinus Nijhoff Publishers, 1995), 823-854.

1 Internal Displacement: an International Problem

In 1998, for the first time, the international community published a world count of internally displaced persons.[1] This recording effort, now prolonged into the maintenance of a database accessible on the World Wide Web,[2] reflects the growing awareness that these uprooted people represent a problem for international politics. Internal displacement issues emerged at the end of the Cold War, as decision-makers' attention turned to state collapse and internal strife. During the early 1990s, new approaches designed to deal with mass displacement were developed and experimented with. Practices such as "in-country protection" or "early repatriation" were part of a fresh emphasis on humanitarian intervention, itself inscribed into a discourse on the new world order. However, renewed humanitarianism also paralleled Western governments' hardening positions vis-à-vis asylum seekers. The international refugee system had been overloaded since the early eighties and industrial states took various opportunities, ranging from the collapse of the Soviet Union to the European construction, to reshape and restrict refugees' access to asylum. Hence both the desire to save populations in danger and the urge to preempt refugee flow were the potential driving forces behind the involvement with people on the move that took place since 1990 in Iraq, Former Yugoslavia, Central Asia and Africa.

The essence of this book is to identify the nature of the interplay between the protection and containment objectives that underlay the early 1990s international policies concerning IDPs. It is widely held that this involvement was propelled by worldwide compassion for the victims of the conflicts. Strategic interests, although acknowledged by most observers as important, are considered an added cause for intervention and their impact on policy remains little explored. Indeed the protection granted to people on the move is assumed to be an end in itself underpinned by a mix of factors, humanitarian and strategic, the exact weight of which is still debated. In contrast, the hypothesis considered by the author is the following: "The protection granted to IDPs is an instrument of containment policies." This assertion is tested through studies of the construction and implementation of measures taken by the international community for people on the move within northern Iraq, Bosnia and Rwanda. Findings are further gauged against the fate of Somali IDPs.

Because internal displacement became the object of coordinated international policies only recently, many concepts are still in the making. Therefore, before presenting the case studies, it is essential to clarify the perspectives and research methods used. In particular, it is necessary to justify the emphasis placed on the containment/protection interplay in IDP policies. There are three simple reasons for this: because it is not being done, because it can be done, and because it should be done. Three reasons, therefore three chapter sections: first, a review of the literature will show that, although research on IDPs expanded dramatically in the course of the 1990s, this issue, the containment/protection interplay, is not adequately explored. Second, an exposition of the research methodology will clarify the conditions under which policies concerning IDPs can be identified and assessed. Third, the chapter's conclusion argues that a clear understanding of the objectives underpinning policies regarding IDPs not only deepens academic knowledge but also provides a stepping stone to engage in sensible policy reforms. Jon Bennett, the first director of the Global IDP Survey, made it clear: "We cannot develop good policy without good theory and these are turbulent times for both."[3]

IDP: an Emergent yet Little-Known Label

IDPs are usually understood to be "those forced to leave their home who, because they remain within the borders of their own country, are not officially recognised as refugees."[4]   In 1992, they were granted a "working definition" by the UN which prevailed throughout the 1990s. They were to be persons

> who have been forced to flee their homes suddenly or unexpectedly in large numbers, as a result of armed conflict, internal strife, systematic violations of human rights or natural or man-made disasters, and who are within the territory of their country.[5]

Six years of experience led the UN General Assembly to amend the above definition and this change will be discussed in the last chapter of this book. For the purposes of this research, the author shall also consider some people who have been refugees only briefly, have returned to their native land but remain unable, or unwilling, to go home. For although these persons have crossed a border twice, and thus can be labelled "returnees," their fate differs little from that of their compatriots who did not cross the frontier in the first place. Besides, in crisis context, border control is often an illusion. Even when local officials know exactly where a border stands, they rarely know how many times it was crossed. Further justifications of this choice will be found later in this chapter. At this stage, it is sufficient to note that the concept of IDP moved from being an unknown abbreviation in the early 1990s to being the object of conferences, books and heated debates.[6] In other words, the literature produced in the 1990s reflected the emergence of displaced persons as a concern in international politics.

Because IDP literature emerged alongside humanitarian crises, many concepts were forged in response to field experiences. In turns, these understandings shaped policy-making throughout the decade, and still do. Hence, reviewing such literature is essential to grasp current debates regarding internal displacement. The review proceeds in three steps. First, the academic backgrounds informing studies on IDPs are depicted. Their diversity suggests a variety of purposes underlying research on displaced persons. Second, the work of three authors who attempt to cross bridges between these fields of studies is evaluated. On the one hand, the value of their contributions is highlighted. On the other hand, their lack of focus on IDP policies and some implications of it are illustrated. Finally, the recent surge of literature specialised on IDPs is assessed. Its wealth of detail is emphasised. However, the fact that the issue of containment is not adequately assessed is also laid on. A closing paragraph outlines the potential insights that an in-depth study of the containment/protection interplay for IDPs may add to current understandings of humanitarian action. The aims of this book in this respect are also defined.

A Term Arising at the Junction of Various Research Areas

Studies on IDPs in international politics originate from a variety of perspectives, namely development, migration, refugee, humanitarian and security studies. Furthermore, they emerged in the context of particular topical debates. For example, IDPs have become central to the debate on the refugee condition. In the course of the 1990s, the United Nations High Commissioner for Refugees - UNHCR - included statistics on internal displacement alongside its data on refugees. Like the United States Committee for Refugees - USCR - and the International Committee for the Red Cross - ICRC - the UNHCR insisted that both issues could not be solved separately.[7] In the same vein, current work on early warning

7

systems seeks to identify the factors at the root of forced displacement and to create models that help anticipate such movements. Debates on "regional security," "weak or failed states," "ethnic wars" and "societal security" have much to do with forced migration issues. Besides, many recent UN peace-keeping and peace-enforcement operations were set up partly to address forced migration issues. As a result, there are numerous researchers who refer to IDPs in the study of international politics. For instance, while analysing Operation Provide Comfort, Howard Adelman discussed the situation of Kurdish displaced persons in northern Iraq.[8] Likewise, Andrew Shacknove, Michael Barutciski and Bill Frelick emphasised how European governments' perceptions of IDPs grounded the evolution of asylum practices in the 1990s. They also assessed some implications of refugee policy changes for displaced persons.[9]

A simplified picture of the state of the literature on IDPs in international politics is summarised in Figure 1.1: several fields of study provide a background from which IDPs' issues are addressed within the context of debates on asylum seeking, intervention etc. It is noteworthy that debates related to IDPs are found on the lines of intersection between research areas.

Figure 1.1: Internal displacement related debates

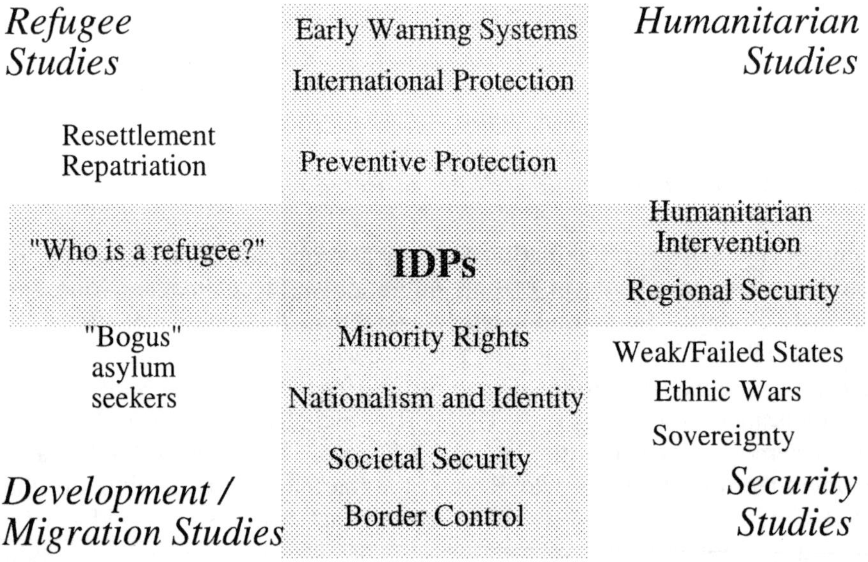

*Refugee
Studies*

Early Warning Systems

International Protection

*Humanitarian
Studies*

Resettlement
Repatriation

Preventive Protection

"Who is a refugee?"

IDPs

Humanitarian
Intervention

Regional Security

"Bogus"
asylum
seekers

Minority Rights

Weak/Failed States

Nationalism and Identity

Ethnic Wars

Sovereignty

Societal Security

*Development /
Migration Studies*

Border Control

*Security
Studies*

This section reviews studies that provide an analytical understanding of some of the issues found at the interfaces between research areas. Among the plethora of writers who now include work on IDP policies in their research, the work of Gil Loescher will be first discussed, partly because he is an inescapable figure in the field of forced migrations and international politics, partly because his work contains several problems often found in literature on IDPs. Barry Posen is considered because he offered one of the first critical and structured evaluation of military responses to refugee outflow. As for Michael Barutciski, he examined in great depth the implications of containment policies in Bosnia and, as such, is the closest to this project.

Gil Loescher pioneered research on the international security dimensions of refugee problems. In studies of American and European refugee policies published in the eighties, he highlighted the strategic objectives underpinning the range of welcoming treatment experienced by asylum seekers who reached the shores of industrial countries.[10] His interest in refugee crises impact on world politics surfaced also in the publication of *Refugees and International Relations*, a co-edited manual reviewing the issues common to both research areas.[11] From the early 1990s onwards, Loescher consistently argued for responses to forced migrations going "beyond charity."[12] In 1996, he wrote with Alan Dowty, a specialist in migration, a paper entitled "Refugee Flows (sic) as Grounds for International Action" in which the two authors argued that mass refugee movements justify a collective or unilateral intervention against the state responsible for or unable to stop the exodus.[13] In this article, the writers also re-assessed some Cold War humanitarian interventions in the light of the refugee movements at stake.[14]

The first piquant aspect of the work of Loescher is the evolution of his research focus. From classical approaches of refugee policies, he went on to highlight international security issues at stake and is now working on defining the conditions under which military intervention to forestall refugee flow is justifiable. Referring back to figure 1.1, Loescher wrote from three perspectives out of four, the refugee, security and humanitarian standpoints. Second, Loescher persistently drew attention to internal displacement. In the early 1990s, he advocated the creation of a "comprehensive strategy" to deal with refugee influxes including the creation of an independent UN monitoring body in charge of the early warning of potential exoduses. According to him, such an institution would require the development of a capacity to intervene in internal conflicts.[15] He also described Operation Provide Comfort as a turning point in international politics given that the United Nation Security Council resolution 688 was especially conceived "to protect internally displaced Iraqi citizens."[16] His work pointed out that forced displacement starts at home, that IDPs' problems are the terrain on which refugee crises develop: hence that understanding internal displacement is instrumental to explaining and anticipating refugee disasters. This insight opened up research perspectives that Loescher and Dowty expanded upon. They highlighted the possibility of re-assessing past humanitarian interventions, even wars, from a strategic standpoint going beyond Cold War power politics. To sum up, Loescher provided mental stepping stones in two ways. First, he linked various fields of studies related to IDPs and second, he insisted that any international refugee policy should address all forms of forced migration. Ironically, these two insights are also the very limits of Loescher's work with regard to IDPs.

Whereas Loescher worked on many topics associated with internal displacement, he did not specifically investigate the policies designed for people on the move. He defined the ways in which refugee flow disturbed international security, studied the processes by which crises were resolved, but consistently abstained from any comment on the construction or implementation of the measures that affected displaced persons. For instance, Loescher and Dowty's evaluation of the three Cold War interventions in Bangladesh (1971), Cambodia (1978) and Uganda (1979) is limited to recording the toppling of targeted regimes and the return home of refugee communities. What happened to the people on the move in the country, either trying to escape or returning, remains unstated. Although the interventions are assessed in terms of international and customary law,[17] there is no discussion or analysis of the precise measures taken to reverse population movements. To be fair to both authors, the reason why they did not focus on them is simply that IDP policies in themselves were not their object. They wanted to clarify the conditions under which international action against a refugee producer state are justifiable rather than study policies on behalf of the uprooted.

Ignoring internal displacement issues in one article is not a problem. However, it becomes one when the omission is systematic in the field. Here, Loescher and Dowty's article illustrates a flaw of the literature as a whole. Because the issue emerged at the crossroads of several fields of study, and in the context of very topical issues such as debates on refugeehood and on the impact of the media, policies towards IDPs were not an object of research *per se* until recently. Academics, including those working on internal displacement and international relations, were more concerned with humanitarian intervention, regional security or the prevention of refugee disasters, than with IDPs. Consequently, action on behalf of displaced persons was not fully assessed. Nevertheless, partial evaluations of decisions regarding IDPs substantiated debates on related topical issues such as aid, intervention, or asylum seeking. In other words, depending on their background and purposes, authors saw in IDPs the "potential refugees,"[18] the "threat to security and stability,"[19] alternatively "the abused," "the vulnerable."[20] IDPs however can be all of the above. Focusing on one feature only may seriously hinder policy-making analysis. For example, neither policy-makers nor observers understood the complexities of repatriating Iraqi Kurds in northern Iraq in May and June 1991. Both failed to consider the fact that most Kurdish refugees were displaced persons even before their rebellion against the regime of Saddam Hussein in 1991 and their subsequent flight before the Republican Guard repression. As a result, the emphasis on returning home, the motto of policy-makers, was reproduced in the main studies of the intervention.[21] This failed to take into account that "home" for most displaced persons were not the towns to which they were to be sent back, but their burnt-down villages, lost in the mountains, from which they had been chased since 1987. The "Memorandum of Understanding", henceforth MOU, signed between the UN and Iraq states that "The measures to be taken for the benefit of the displaced persons should be based primarily on their personal safety and the provision of humanitarian assistance and relief for their return and the normalization of their lives in their *places of origin.*"[22] But it does not specify what the latter are. UNHCR did not question the concept of "home" either.[23] Whereas it was widely acknowledged that the forced migration of displaced persons was the cause for intervention, strategic analysis of policies towards IDPs stopped at the end of Provide Comfort in July 1991. As a result, summer displacements were largely ignored by regional security and refugees experts. Instead, they were dealt with by area specialists. To date, there is no comprehensive study of international policies towards displaced persons in northern Iraq but many incomplete, truncated analyses written to substantiate debates over related issues.

The above example also illustrates a second problem in Loescher's work regarding people on the move. Whereas it is crucial to highlight the links between refugees and IDPs, it is a mistake to equate both policies systematically. International action towards displaced persons is not necessarily the same as that for refugees. Measures taken may differ, the policy may not coincide in time. In addition, the resolution of a refugee crisis can mean an increase in IDPs. The return of most Kurdish refugees to northern Iraq dramatically increased internal displacements problems. Mass repatriation also yielded substantial repercussions in Rwanda in 1994 and 1996 and in Bosnia since the signature of the Dayton Peace agreements. This explains why, following the position of the International Organisation for Migration, the IOM, this study includes some returnee populations who remained displaced within their country of origin.[24] Assuming that refugee and IDPs crises always occur simultaneously is a mistake. Presuming that international policies exist only for IDPs as "potential refugees" makes sense but remains an assumption. The author has found, so far, no comprehensive and compelling study of *when* IDPs are cared for by the international community. The above examples suggest that distinguishing IDPs from refugees is a worthwhile endeavour, an issue which shall be further discussed in the methodology section.

Indeed, although ground-breaking, Loescher's work is not focused on IDPs and often assumes displaced persons to be a dependent entity, whose problems are raised and dealt with alongside refugee crises. This epitomises the majority of the work on IDPs. Two reasons explain this absence of focus. As already mentioned, writers are not interested in IDPs as such. Their research focuses on refugee policies or humanitarian intervention; thus displaced persons themselves are of secondary importance to them. This is compounded by the fact that policies for the uprooted are a new subject matter in international politics. As a result, researchers rely heavily on the material provided by international organisations who, themselves, emphasise the features of displacement best suited to their work.

Let us now turn to an article by Barry Posen,[25] a specialist in security studies. In contrast to Loescher, Posen *did* focus on the analysis of policies that affected the uprooted. After identifying five causes of refugee flow, he discussed the advantages and limits of the military options available to the international community. The alternatives highlighted were strategic bombing, the creation of a large "safe zone" where life could carry on, and the establishment of "safe havens", i.e. small places of refuge, enforced truce or an offensive war. The originality of Posen's argument lies in the application of the strategic deterrence/compellence model of analysis to evaluate the efficiency (outcomes versus costs) of the options and determine the conditions under which they can be used. He distinguished three types of protagonists, the "assailants," the "threatened populations" and the "rescuers," and argued that "in general, rescuers will find

12

themselves practising coercive diplomacy, that is compellence."[26] His conclusion is a warning against the belief that the use of military resources for humanitarian purposes would fall short of war. In essence, "what good hearted people are proposing is war."[27]

Posen's analysis is enlightening, first because it is an effort to compare policy options, whereas other studies in the same field tend to focus on, say, "the construction of safe areas." This is why focus is placed on Posen rather than on Tiso, Chimni, Landgren or Frelick who have produced excellent criticisms of safe haven policies. By systematically matching and discussing military moves and situations, Posen acknowledged the fact that options were chosen depending on contexts and alternatives. Furthermore, he proposed a dissuasion/coercion grid of analysis which clarified field experiences. His suggestion that policy makers wrongly saw military humanitarian action as "deterrence" shed light on some of the decision-making processes, for instance in Somalia.[28] Besides, his adaptation of Schelling's strategic model to the study of humanitarian wars allowed him to combine issues of logistics, capacities and practical circumstances with the problems of motivations and interests. In short, Posen offered a theoretical account of why operations in Bosnia or Somalia went wrong. Finally, he did not shy away from dilemmas, but instead spent a whole section of the paper highlighting the limits of each "remedy." As a whole this represents a genuine attempt at modelling recent humanitarian interventions.

However, Posen's insights into policies for the uprooted remain limited on two counts. First, he ignored mechanisms of co-operation that humanitarian, refugee and military agencies tried to set up after "Operation Provide Comfort." Today's responses to complex emergencies are a mixture of humanitarian activities, such as the provision of food and basic necessities, diplomatic measures like conflict management, negotiations, mediation, and, often as a last resort, military measures as outlined by Posen. In addition, positions with regard to border control, migration and refugees are to be taken into consideration. Although Posen must have been aware of these interactions, he chose to set apart militarised options and focus on them only. As a result his categories are neat but unrepresentative of much field experience. For instance, "safe areas" are procedures of humanitarian law that can be non-militarised. The ICRC tried to implement them during various conflicts in parallel to military actions led by other institutions.[29] Besides, relationships between humanitarian agencies and the military, increasingly in charge of the protection of humanitarian aid, can be ridden with conflicts that affect the work of both. Assessing solely militarised operations can lead to inconclusive judgements. On the one hand Posen declared the safe area policy in Bosnia to be a semi-success given that four out of six survived despite under-staffing by blue helmets. One the other hand, he mitigated his appraisal by mentioning the low level of safety and the deprivations that people, trapped in safe areas, endured during years of war.[30] Furthermore, in the theory section of his paper, Posen acknowledged the importance of logistical issues and that of the provision of ground troops by locals. However, he hardly considered aid workers' dilemmas in Bosnia. Likewise, in his assessment, he omitted to mention the role of the Bosnian army in defending places such as Tuzla or Bihac. Consequently, although Posen's model is interesting, his evaluation of one precise case, the Bosnian safe areas, turns out to be incomplete. To measure the success of the Bosnian safe areas, one cannot rely on evaluating military action only but should discuss the mechanisms of co-operation with humanitarian agencies and locals. After all, the original mandate of UNPROFOR was to support the UNHCR.

Second, the evaluation of international action in response to refugee crises also requires a serious assessment of the aims of policy-makers. For Posen however, "the most important question about any humanitarian intervention is whether it is fundamentally an act of deterrence or compellence."[31] Although the "deterrence/compellence" dichotomy does enlighten some aspects of the policy, it hardly clarifies in itself the objectives of decision makers. Hence it does not help evaluation. Posen, in fact, took for granted the aim of policy makers. When warning against taking military action lightly, he wrote:

> The complexity of the problem resists broad conclusions but most plausible remedies are serious military operations that require substantial, diverse capabilities. If "rescuers" cannot in fact, muster such capabilities and the will to use them, it is improbable that scattered air attacks and diffuse threats will convince the assailant -the party whose actions precipitated the refugee flight - to cease its depredations.[32]

Beneath this statement lies the assumption that stopping human rights abuses was the intermediate aim of policy makers. For Posen, interventions were mainly about protecting people so as to forestall their exodus, either by creating protected zones or by pressuring abusive powers into stopping persecutions.[33] Here, he reproduced a conventional justification of international humanitarian interventions without questioning

14

it. Posen did not allow for complex motives. He gave no space to media-led actions. Neither does he contemplate the possibility that intervention was a direct way of containing people within the confines of troubled states. As a result, he sometimes provided inaccurate depictions of humanitarian action. Consider this statement:

> Turkey had made it clear that it was unwilling to take Kurds in, but at the same time it did not want the ill-will of the United States and its European NATO allies, which it would have earned if it allowed the Kurds to die on the border in full view of television cameras.[34]

In fact, Turkey did leave some Kurds to die on the border in full view of CNN. The Turkish government simultaneously attempted to contain and, to some extent, protect displaced persons. The complexities of such an ambiguous position were not grasped by Posen. In the same vein, his analysis sometimes fell short of explaining some of the problems he himself recorded. For instance, he pointed out the danger that safe areas turn into dangerous jails.[35] However, he provided neither explanation nor even a specific illustration of such a claim although the reference to "ethnic cleansing" suggests that he was thinking of Bosnia. There are two reasons why Posen does not convincingly explain this statement. To the author's knowledge, there is no comprehensive study of the extent to which safe areas in Bosnia were turned into "prisons" for their residents. Second, Posen failed to clarify the objectives underlying action in Bosnia and the interplay between them. He struggled with this underlying problem of purpose throughout the essay. Occasionally, he touched on the issue. When discussing safe areas, he did mention two potential aims. "The purpose may be brutally pragmatic as forestalling a wholesale departure ... or the purpose may be to help the refugees stay close to their original homes." However, a few lines later, Posen referred to the impossibility in some conditions of using "air power to protect the victims"[36] thus assuming one aim rather than another. In effect, it is very difficult to assess international policies sensibly without a clear grasp of their objectives and of the articulations between them. Posen himself confirms this difficulty when writing "it seems unlikely that defended safe havens would work (although under some circumstances, *depending on the motives of the actors*, negotiated safe havens ... are a possibility)."[37]

Clearly, Posen is entitled not to write an essay on international actors' motivations to intervene in internal conflicts. However, he worked on unclear assumptions. He did not explain his acceptance of international organisations' justifications for action. Neither did he acknowledge his position, i.e. "international protection is developed to preempt refugee disasters," as a working assumption. His analysis displayed an experience of theoretical strategic models and proposed an interesting grasp of the essential issues surrounding the use of the military. Nevertheless, the study remained limited because the purposes for action were not qualitatively explored,[38] and because the issue of co-operation was ignored. Somehow, Posen seemed reluctant to go beyond his model and really grasp the mechanisms rooted in the events. Although he showed interest in policy analysis and therefore was more eager than Loescher in working out what happened, it was discussing military strategies that mattered to him. Once more, although policies for IDPs were part of the analysis, they were not its focal point.

In a fascinating study of international refugee policy in Bosnia, Michael Barutciski discussed the implications of containment approaches. The essence of his argument is the following: "Recent preoccupation with in-country protection is intended to reinforce state policies that deny entry to asylum seekers ... the office of UNHCR is assigned these interventionist activities in order to indirectly subvert its original palliative role."[39]

Barutciski started with highlighting that in-country protection was a convenient concept for affluent states reluctant to accept refugees. He then dismantled the concept of "preventive protection" promoted by the UNHCR and its financial backers in Bosnia and showed how it led to limited admissions, denial of access and reduced protection for asylum seekers.[40] Lastly, he turned his attention to UNHCR programmes and pictured safe areas for war victims as "consolation," the foundations of which were to be found, at least partially, in containment approaches.[41] In particular, UNHCR, despite being ill-equipped to act amidst conflict, encouraged people to stay in Bosnia.[42] Hence the ambiguities of the concept of "right to remain." Barutciski argued that, because internal protection was rooted in containment policies, it became a process applied selectively which progressively undermined the credibility of UNHCR. The article concluded with a critical assessment of new modes of interventionism which Barutciski found lacking in vision and responsibility.

This short summary cannot do justice to the sophistication and depth of the article. Discussions concerning the right - or as he called it - the "duty to remain" are especially worth reading. Insights into the politics of safe areas are also remarkable as the author made clear that they were both about containment and protection.[43] However, he did not try and articulate the interplay between protection and containment further. In fact, as both his introduction and conclusion made clear, Barutciski's ultimate concern was the evolution of international refugee law. Thus, although he devoted a substantial part of his paper to assessing in-country protection, understanding policies for IDPs was not an object *per se* but was instrumental in his analysis of the evolution of asylum practices. Barutciski did not systematically study practices for displaced persons and, as a result, its conclusions may not necessarily apply to them. For instance, the paper ends with the claim that internal assistance was a cover-up for sinister asylum denial practices: "The grim truth is that these concepts [preventive protection, the right to remain] simply provided cover for more insidious development in immigration control."[44] The idea of cover-up upholds mainstream thinking regarding the impact of the media on international protection for war victims. Barutciski himself made the point that war victims in general, and displaced persons in particular, only receive substantial protection when their plight is "visible," that is, when they take centre stage on TV screens. Still, in essence, the above claim contradicts his own argument. For it dissociates protection from containment aims. In fact, relationships between containment, protection and the role of the media are simply not explored. In particular, it is never clear from the study itself whether assistance in Bosnia was a tool to promote containment or a simple indifference cover-up exercise. While this book builds, to a great extent, on the insights gathered by Barutciski, it seeks to explore further the containment/protection interface for the uprooted. Besides, it focuses on IDPs rather than on refugee law. It also extends the research to a set of cases. But before exposing the methodology, this literature review will close with comments on the recent surge of literature on displaced persons.

Recent Policy Surveys: Pictures over Analysis

Whereas Loescher, Posen and even Barutciski worked on IDP policies in order better to grasp changes in refugee law or military ventures, IDPs recently acquired a status of their own in the context of humanitarian studies. In addition to the global IDP Survey, two studies, *Masses in Flight* and *The Forsaken People*, were published in 1998 and represent a far-reaching effort to shed light on internal displacement.[45] *The Forsaken People* is an edited volume collecting country studies in which field experts mixed analysis and recommendations. However, as a book, *The Forsaken People* offers no comparison across the ten case studies. Thus the reader is left to put into analytical perspectives the wealth of material and knowledge gathered in 500 pages by specialists. This, however, is the way the book was intended to be, given that its companion volume, *Masses in Flight*, is a thematic analysis of forced migration. Its authors, Cohen and Deng, set out to describe systematically the state of international affairs regarding IDPs. Being particularly concerned with legal and institutional responses to crises of forced migration, they provided a detailed account of the legal framework and problems faced by various institutions struggling with the issue. Besides, given their interest in policy making - Francis Deng being the UN High representative for IDPs - the authors ended the book with a set of strategies and recommendations. A number of fascinating problems are raised, such as the links between sovereignty and responsibility or the unintended consequences of humanitarian action. Not only did Cohen and Deng focus on the topic of policies for IDPs but they also displayed the complexity of trying to grasp a subject matter in rapid evolution.

The authors however did not discuss the interplay between the desire to protect and that to contain as motors for action. Nor did they assess the potential impact of the latter on humanitarian practices. In their initial review, they asked "Why do IDPs not become refugees?" In response, they pointed out that the absence of an alternative, in other words, closed borders policies, had an impact on the growth of IDP numbers in relation to that of refugees, as well as on policies towards both groups.[46] A similar statement can be found in UN official documents regarding IDPs also drafted by Francis Deng.[47] Such a claim however, remains stated rather than discussed. Furthermore the latent impact of containment policies remains unexplored. By neither justifying nor examining the potential implications of the mixed aims of intervention, Cohen and Deng remain within conventional literature assumptions. Closed border policies are presented as an additional factor for intervention, the impact of which is assumed to be limited to the early stages of action. Beneath the absence of focus on the potential impact of containment objectives lies the assumption that once the humanitarian machine was launched, it had its own logic. Somehow, initial aims no longer mattered. In short, Cohen and Deng ignored questions such as "are protection and containment two independent factors for action?" Or indeed, if containment is a cause for action, "what are its implications on humanitarian practices?" The absence of clarity regarding the objectives of international engagement concerning IDPs and their potential impact leads to vagueness in the evaluation of policies, a problem reminiscent of Posen. For instance, the authors recorded the abuse and limits of the notion of safe areas. However they also wrote:

The fact that the safe areas in Bosnia, Rwanda and Iraq have failed to provide full protection for internally displaced and other populations should not occasion the rejection of safe areas as a protection strategy but rather its refinement.[48]

From this follows a set of conditions which, to be fair, includes the idea that UNHCR should denounce the procedure should it see in it a pretext to deny asylum.[49] While all energies are focused on working out the right processes for the right circumstances, little attention is devoted to purposes, to "why?" or "for what?" questions. Somehow it is assumed that the protection of persons was the ultimate aim of safe areas policies. Consequently, despite a wealth of details difficult to match, the strategies and recommendations that end the book build less on the tremendous insights found in some of the case studies than on mainstream humanitarian wisdom. In other words, the dominant assumptions remain that aid workers' dilemmas were created by the new features of civil conflicts - collapsed states and populations as targets - and by the absence of Western political will. This leaves space for comparative studies questioning the purposes and nature of international action for displaced persons.

By contrast, Jon Bennett, himself a practitioner, did challenge mainstream views on policies for the uprooted. His short articles contain some of the most radical insights into the issue of containment, sovereignty and intervention regarding IDPs.[50] He stated for instance: "Intervention is disengagement, for it is associated with containment which support populations in war zones, discourages refugee flows and internalises causes and consequences."[51] Further, he also claimed that the concept of IDP strengthens sovereignty by vindicating government responsibility towards its own citizens.[52] He also briefly highlighted some implications of novel approaches affecting the uprooted. For him, "Within an arena of unresolved conflict, attention is drawn not to inequality *per se*, but to a study of human development concerned instead with how people can be helped to cope with inequality."[53] Beneath Bennett's short texts, one can feel not only a tremendous experience but also the ability to look at IDPs issues with critical distance. However, he still did not expand on how and why intervention and containment were - and still are - about disengagement. There is no doubt that Bennett has much more to say. Somehow the papers referred to are too short, too dense for him to lay down all examples and experiences that led to his fairly radical positions.

The essence of this book is to investigate the premises that underpin his claims.

In summary, literature on IDPs in world politics emerged at the conjunction of various fields of studies. Still, whereas IDPs issues were part of many debates, they were the focal point of none. Most writers researched some aspects of the construction or implementation of policies concerning displaced persons in order to discuss humanitarian intervention, failed states, refugee crises or other topical issues. Loescher, Posen and even Barutciski provide examples of this. The three authors asked fascinating questions related to IDPs, but ultimately, were interested in other matters. By contrast, recent work that is well focused on IDPs consists mainly in gathering field reports into case studies which, although fascinating, provide little analytical and comparative grasp of the policies. Overall, we face a field of study in construction where numerous grass root insights have not yet been matched up, where abundant theoretical assumptions still need to be questioned. In this context, each new study, while missing some perspectives, may bring forth unusual vantage points.

This book seeks primarily to place the focus on understanding policies designed for IDPs *per se*. Hence already existing literature is drawn upon and is substantiated with the author's own research. Clearly one cannot address all issues at stake. Two complementary axes of research are needed to improve understanding of policies regarding IDPs. The first path is to focus on *when* international policies towards these uprooted populations occur through an extensive study of all international action and non-action in response to internal forced migration. This would be a comprehensive exploration of the relations between IDPs and refugees. This work will focus on the second option, which is to work on the mechanisms at work in IDP policies, when they occur. The author wants to probe the main assumption underlying the work of Barutciski and Posen: international policies towards IDPs aim to protect people *in order to* forestall their exodus.[54] Besides, exploring the interplay between protection and containment may help to check out Bennett's intriguing claims. Added to a comprehensive study on intervention and non-intervention on behalf of IDPs, it would further explain the extent to which they matter in world politics. Two questions remain to be answered though. First, "is such a project feasible?" and second, "how useful, how right is it to distinguish IDPs from other war victims?" The ensuing discussion of concepts and methodology tackles the first question and the chapter's conclusion the second.

Questioning Policy towards IDPs

This book seeks to clarify what the international community was trying to achieve with regard to IDPs in the early 1990s. The following paragraphs detail the approach used in a series of discussions of the concepts, the hypothesis, the choice of case studies and of testing procedures.

Neither Refugee Work nor Mere Humanitarianism

IDPs represent only a subset of the civilians on behalf of whom the international community becomes active during humanitarian operations. Other categories of recipients are "refugees" and "war victims," for instance the inhabitants of besieged cities. As Western engagement unfolded in the 1990s, few measures were specifically targeted at IDPs. Most decisions affecting them were inscribed in overall plans such as "Provide Comfort" and "Restore Hope." One can therefore challenge the very concept of policies designed to address IDPs' specific situations. Nevertheless, displaced persons are in a particular situation vis-à-vis the international community. On the move, though not legally protected by refugee conventions, they create problems and engender measures that are worth studying in their own right. Provided IDPs themselves are identifiable, it becomes possible to assess decisions that applied to them, whether the latter were specific measures or were part of a larger humanitarian endeavour. Below are highlighted both the specificity of policies regarding IDPs and the conditions under which they can be evaluated.

IDP policies cannot be equated with refugee policies. First, displaced persons do not enjoy the protection of refugee conventions. Although it may be convincingly argued that refugees in Turkey, Croatia, Zaire or Tanzania were not given much of a chance to apply for asylum or resettlement, their status nevertheless imposed constraints on the international community. Host states and the UNHCR had to define new modes of protection and repatriation somewhat consistent with the 1951 Refugee Convention. Second, in the early stages of crises, the agencies involved with displaced persons and refugees were different. In Iran and Turkey in April 1991, the needs of most refugees were covered by local and national initiatives, whereas the international community focused its work on populations stranded in the Iraqi mountains and later, on the newly returned communities. The only institution working legally in Iraq in the aftermath of the Gulf War, the ICRC, also played a prominent role in the early days of the crisis. UNHCR by contrast was very reluctant to get involved in the safe haven, and did not officially take over the Zakho camps before June 1991.[55] In the first months of the Bosnian conflict, despite the fact that UNHCR was in charge of overall operations, tasks were divided in ways that left Bosnia to the ICRC.[56] This changed after the establishment of the airlift to Sarajevo. In Rwanda, only the ICRC stayed in Kigali throughout the 1994 genocide and, with the help of the WFP, tried to prevent mass killings and displacements. Besides, military troops, when becoming involved in building and securing camps (Iraq; Rwanda) or ensuring food deliveries within disintegrated states (Bosnia; Rwanda) became actors to be reckoned with. The third important - and already mentioned - reason for dissociating refugee from IDP policies is the fact that refugee and IDPs flow, thus policies, are not concurrent. By closing its border to Kurds in April 1991, Turkey limited its own refugee crisis while engineering an internal displacement deadlock just on the other side of the border. Six weeks later, more than one million Kurds from both Turkey and Iran crossed the frontiers back to Iraq, yet many fell short of returning home, generating for the agencies in charge a displacement problem of vast dimensions.[57] In Bosnia, only refugees were cared for in the first three months of the war until the UNHCR drew up new plans of containment in July 1992. After 1995, the return of Bosnians from Croatia and Germany led to an increase in displaced persons in Bosnia proper. In Rwanda, international action was focused on refugees late April early May 1994, then IDPs in the course of May and June then refugees again in July as people fled to Goma. In February 1995, a regional conference on refugees in the Great Lakes area produced a Plan of Action which included the idea that refugees should return to stable areas of Rwanda, if not their homes. This approach was to transform refugees into IDPs.[58] Hence policies that reduce refugee dilemmas using containment or early repatriation operations can create mass internal migration problems. Questions such as "Who is living in my house?" are relevant to Bosnian and Rwandan returnees/IDPs alike.[59] To sum up, IDP policies have timings and constraints that, although crucially related to refugee policies, differ significantly. The above examples suggest that whereas refugees and IDP policies are connected, the links are complex. A study of IDP policies might help understand these ties better.

Policies towards IDPs cannot be equated with those for war victims either. In addition to food, water and fuel for heating, displaced persons need tents, building material, blankets as well as articles for a basic household. Even from a strictly humanitarian perspective, vulnerability and needs are usually greater. Francis Deng claimed that, in times of emergencies, the death rate of displaced persons could be up to 60 times that of non-displaced.[60] Consequently, IDPs use more international attention and resources than resident war victims. More importantly, they require space, a place where to stay, if only temporarily. "Where to settle, direct or evacuate IDPs?" "For how long?" are matters of much contention between intervening agencies, national authorities and the uprooted themselves. Even basic questions such as building a camp or installing a permanent water supply become political decisions, as they may affect settlement and return. When designing policies of "preventive protection" in Bosnia, UNHCR and its European partners talked of "preventing or containing" the exodus. Potential ethnic cleansing targets were to be "preventively protected." People already on the move were not only to be protected but also contained.[61] Indeed, forced displacement creates a particular set of policies where needs are addressed in combination with issues of space, territory and political order. Because of their political dimensions such policies are worth a study of their own.

Since policies to deal with forced displacement exist and cannot be totally merged with the study of refugee programmes or humanitarian endeavour, focusing on them is justified. However, because such measures are part of humanitarian packages, caution is required. In order to study humanitarian intervention affecting IDPs, it is necessary to be able either to determine how humanitarian measures apply to IDPs specifically or highlight cases in which all or most of the people dealt with are displaced persons, not only "people in need," and not "refugees." This will be a determining criterion in the choice of case studies.

Hypothesis: Focus on the Protection/Containment Interplay

A hypothesis can be defined as the suggested explanation for a set of facts which provides a basis for further verification. In the context of this research, the phenomena studied are international interventions within collapsing states, officially to protect uprooted civilians and to dissuade them from fleeing abroad. Protection policies include the provision of humanitarian aid, human rights monitors, conflict mediators, the creation of no-fly zones or safe areas as they apply to people on the move. Policies of containment encompass all measures taken to prevent refugee outflow, from closing borders to enforcing returns to particular regions of the countries under intervention. The hypothesis is the following: "The international protection granted to IDPs is an instrument of containment policies." It is tested through a study of the construction and implementation of measures taken by the international community for people on the move. With regard to the construction of policies, the study checks whether international protection is promised in order to contain IDPs within the borders of their country of origin. As far as implementation goes, the research checks whether international actors give priority to containment over people's safeguard or vice versa.

In this research, "protecting IDPs" and "containing IDPs" are the two variables whose interplay is to be assessed. Two justifications are required. To start with, one might ask about the relative weight of other factors in explaining policies regarding IDPs. Indeed, numerous potential causes for intervention on behalf of the uprooted can be brought forward: concerns about regional stability, TV news, general human rights concerns, or anxieties regarding increased migrations. Although this is true, these factors do not play a direct part in the study. For these potential motives do not interfere at the level of the research but instead are channelled into the formulation of the two policy objectives discussed: protecting and containing populations. Figure 1.2 illustrates this point.

Figure 1.2: Purpose of humanitarian action

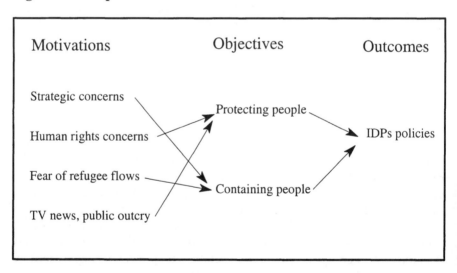

To take an example, although strategic concerns influence actions towards IDPs, they do so through giving weight to either or both aspirations. Protection and containment are the public justifications

24

grounding all IDP policies. They are the policy aims enclosing all motives for engagement, including media-induced pressure. This study is about assessing the relationship between objectives rather than trying to unravel a complex web of motivations. Indeed, examining thoroughly all factors having, at some stage, some influence on policy could turn into an endless quest. What about the psychological factors informing strategic fears? What of cultural environments underpinning faith in human rights? One is limited, and so is research. Through the study of policy objectives and outcomes, some insights might be gained regarding the concerns and motivations of international actors. However, these will be suggestions for further investigation rather than systematic conclusions.

More challenging is the suggestion that it would be difficult to assess the weight of each variable given that the two seem linked in policy making. In fact, the above picture represents conventional wisdom which, to a great extent, relies on the assumption that protecting and containing people are two independent objectives grounding action on behalf of people on the move. This is the assumption framework that underpins the work of Roberts, of Dowty and Loescher, of Posen and Sadako Ogata herself.[62] Much debate is indeed focused on the relative weight of the causes for involvement. However, such setting relies on the idea that the two variables are independent, whereas there is evidence that they are linked. In the rhetoric justifying interventions on behalf of IDPs, the emphasis is frequently placed on protection rather than containment. In addition, the prevention of exodus is usually described as the natural consequence of the protection of the uprooted. In other words, politicians often say "let us protect them and they will not flee." The logic of this discourse is represented in Figure 1.3:

Figure 1.3: Common reasoning behind intervention

Active policy towards IDPs ⟶ Protection increases ⟶ Exodus decreases

Alternatively, institutions dealing with IDPs occasionally seem to advocate a different rationalism. It is usually assumed that, by definition, powerlessness and destitution increase with a flight. In the words of an aid worker, people in a refugee situation "are told or ordered where to live, what to eat and what they can do. Refugees suddenly become disempowered and dependent on others. There is very little room for either individual or community choice in emergency situations."[63] Given that a forced move entails a loss not only of material belongings but also of social and family ties, community protection and support, it is sometimes claimed that the prevention of movement is itself a form of protection. In this context, containment can be taken to "mean" protection. Indeed, the links between protection and containment are manifold, possibly changing, depending on institutions and circumstances. This paragraph gives only a taste of the possible interplay between the two.

Contrary to mainstream approaches, this study starts from the assumption that both concepts are linked and seeks to unravel their relationships. By providing a clearer picture of the articulation mechanism, it will hopefully complement understanding of policies for IDPs. It may also highlight potential problems in conventional understandings of policies regarding displaced persons. Caution is required though. Since both the increase of people's protection and the prevention of exodus are desirable outcomes, it may seem difficult to assess the part of each in the decision-making processes whenever the increase of one is to boost the other. This said, the international community faced numerous emergencies during which protection and containment were at odds. In circumstances such as in Iraq in April 1991, in Bosnia in summer 1992 and Rwanda in June and August 1994, the danger and the emergency made it difficult for interveners to step up protection with traditional peace-keeping instruments - mediation, confidence building measures, the monitoring of human rights, etc. The alternatives faced were stark: immediate military involvement to enhance protection rapidly or large scale evacuation. The extent to which international organisations chose either option or tried to mitigate the situation gives clues as to what they hoped to achieve regarding the uprooted. Indeed, the compromises during emergency situations help to assess where priorities lie. This highlights the fact that, if one wants to grasp the protection/containment interplay, the case studies must be crisis points.

Case Studies: Mass Responses to Displacement Emergencies

Given that the research assesses the mechanisms at work in policies towards displaced persons, cases must be explored to a certain depth. Thus their number will be limited to three plus one test case. Criteria for their selection are the following: a post-Cold War context, an intervention involving numerous players, the visibility of IDPs and of the policies affecting them.

A similar international relations background eases comparisons. Consequently, the study should be limited to a short period of history. The author decided to focus on recent events, namely post-Cold War crises, for two reasons. Although much remains to be written on previous forced migrations, IDPs have emerged as an issue in world politics only recently. The end of the Cold War prompted a redefinition of agendas and of UN activities. This collided with the crisis of the refugee regime owing to an increased number of forced migrants and the disappearing hospitality of industrialised nations. The second, and important, reason of this concentration on the 1990s is that, ultimately, the author is interested in policy-making with regard to displaced persons.

Given that here we study the mechanisms at work in intervention, as opposed to *when* intervention occurs, such an involvement must take place. This common-sense criterion eliminates numerous occurrences of forced migrations. Although many countries already have high numbers of IDPs, numbers alone do not create involvement. Interestingly enough, only new movements seem to attract international attention. A build-up of persons does not engender concerns whereas a flux does. This said, in many cases of new movements, little interest was shown: for instance in Former USSR, Georgia and Chechnya, or in some parts of Africa such as Sudan, Liberia, Burundi. In those countries, only the ICRC, a few NGOs and occasionally some UN bodies were active. This hardly amounts to an engagement of the international community.

The larger the operation, the better the chances are to be able to compare the positions of actors across cases. Thus to ease comparisons, the operations chosen show a significant involvement of governments, UN institutions and NGOs. Prominent interventions in the 1990s started with UNHCR's work in Sri Lanka. However, only the UNHCR and some NGOs were involved. In Iraq by contrast, the US and other NATO states were massively engaged, preceded by NGOs and joined later by the UN. After the Former Yugoslavia had disintegrated, the UN sent troops to Croatia in 1992. They were to oversee both the cease-fire and the return home of Croat displaced persons and refugees. The latter did not take place until 1995. Because of their work in Croatia, UNPROFOR troops were stationed in Bosnia from the start of the conflict. So were most UN and NGOs humanitarian bodies, followed later by NATO. As in Iraq, the Bosnian crisis was the object of numerous debates on refugee definitions and approaches to intervention and protection. In Somalia, a plethora of humanitarian organisations and multinational troops participated in the fight against the effect of the famine. A similar mass phenomenon took place in Rwanda and Zaire in the aftermath of the 1994 genocide. In the intervention to restore democracy in Haiti, by contrast, only the US, the UNHCR plus the ICRC became involved. Therefore, as far as international involvement matters, Sri Lanka, Haiti and Croatia were on a smaller scale than the other cases and thus are not to be studied as a priority.

As pointed out in the previous section, IDP policies must be identifiable. In Iraq, Sri Lanka and Rwanda displacement was geographically localised and involvement was clearly related to people on the move. Northern Iraq, with around 400,000 persons stranded, not allowed to cross the Turkish border, is relatively straightforward to study. In Rwanda, despite the confusion between genocide targets and people fleeing the war front, debates in the UN circles clarified the dispositions intended for persons on the move. By contrast, in Haiti, Somalia, Bosnia and Croatia, displaced populations moved from countryside to villages and from villages to towns, thus mixing with local city dwellers, themselves besieged and sometimes starving. Given that all were in need of help, interveners often talked about the "protection of civilians." This, in addition to the fact that interventions encompassed large territories made it difficult to separate IDP policies from wider agendas such as the re-establishment of political authorities. In this context however, Bosnian IDPs were easier to identify than Croat, Somali and Haitian displaced persons. Because in Bosnia eviction took place under international scrutiny with the occasional direct involvement of humanitarian agencies, displacement dilemmas were better recorded. Besides, some situations involved mainly displaced persons. The fall of various towns during the war, from Zvornick in the first days of April 1992 to Srebrenica and Zepa in 1995, provoked streams of displaced persons to be rescued. Policies concerning Srebrenica in 1992-93 were, to a great extent, for displaced persons. For the pre-war town population of 6,000 had swollen to between 30,000 and 50,000 by civilians fleeing the surrounding countryside.[64] To sum up, as far as the visibility of policies for IDPs goes, Iraq, Rwanda and Sri Lanka are straightforward cases. Bosnia supplies interesting dilemmas, provided one is cautious enough to determine circumstances where IDPs issues dominate. Somalia, Croatia and Haiti come last, given that less reference was made to forced displacement in these cases.

In short, the first two criteria broadly determine recent humanitarian intervention linked to mass population movements. Equally important, the last two criteria determine, amongst the seven cases, which are better suited for the study. The most important interventions affecting people on the move were 1) Bosnia, 2) Iraq, 3) Rwanda and Somalia, 4) Croatia and Sri Lanka, 5) Haiti. The evidence of action for the uprooted was greater in 1) Iraq and Sri Lanka 2) Rwanda, 3) Bosnia, 4) Croatia, 5) Somalia, 6) Haiti. Thus prominent cases are first Iraq, Bosnia and Rwanda. Sri Lanka, Somalia, Croatia and Haiti all have relevant features. However, none of the latter set combines a mass intervention with a clear emphasis on the uprooted. Engagement in Haiti was limited to a few actors with no clear agenda for IDPs. Action in Sri Lanka, although clearly focused on IDPs, was limited in scope. In Croatia, intervention took place after people had left and its chief purpose was to encourage their return both from other areas of the country and from abroad. For the above mentioned reasons these three cases will not be considered. As for Somalia, whereas international engagement was extensive, little if anything was said about internal displacement. In addition, Somalia is often heralded as an example of media-induced action, which makes it an ideal control case for the research.

Indeed, one can suggest that all chosen cases studies present a disturbing similarity affecting the scope of the findings. In Iraq, Bosnia and Rwanda international media are still understood to have played a major role in promoting humanitarian engagement. Thus, any finding of the research regarding the impact of containment on protection activities could be opposed by the idea that, far from being an implement of containment approaches, action for IDPs was a direct response to media-induced pressure. As already clarified, the book only makes indirect claims about motivations for action. It is concerned with the interaction between containment and protection as policy objectives. Someone, however, could seek to challenge the links between motivations, policy objectives and outcomes which were pictured above and instead, to present containment as simply another cause for engagement to be assessed against alternatives. There are three lines of reply to this potential criticism. First, to defend the model, one must show that containment was an explicit policy objective. In other words, that international actors clearly stated their desire to pre-empt refugee outflow. Second, with regard to the findings, one must bear in mind the role of the media at times when decision regarding IDPs were taken, and be ready to qualify one's conclusion if media pressure is constantly associated to action to protect IDPs. Finally, one can test the findings using a case where news media rather than mass displacement are conventionally understood to be the cause for action. No event would better fit this description than the 1992 intervention in Somalia. As the following section makes clear, all three approaches will be used in the study.

Testing Procedures: Checking Predictions

For the sake of a clear argument, the hypothesis is tested in two steps: the construction and the implementation of international decisions for displaced persons. In other words, two sub-claims are derived from the main hypothesis. As far as the construction of policies is concerned, the sub-hypothesis is that "promises of safety for IDPs are contingent on fears of mass exodus." Regarding the implementation of such protection pledges, the assertion tested is that "safety for IDPs is subordinated to containment objectives." Chapter II deals with the construction of policies and Chapter III with their implementation.

Testing the claims starts with setting up a framework of statements to be systematically investigated. By "generating as many observable implications as possible" that are available to empirical verification, one can check the extent to which an hypothesis is grounded.[65] The statements are derived from the sub-hypothesis and chosen for their pertinence in disclosing the relative roles of protection and containment. Built to enlighten the relation between rhetoric and action regarding IDPs, they highlight the timing of operation, the actors first involved, the options discussed etc. Both chapters II and III start with an exposition of the postulates to be checked against the three cases. Here are a few examples: regarding the emergence of interest for IDPs, the following statements will be assessed. "*The protection of IDPs is not an issue in the absence of mass cross border displacement*" also called the "*no protection without exodus*" clause. By contrast, "*the protection of IDPs is always an issue when a cross borders exodus takes place,*" in other words an "*exodus generates protection debates*" stipulation. As for the implementation of safety pledges, the statements considered will include an "*irrelevance of need*" proposition: "*safety provision does not vary according to displaced population needs,*" a "*containment first*" postulate: "*containment objectives always take priority over protection aims.*" A "*protection withdrawal*" suggestion will also be considered: "*The international community may use threats, the refusal to provide safety or its withdrawal to pre-empt exoduses or to promote departures and returns.*" The latter statement is of particular relevance, given that the hypothesis suggests that the safety granted by the international community is instrumental in migration objectives. The introductions of chapters II and III contain all postulates to be investigated.

Building from secondary sources and personal research, the chapters then proceed by checking the statements against the case studies and comparing the findings. Whenever a statement does not match up to the test of evidence, findings will have to be qualified. One might want to check whether other factors are at work, whether there are differences among the cases studies that affect and explain such results. If patterns confirming the hypothesis emerge, then the findings need to be tested against a hard case in order to determine the limits of the hypothesis - in other words, the extent to which a strong claim can be articulated. This will take place in chapter IV and, for reasons outlined above, the hard case considered is the 1992 intervention in Somalia. Only after such a review has occurred, can one conclude the project by comparing the overall findings to mainstream literature in chapter V. Implications of the study will help to draw propositions for future research. But before unfolding the essence of the argument, one must explain why it is important to focus on policies for IDPs.

Why Focus on Internal Displacement?

Two reasons have been proposed so far. First, it is important to focus on approaches to IDPs because they are not studied comprehensively. Such work could therefore add to the debates mentioned in the opening of this chapter. It may provide a better grasp of some continuities and complexities of humanitarian work. In particular, it could help to determine whether general understandings of international involvement in northern Iraq, Bosnia or Rwanda apply to displaced persons. Besides, the containment/protection interplay could be used in discussions regarding the exact role of the media over humanitarian action. Furthermore, given that IDPs are themselves an integral part of the "people of concern," a better grasp of action concerning them can provide insights into the ways in which the international community categorises groups of people it cares for. The second reason for studying IDP policies is that the current lull in literature is not the result of methodological difficulties. One can identify and assess policies for IDPs. They are a unique blend of decisions drawn from migration, development and international security considerations. Although linked to refugee emergencies, they cannot be completely merged with the study of refugee policies or humanitarian action. They have their own timings and bring about their own constraints. For these two reasons, studying international approaches to IDPs remains primarily a matter of filling gaps in the study of forced migration.

However, the author would contend that understanding the interplay between protection and containment is crucial not only for academic research but also for policy purposes. One cannot hope to sustain or improve protection mechanisms if their roots are not properly grasped. Thus there is room for perspectives which both complement and challenge mainstream approaches. In particular, by suggesting a dependency relation between protection and containment, the hypothesis may enlighten us regarding the roots of current humanitarian shortcomings. If protection were to be a containment device, then the deadlocks faced by field workers vis-à-vis ethnic cleansing or the "protection drift"[66] would be grounded in overall "new order" policies rather than solely in the nature of new civil wars. As a result, humanitarian dilemmas could not be adequately tackled unless global approaches to international disorder, especially the reform of asylum, migration and development policies were themselves questioned. Given the current emphasis on reforming humanitarianism, all efforts to understand these problems can be of use.

Nonetheless, before claiming that this study might enhance policy reform to the benefit of uprooted people, a choice needs to be justified. Paul Garde said about the war in Bosnia: "Nommer quelque chose, c'est déjà choisir son camp" "labelling itself, already entails taking sides."[67] Emphasising IDPs might deepen categorisations that are not helpful to these persons or to other vulnerable populations. In Columbia, IDPs try their best not to be known as such to avoid further discrimination and persecution.[68] The question is: can policy makers, or academics, pretending to work towards the well-being and emancipation of uprooted persons, insist on placing them into separates categories, that might be damaging in themselves? In particular, a researcher's adoption, or reiteration, of harmful frameworks for analysis might lead to neat yet profoundly destructive studies which, for the sake of academic clarity, instrumentalise the persons studied. People would remains means, not ends. The following section seeks to spell out the advantages and limits of placing the research emphasis on IDPs.

In their study of humanitarian action in Former Yugoslavia, Pasic and Weiss claim that distinguishing IDPs from other vulnerable populations made no practical sense.[69] What was needed, and what the UNHCR set up, was a policy focused on needs rather than on displacement statuses. Here both authors illustrate an emerging wisdom in humanitarian circles. From a grass root perspective, distinguishing IDPs from refugees or other vulnerable groups is not only difficult, given the chaos in which aid workers often have to take decisions, but is also irrelevant. Priorities lie in needs: need for food, for medical equipment or shelter and beyond for legal and social protection, whether or not these requirements have been caused by displacement. In this context, uprooting, although dramatic, is not always the sign of ultimate vulnerability. In the spring of 1994, being a Tutsi in Rwanda was far more dangerous than being on the move. Later, in the same country, being a widow had far more social implications than being displaced, for women could not inherit land. From 1992 onwards, Muslim and Croat resident minorities in Banja Luka lived through daily persecutions which the presence of three isolated UNHCR protection officers could not offset.[70] They were more vulnerable than Serb displaced populations living in the same region. In the same vein, separating displaced persons from their hosts can lead to seriously flawed aid and reconstruction programmes.[71] Gender, religious and social distinctions such as age may be more reliable indicators of need than displacement itself. In short, one cannot assume that forced migration is automatically the dominant cause of distress. Neither can one hold that IDPs are, by definition, the persons most in need of immediate protection. Thus, as far as the reform of humanitarianism is concerned, a study focused on displacement can, at best, complement work on need. On its own, it is insufficient to grasp the complexities of humanitarian emergencies.

This said, the author also holds that studies of humanitarian need should be complemented by a good understanding of displacement dilemmas. An approach that focuses on needs only presents two problems. First, in the early 1990s, the humanitarian community itself participated in the enthusiasm regarding work with IDPs and thus in the creation of a label that, now, has a life of its own. If this was a mistake, then practitioners, academics and displaced persons need to reflect on what happened before we can move on, in the best interests of the uprooted. Second, given that nowadays IDPs are usually identified as such, the focus on need as a humanitarian concept may, in fact, increase their vulnerability, for it maintains an artificial focus on assistance as opposed to political protection, whereas the latter is often what the displaced persons want most. Both these points require expansion.

The international humanitarian community participated enthusiastically in the creation of the tag "IDP" to identify specific groups of persons in need of international attention. In the course of the 1980s, the UNHCR acknowledged the structural crisis of the refugee regime and brought IDPs on the world political agenda. It established a working group on internal displacement and international protection from 1983 onwards, the work of which became topical in the early nineties. The refugee institution claimed that it could no longer ignore the links between internal and external displacements. As the end of the Cold War offered renewed scope for multilateral interventions, the international community involved itself with uprooted people in Cambodia, Sri Lanka, Iraq, Croatia, Somalia, Bosnia, to name but a few. After the Gulf War, a UN Department for Humanitarian Affairs - UNDHA - was created to co-ordinate such operations. In 1992, Francis Deng was appointed representative of the UNSG for Internally Displaced Persons. Since then, UN agencies have continued to produce reports on international politics towards people on the move. Humanitarian organisations such as MSF or the ICRC, accustomed to dealing with people on the move, also publish literature on displacement. Nevertheless, as far as UN organisations were concerned, IDPs became an issue because they were considered part of the global refugee crisis. The emergence of attention given to early warning systems to avoid refugee crises since the early 1980s was extensively discussed by Luise Drüke, herself a UNHCR staff, in a thesis published in 1993.[72] However, in the study, IDPs were a simple add-on to the real problem: refugee flows. In the same vein, Ogata declared: "I see them as potential refugees, and an effective response to the refugee problem cannot ignore their plight. By meeting their protection and assistance needs we could preempt a refugee exodus, and even perhaps help to reduce internal displacement."[73] For humanitarian NGOs, IDPs were important as bearers of particular needs. In all cases, understandings of IDPs were shaped by agencies' missions and the problems that they had to solve: refugee crises for some, cholera emergencies for others. Thus although the concept of IDPs emerged, problems of displaced persons *per se* remained only partially explored.

Furthermore, much of the material compiled by agencies informed the work of academics. Interestingly enough, internal displacement issues were raised on the academic agenda by persons working for international organisations: Fred Cuny for the US government, Bill Frelick with USCR,

Rony Braumann, François Jean for Médecins sans Frontières (MSF), Mendiluce and Landgren for UNHCR. These humanitarian perspectives dominated academic approaches to internal displacement. Given that both IDPs and "war victims" were "persons of concern", writers adopted the term IDPs, yet failed to distinguish between policies for both types of people. In fact, most humanitarian literature focuses on debating the legality of interfering within the confines of sovereign states or the practicabilities of reaching people with aid (war victims and displaced alike). Likewise, specialists of forced migrations tended to include IDPs in refugee studies. Loescher and Dowty, Weiner or Adelman considered "people on the move" as if the relationship between refugees and IDPs was straightforward.[74] Even Frelick or Shacknove who focus on the containment versus asylum debate rely on the unexplored assumption that displaced persons are refugees in the making.[75] Although most authors reflected on the implications of new policies, few questioned the concepts at stake. In short, a label was created; yet the particulars of policies for displaced persons were rarely investigated. This is because the notion of IDP originated in the need of UN organisations to solve refugee and/or humanitarian crises, which suited the background of academics. In the process the complexity of the situation of IDPs was often overlooked and so were the requests of the people. Both researchers and practitioners share responsibility for this, although the fact that the field is new, prompted by fresh humanitarian experiences, also explains gaps in the literature. This highlights the necessity to establish a real dialogue in which field workers and observers can share their expertise as well as reflect on the origins of the concepts they use. With the publication of the Global IDP Survey and the Guiding Principles, this is now happening. In this context, it might be right to acknowledge that IDPs is not a helpful label. However, because of their participation in its rise, neither practitioners nor humanitarian intervention specialists can now dismiss or reform the concept without reflecting on why and how they created it in the first place. Among other things, this entails analysing closely interventions in the early 1990s.

Weiss and Pasic's emphasis on "need" also derives from the reflection of the international community on its failure to solve the Somali, Bosnian or Rwandan crises. The ethical and humanitarian dilemmas in which aid workers became entangled when trying to negotiate aid distribution, protection measures and access to people led many to advocate a stronger separation between humanitarian duties and political negotiations. Hence the idea that displacement stories are irrelevant on the war field. Only needs count. It is readily accepted that, in recent crises, humanitarian missions were abused. However, grasping the roots of humanitarian disasters does not necessarily entail compromising on the priority given to people's needs. Some abuses of humanitarian missions that were witnessed in Bosnia or Rwanda, for instance, aid diversions, blackmails or the refusal to give asylum under the pretext that ethnic cleansing should not be encouraged, came from the combination of local and Western political agendas regarding civilians. A lack of exploration of the political contexts and constraints imposed on humanitarian work would not help aid workers to make a positive difference next time.

Here also comes the second problem with an approach emphasising need only. De-politicising vulnerabilities is not a straightforward process. Although there are ethical and practical reasons for refusing to bargain people's safety amid conflicts, policy makers and academics should not lose sight of the inherently political roots of the dilemmas witnessed. In analytical terms, de-politicising needs entails assuming a distinction between forced migration and vulnerability that is not warranted. Although displacement does not explain all miseries, it gives clues as to the origins and the nature of the needs faced, in particular that of needing protection against political persecution. Ignoring displacement issues would maintain an artificial separation between assistance and political protection as well as the temptation to focus on the former only. In Bosnia, it was precisely treating need as an entirely humanitarian issue that led the international community, in an almost obscene way, to focus on feeding people who were then slaughtered. What the people in Srebrenica needed most was not food but an end to the bombing. Such were their anxieties that cigarettes were the goods most sought after, not food cans. In fact, this artificial distinction between assistance and protection served the purposes of many participants in the Bosnian conflict (warring parties but also some mediators) who did not want the issue of protection to be dealt with comprehensively. Although such experienced academics as Weiss and Pasic certainly include political protection in their understanding of need, on the ground, the concept itself is often narrowed down to immediate physical needs only. Given that reform debates currently focus on the necessity to go beyond assistance and to deal with the overall safety of persons,[76] it is essential to consider seriously the roots of recent action associated with internal displacement.

To sum up, because IDPs are now identified as such, the suggestion to de-politicise their needs places them in a no-win situation. On the one hand, they are identified as political problems - given that displacement is the main indicator of social disorder. On the other hand, only their needs for food or shelter might be adequately cared for. This approach, which might dramatically increase the helplessness of the uprooted, is the result of two combined trends: policy makers are now using the concept "IDPs" as a given while academics dispute it, but only because of its operational uselessness. Clearly, the label IDP is conceptually problematic and, by now, policy makers should be cautious about using the term. A similar prudence is required from researchers who pretend to work for the benefit of people on the move. IDPs are interesting. They are this particular group of people, a focus on whom might highlight inherent contradictions within international policies. Still, to avoid making them an instrument of academic enquiry to their own detriment, the use of the term must be scrutinised and its problems acknowledged. Questions such as "Why use this concept?" "Are displaced persons themselves satisfied to be recognised as such?" "How does it serve their purposes?" need to be asked. Otherwise, Wood and Zetter's warning that "labelling is a way of referring to the process by which policy agendas are established and more particularly the way in which people, conceived as objects of policy are defined in convenient images"[77] would be entirely lost. Researchers as well as practitioners need to take responsibility for their work. This research examines international approaches towards people on the move in the early 1990s. It uses the concept of IDPs precisely because the latter emerged as a separate category in international discourses at that time and because the research seeks to assess the nature of international approaches to internal displacement. As already mentioned, grasping why and how the label emerged is essential before researchers can decide on the extent to which it is detrimental to humanitarian practice. Besides, critical self-reflection is owed to the Bosnians, Kurds or Rwandans who, for better or worse, were labelled IDPs.

In conclusion, although the concept lacks operational appeal and thus may be questionable, it cannot be disregarded easily. It would be dangerous to adopt entirely the current domination of humanitarian perspectives, for they often obscure understanding that forced displacement crises are political in their roots and humanitarian only in their consequences. As a result, discourses focusing on humanitarian issues can blur political mechanisms at work, hence the responsibilities of local and international actors. In order to avoid this, a dialogue is needed that clarifies the objectives of each partner in the action, whether displaced person, policy maker or researcher. In fact, a comprehensive study of international action for IDPs cannot emerge without such an exchange. Although the present researcher is neither a practitioner nor a field specialist, she hopes that deliberate focus on IDPs, however incomplete, might help to strengthen current discussions. The book's main findings are outlined next.

"Flocks without Shepherds" but a World Busy Mending Fences

Chapter II examines the ways in which IDPs issues emerged on the international agenda and discusses the reasons for which the international community promised protection. In all three case studies, protection for IDPs became topical only when masses of people threatened to overrun borders and international authorities believed that promises of in-country protection would convince the uprooted to remain within their collapsed home state. Thus granting safety was conceived as a means of achieving containment objectives. Chapter III assesses the implementation of the pledged protection. It shows that measures enhancing the safety of displaced persons were shallow and were always subordinated to containment aims. Apart from isolated exceptions, safety never took priority over international views regarding where people should stay or return to. Chapter IV summarises the findings of chapters II and III and tests them against the 1992 intervention in Somalia. It concludes that, even in Somalia, containment objectives were present from the start and underpinned UN policies, affecting the safety effectively granted to Somali IDPs. Chapter V, the conclusion, holds therefore that the hypothesis not only is valid but also provides a strong reading of action for IDPs. Chapter V also highlights that the findings represent an alternative standpoint to mainstream literature. They question the humanitarian narrative usually focused on suffering and on media influence. Understanding protection as a migration policy device can provide a backbone for further studies of action for people on the move. It should also be born in mind when reforming current humanitarian practices. Cynthia Enloe, the feminist writer, once reckoned that, to understand institutions, one needed to look at what they were afraid of. "Look at what they are nervous about," she said.[78] Indeed, it is telling that Francis Deng referred to IDPs as "flocks without shepherds."[79] This book suggests that Western governments and UN institutions sought to raise shepherds or become one themselves. However, these were shepherds seeking to contain, direct and control the "flocks." In short, barrier-mending shepherds. So far, the international community has shown itself a shepherd less worried by the plight of the "flock" than by the absence of order, of leaders in control and by the collapse of borders. In

38

reforming itself, it might want to reflect on whether it wants to be a "shepherd" and, if so, what kind of shepherd it should be.[80]

Notes

[1]   Hampton, Janie, ed., *Internally Displaced Persons: A Global Survey* (London: Earthscan Publications Ltd., 1998).

[2]   See http://www.idpproject.org

[3]   Bennett, Jon, "Internal Displacement in Context: The Emergence of a New Politics," in Davies, Wendy, ed., *Rights Have No Borders, Worldwide Internal Displacement* (Geneva/Oslo: Global IDP Survey/Norwegian Refugee Council, 1998), 15-29, 15.

[4]   Loescher, Gil, *Refugee Movement and International Security*, Adelphi Paper No. 268, Summer 1992 (London: Brassey's for the International Institute for Strategic Studies -IISS- 1992), 2.

[5]   Quoted in Frelick, Bill, "Aliens in their Own Land: Protection and Durable Solutions for Internally Displaced Persons" in, United States Committee for Refugees, *World Refugee Survey 1998* (on-line: http://www.refugees.org/world/articles/internallydisplaced_wrs98.html, no pagination).

[6]   See for instance the debate between Michael Barutciski, Bonaventure Rutinwa, Michael Kingsley-Nyinah, Jon Bennett and Marc Vincent in, *Forced Migration Review*, No. 4 (April 1999), 29-35.

[7]   UNHCR, *The State of the World's Refugees 1995* (New York: Penguin Books, 1995), 20 and 40.

[8]   Adelman, Howard, "The Ethics of Humanitarian Intervention: The Case of the Kurdish Refugees," Vol. 6, No. 1 (1992), *Public Affairs Quarterly*, 61-87.

[9]   Shacknove, Andrew, "From Asylum to Containment," Vol. 5, No. 4 (1993), *International Journal of Refugee Law*, 516-533; Frelick, Bill, "'Preventive Protection' and the Right to Seek Asylum: A Preliminary Look at Bosnia and Croatia," Vol. 4, No. 4 (1992), *International Journal of Refugee Law*, 439-454; Barutciski, Michael, "The Reinforcement of Non-Admission Policies and the Subversion of UNHCR: Displacement and Internal Assistance in Bosnia-Herzegovina (1992-1994)," Vol. 8, No. 1/2 (1996), *International Journal of Refugee Law*, 49-110.

[10] Loescher, Gil and Scanlan, John, *Calculated Kindness: Refugee Problems in America's Half Open Door, 1945 to the Present* (New York: Free Press, 1986); Loescher, Gil, "The European Community and Refugees," Vol. 65, No. 4 (1989), *International Affairs*, 617-636.

[11] Loescher, Gil and Monahan, Lisa, eds., *Refugees and International Relations* (Oxford: Oxford University Press, 1989).

[12] Loescher, Gil, *Beyond Charity, International Co-operation and the Global Refugee Crisis* (Oxford: Oxford University Press, 1993).

[13] Dowty, Alan and Loescher, Gil, "Refugee Flows as Grounds for International Action," Vol. 21, No. 1 (1996), *International Security*, 43-71. Although the word "flow" has no possible plural in English, the term "flows" is used by Dowty and

39

Loescher, Bennett and Weiner among others. It is therefore occasionally used in this book as well.

14 Ibid., 62-65.

15 Loescher, *Refugee Movement*, 58-59.

16 Ibid., 59.

17 Dowty and Loescher, "Refugee Flows," 62.

18 In addition to the work of Loescher already quoted, see Tiso, Christopher, "Safe Haven Refugee Programs: a Method of Combatting International Refugee Crises," Vol. 8, No. 4 (1994), *Georgetown Immigration Law Journal*, 575-601; Mendiluce, Jose-Maria, "Meeting the Challenge of Refugees: Growing Co-operation between UNHCR and NATO," Vol. 42, No. 2 (1994), *NATO Review*, (on-line edition: http://www.nato.int/docu/review/articles/9402-5.htm, no pagination); Onishi, Akira, "Global Early Warning System for Displaced Persons: Interlinkages of Environment, Development, Peace and Human Rights," Vol. 31, No. 3 (1987), *Technological Forecasting and Social Change*, 269-299; Independent Commission on International Humanitarian Issues, *Refugees: the Dynamics of Displacement: a Report for the Independent Commission on International Humanitarian Issues* / Foreword by the co-chairmen Sadruddin Aga Khan, Hassan Bin Talal (London: Zed Books, 1986).

19 See Adelman, "The Ethics of Humanitarian Intervention," and Roberts, Adam, *Humanitarian Action in War*, Adelphi paper, No. 305 (Oxford: Oxford University Press, 1997). See also Roberts, Adam, "Humanitarian War: Military Intervention and Human Rights," Vol. 69, No. 3 (1993), *International Affairs*, 429-449.

20 Braumann, Rony, "Contre l'Humanitarisme," No. 177 (1991), *Revue Esprit*, 77-85; Jean, François, ed., *Populations in Danger 1995*, A Médecins Sans Frontières Report, (London, 1995); Landgren, Karin, "Safety Zones and International Protection: A Dark Grey Area," Vol. 7, No. 3 (1995), *International Journal of Refugee Law*, 436-458; Minear, Larry and Weiss, Thomas, *Mercy under Fire, War and the Global Humanitarian Community* (Boulder Colorado: Westview Press Inc., 1995).

21 For instance in the articles of Roberts "Humanitarian War" and Adelman, "The Ethics of Humanitarian Intervention " quoted above.

22 S/22513, 21 April 1991, Letter from the Minister for Foreign Affairs of Iraq addressed to the Secretary-General, 21 April 1991 (Contains the Memorandum of Understanding signed on 18 April 1991) reproduced in Weller, M., ed., *Iraq and Kuwait: The Hostilities and their Aftermath*, Cambridge International Document Series, Vol. 3, (Cambridge: Grotius Publication Limited, 1993), 615-616, 616 (author's italics).

23 Statement of the High Commissioner for Refugees at the Donor Information Meeting, Geneva, 15 May 1991, UNHCR Information Service, in Weller, ed., *Iraq and Kuwait*, 617.

24 International Organisation for Migration (IOM), *Internally Displaced Persons, IOM Policy and Programmes*, Geneva, April 1997, 4.

25 Posen, Barry, "Military Responses to Refugee Disasters," Vol. 21, No. 1 (1996), *International Security*, 72-111.

26 Ibid., 85.

27 Ibid., 111.

28 Ibid., 79.

29 Landgren, "Safety Zones and International Protection," 438-440.

30 Posen, "Military Responses," 103-104.
31 Ibid., 79.
32 Ibid., 73.
33 This assumption runs throughout the paper. Ibid., 77-78, 83, 86, 98, 108.
34 Ibid., 95.
35 Ibid., 101.
36 Ibid., 98.
37 Ibid., 101 (author's italics).
38 In fact, the "deterrence/compellence" model cannot address some of the problems Posen outlines. For motivation in this model is taken into account only quantitatively - how much more than one's enemy does one wants something? This is too limited to evaluate the interplay that led to the creation of, for example, the Bosnian safe areas.
39 Barutciski, "The Reinforcement," 50.
40 Ibid., 72-80.
41 Ibid., 84.
42 Ibid., 95.
43 Ibid., 105.
44 Ibid., 109.
45 Cohen, Roberta and Deng, Francis, *Masses in Flight, The Global Crisis of Internal Displacement* (Washington D.C.: Brookings Institution Press, 1998); Cohen, Roberta and Deng, Francis, ed., *The Forsaken People, Case Studies of the Internally Displaced* (Washington D.C.: Brookings Institution Press, 1998).
46 Cohen and Deng, *Masses in Flight*, 29-30 and 282-283 on safe areas. During the 1990s, numbers of IDPs soared whereas official refugees numbers stagnated. However, it may be that many IDPs were counted for the first time as international bodies became more interested in their plight.
47 E/CN.4/1995/50, 2 February 1995, *Internally Displaced Persons*, report of the representative of the Secretary-General Mr. Francis Deng submitted pursuant to Commission on Human Rights resolutions 1993/95 and 1994/68.
48 Cohen and Deng, *Masses in Flight*, 283.
49 Ibid., 283.
50 Bennett, "Internal Displacement in Context," in Davies, ed., *Rights Have No Borders* and Bennett, Jon, "Forced Migration within National Borders: The IDP Agenda." Vol. 1 (January-April 1998), *Forced Migration Reviews* 4-6.
51 Bennett, "Internal Displacement in Context," in Davies, ed., *Rights Have No Borders*, 16-17.
52 Ibid., 23.
53 Ibid., 22.
54 Although, as detailed above, Posen remains unclear, wavering between assumptions.
55 Interview with John Fawcett, head of the International Rescue Committee (IRC) team in northern Iraq during the spring of 1991. February 1997.
56 Mercier, Michelle, *Crimes without Punishment* (London: Pluto Press, 1995), 52.
57 These were acknowledged by Sadako Ogata, UNHCR, in Ogata, Sadako, *Refugees, a Multilateral Response to Humanitarian Crises*, Elberg Lecture on International Studies, University of California, Berkeley, 1 April 1992 (on-line: http://www.unhcr.ch/refworld/unhcr/hcspeech/1ap1992.htm, no pagination).
58 Rutinwa, Bonaventure, *Short Notes on the Plan of Action for Voluntary*

Repatriation of Refugees in the Great Lakes Region, Paper presented at the International Workshop on the Refugee Crisis in the Great Lakes Region, Arusha Tanzania, 16-19 August 1995, 5 pages, 3.

59   *Who is Living in my House? Obstacles to the Safe Return of Refugees and Internally Displaced People*, Amnesty International report on the repatriation programme in Bosnia-Herzegovina, 19 March 1997, AI index EUR/63/01/97.

60   A/50/558, Annex: *Report on Internally Displaced Persons* prepared by the Representative of the Secretary General Mr. Francis Deng, 20 October 1995.

61   HCR/IMFY/1992/2, *A Comprehensive Response to the Humanitarian Crisis in the Former Yugoslavia*, 24 July 1992, 3.

62   Ogata, *Refugees* (on-line, no pagination).

63   Reynolds, R., *Development in a Refugee Situation: the Case of Rwandan Refugees in Northern Tanzania*, June 1994, Consultancy report for Christian Outreach and Tear Fund. A Copy can be found in the Documentation Centre, Refugee Studies Programme, Oxford, 2-3. For in-depth reflections on these issues, see Harrell-Bond, Barbara, *Imposing Aid* (Oxford: Oxford University Press, 1986), especially 283-284.

64   Interview with Louis Gentile, UNHCR, London 11th September 1998. For detailed accounts of the history and fall of Srebrenica during the war see Both, Norbert and Honig, Jan Willen, *Srebrenica Record of a War Crime*, (London: Penguin Book, 1996), as well as Rohde, David, *End Game, the Betrayal and Fall of Srebrenica: Europe's Worst Massacre since World War II*, (Boulder, Colorado: Westview Press, 1997).

65   King, Gary, Keohane, Robert and Verba, Sidney, *Designing Social Inquiry: Scientific Inference in Qualitative Research* (Princeton New Jersey: Princeton University Press, 1994), 21 and 109.

66   "Protection drift," a term coined by Jon Bennett, is the tendency to ensure the protection of aid and humanitarian personnel rather than that of local civilians. Bennett, "Internal Displacement in Context," in Davies, ed., *Rights have no Borders*, 25.

67   Garde, Paul, *Journal de voyage en Bosnie Herzegovine* (Paris: La Nuée Bleue, 1994), 16 (author's translation).

68   Obregón, Liliana and Stavropoulou, Maria, "In Search of Hope: The Plight of Displaced Colombians," in Cohen and Deng, eds., *The Forsaken People*, 399-454, 401.

69   Pasic, Amir and Weiss, Thomas, "Dealing with the Displacement and Suffering Caused by Yugoslavia's Wars," in Cohen and Deng, eds., *The Forsaken People*, 175-232, 178-180.

70   Interview with Louis Gentile, UNHCR protection officer in Banja Luka 1993-1994. London, 11 September 1998.

71   Pottier, Johan, "Agricultural Rehabilitation and Food Insecurity in Post-war Rwanda, Assessing Needs, Designing Solutions", Vol. 27, No. 3, *IDS Bulletin*, 1996, 56-75, 57. The need to take into account host families in aid programmes was also emphasised by WFP in Bosnia, *WFP in Former Yugoslavia, Assistance to Refugees, Displaced Persons and Other War Affected Populations*, Situation Report No. 2, March 1993, 39 pages, 5.

72   Drüke, Luise, *Preventive Action for Refugee Producing Situations*, European University Studies Series XXXI, Political Science, Vol./Bd. 150, (Peter Lang, Frankfurt am Main, 1993).

73   Ogata, UNHCR, *Refugees* (On-line, no pagination).

74   Dowty and Loescher, "Refugee Flows," Adelman, "The Ethics of Humanitarian Intervention," Weiner, Myron, "Bad Neighbors, Bad Neighborhoods, An Inquiry into the Causes of Refugee Flows," Vol. 21, No. 1 (1996), *International Security*, 5-42.

75   See Frelick, "Preventive Protection," and Shacknove, Andrew, "From Asylum to Containment," Vol. 5, No. 4 (1993), *International Journal of Refugee Law*, 516-533.

76   For a clear insight into the issue, see Keen, David, *The Kurds in Iraq: How Safe is their Haven Now?* A report for Save the Children Fund, London, June 1993, especially Chapter 4, "The Links between Assistance and Protection," 56-64.

77   Wood quoted in Zetter, Roger, "Labelling Refugees: Forming and Transforming a Bureaucratic Identity," Vol. 4, No. 1 (1991), *Journal of Refugee Studies*, 39-62, 44.

78   Professor Cynthia Enloe visited the Politics Department at Bristol University in October 1997 as a Benjamin Maker professor. She made this comment in the course of a research seminar.

79   Deng, Francis, "Flocks without Shepherds: The International Dilemma of Internal Displacement," in Davies, ed., *Rights Have No Borders*, 1-13, 1.

80   Here however, it is necessary to emphasise that the purpose of this work is to establish whether a means/end relation between protection and containment policies can be shown, and not whether such link, if it exists, is right or wrong. As was pointed out, a containment policy itself can spring from several motivations and this book does not seek to discuss or judge them. Nevertheless, the author is aware that, to a reader versed in humanitarian literature, the very suggestion that protection is a strategic tool may appear to entail a condemnation of Western "hypocrisy" and thus be a normative position in itself. Furthermore, the methodology showed that, in order to test the hypothesis, one must focus on difficult issues, on deadlocks and crises, when compromises were accepted. As a result, the research focuses on suffering, and it often links hardship to Western decision-making processes. At times, this might create a tone of moral reprobation which the author found difficult to avoid. However, the work posits nothing regarding Western claims to relieve suffering. In fact, it will show that Western protagonists did not hide their migratory concerns. What the study does is to offer an explanation for some of the failures of post-Cold War humanitarian engagement. This explanation, i.e. the confirmed hypothesis, raises normative questions regarding choice and responsibility, some of which are discussed in conclusion. The latter provides no policy recommendation but, arguably, suggests one normative position: given the findings, the questions of clarity in policy designs and responsibility should be addressed. In other words, the international community must clarify what kind of "shepherd" it wants to be.

2 Behind Safety Promises, the Quest for Stability

I sat down on the floor with Munevera who had just arrived with her two children, a daughter of seven and a son of five. She had come on foot from Foca, a Bosnian town that's about a six-hour drive from Split, in normal times. She had to leave Foca in the middle of the night, when attacks by bands of Serb paramilitary soldiers became too frightening, and then she had to sneak from one safe village to the next, never in a direct line, avoiding roads, walking through forest and mountains, sneaking past Serb villages, occasionally being shot at. ... She could rest for no more than a day at safe villages, because other refugees were arriving and food was running out. I asked how long it took to get from Foca to Split.

"Forty-five days" she said.

"Excuse me?"

"Forty-five days"

"You've been walking for forty-five days?"

"Yes but only at night. It was too dangerous to walk during the day."

I wrote it down in my notebook but I didn't believe it.[1]

With hindsight, most of us would believe Munevera. We also know that she was fortunate to have fled and reached Croatia in the first months of the war. She made the right choice. For Gorazde or Sarajevo were closer to Foca than Split, and some of her neighbours sought refuge there. As a result, they became the inhabitants of besieged cities whereas she was a refugee. Newly established borders made a statutory difference between forced migrants. Whereas under the 1951 Refugee Convention the international community must care for refugees, its duties towards internally displaced persons are moral rather than legal. IDPs fall under humanitarian law usually upheld by the ICRC.

Nevertheless the international community did intervene on behalf of displaced persons not only in Bosnia but previously in northern Iraq, and in Rwanda after the 1994 genocide. IDPs received aid distributed not only by NGOs or the UNHCR but also by national and multinational military troops such as the US in northern Iraq, France and UNAMIR in Rwanda, UNPROFOR in Bosnia. No-fly zones were proclaimed, human rights observers dispatched, safe areas established on behalf of threatened civilians, many of whom were displaced persons. However, alongside these measures, barriers to forestall refugee outflows were raised. Closed borders, the reestablishment of visa requirements and the refusal to evacuate civilians prevented populations from seeking safety abroad.

This chapter studies the construction of international action regarding displaced persons in northern Iraq (1991), Bosnia (1992-93) and Rwanda (1994). Exploring the ways in which forced migration issues emerged on the UN agenda, it assesses the claim that international protection policies for IDPs were promised in order to contain them within the confines of their home states. Consider the following propositions:

1. "No protection without exodus." The protection of IDPs was not an issue in the absence of mass cross-border displacement.
2. "Exodus generates protection." The protection of IDPs always became an issue when mass cross-border displacements took place.
3. "Neighbouring states care." IDPs issues were raised by institutions with a vested interest in avoiding refugee crises.
4. "Distant states do not care." States facing no risk of mass refugee arrivals were reluctant to act over IDPs.
5. "Protect to contain." Measures to protect IDPs were discussed in terms of their containment potential.
6. "No escape route." Protection policies advocated by the international community excluded measures that would increase refugee outflows (dropping border controls, creating exit routes, evacuating) despite the fact that the latter would enhance immediate safety.

The extent to which the above statements apply to the case studies gives a measure of the validity of the hypothesis. Although the text is not structured following the above list, each proposition is assessed in the course of the chapter. This introduction is followed by a section presenting each case's background and the early stages of the crises. A study of the first movements of the populations and initial responses of members of the UNSC, states and international organisations shows that, as a whole, the international community ignored the fate of IDPs. The author then focuses on the emergence of international concern on behalf of forced migrants. Attention to timing and to the positions of international actors allows one to highlight several points: first, all debates on the protection of IDPs appeared in the wake of refugee crises. Second, the issues were raised by UN organisations or neighbouring states, whereas other countries responded slowly. Third, in some cases, although not all, institutions championing IDPs' safety concurrently took measures preventing people from escaping danger. Finally, diplomatic debates concerning IDPs and the implementation of the first measures taken on their behalf are investigated. Working on the propositions "protect to contain" and "no escape route," discussions and justifications for adopting one safety measure rather than another are examined. Paying special attention to evacuations and humanitarian corridors since these operations can challenge the hypothesis, we argue that policies were justified and constructed so as to anticipate, stop or reverse an on-going exodus. Given these findings, the chapter closes suggesting that understanding protection of IDPs as a containment device is justified.

Tales of Exodus and Indifference

Three Wars

Attention to background is required not only to familiarise the reader with the particularities of each case but also to highlight changes in attitude towards people on the move. To give an account of international policies towards displaced persons prior to the events studied, the study relies on the work of area specialists: Chaliand, Van Bruinessen and MacDowall for the Iraqi Kurds,[2] Silber and Little, Malcolm, Cigar, Bennet for Yugoslavia.[3] As for Rwanda, de Waal, Prunier, Lemarchand, Franche and de Heusch are the sources most used.[4] The next paragraphs briefly picture the characteristics of forced migration issues for each case study, starting with northern Iraq.

Northern Iraq, south-east Turkey and north-west Iran, form Kurdistan. Although numbering 20 million persons with their own languages and customs, the Kurds have never achieved modern statehood and remain divided among the three above states. As host states struggle against Kurds' irredentism, the minorities endure permanent military rule. Since the 1970s, Turkish and Iraqi Kurds have also suffered intense campaigns of repression in between times of negotiation. In addition, governments competing for regional power, occasionally try to destabilise the Kurdish minorities in neighbouring countries, for instance during the 1980s Iran-Iraq war, as well as play on the disunity of Kurdish movements of resistance. Feuds that constantly divide Kurdish opposition groups, come partly from social and religious differences, partly from the permanent exploitation of disagreements by state rulers. The latter also frequently used forced displacement as an instrument of policy. In the 1920s and 1930s, both Ataturk in Turkey and Reza of Iran organised the deportation of Kurdish elites in an attempt to break the social structures of their troublesome minorities.[5] Such endeavour to force the Kurds into accepting the rule imposed on them were repeated over the years.[6] In Iraq, since the Ba'ath party led by Saddam Hussein took power in 1969, the Kurds entered a recurrent war against the government.[7] Despite the recognition of an autonomous Kurdistan,[8] violent repression provoked the flight of thousands of refugees to Iran and Turkey in 1975, 1983 and 1988 as well as the internal displacement of many more. Further, the Iraqi government undertook to Arabise Kurdistan[9] and to redistribute the Kurdish population so as to better control it. Rural communities in particular were forced into newly built "Saddam cities." Chaliand claims that 250,000 persons were forcefully relocated in 1978-79.[10] Since the mid-eighties, another such crusade, "the Anfal Campaign" yielded the following results:

> By 1988 ... 3000 Kurdish Villages had been destroyed. A third of the Kurdish area had become uninhabited ... In September 1988 the "resettlement" campaign intensified. Iraqi forces created a 30 km wide uninhabited "security zone" along the border with Turkey and Iran. Some 300,000 people were moved from those areas in the next year; The government claimed they were provided with better facilities.[11]

Indeed, both Iraq and Turkey saw physical control of territorial frontiers and of population movements as crucial to the creation and enforcement of national identities. Since their mountainous borders traced by colonial powers are not easily controllable, both governments tried and isolated their Kurdish minority through establishing unpopulated buffer zones alongside the border. In that context, cross-border displacements can be a major source of disturbance of the order governments intend to create.

Despite an appalling Iraqi human rights record including, in 1988, the use of chemical weapons against villages and towns in northern Iraq, Western states supported the regime of Saddam Hussein until 1990. According to Noam Chomsky, the US and the UK in particular helped to prevent UN sanctions for Iraq's aggression of Iran in 1983 as well as armed the country during this war.[12] Neither the use of chemical weapons against civilians nor the political terror instigated by Baghdad were denounced by either the US, Britain, France or Turkey.[13] Forced displacement, when controlled and contained, was accepted as a normal practice for a sovereign state.

In contrast to northern Iraq, the roots of the Bosnian conflict are to be found in recent political events, namely in the disintegration of Yugoslavia. The Yugoslav state imploded as president Milosevic waged war to prevent Slovenia and Croatia from quitting the federation. Both republics, the richest in Yugoslavia, had opposed Milosevic's recentralisation policy. Facing inflexibility, Slovenia and Croatia declared their independence and endured the wrath of Belgrade. Slovenia escaped with little damage thanks to its geographical location and to the fact that few Serbs lived there. Croats however, with a significant Serb minority, itself a majority in Knin or eastern Slavonia, fought against the Yugoslav National Army (JNA) and Serb paramilitary.

The term "ethnic cleansing" became known as local Serb militias and the JNA drove non-Serbs out of the areas under their control.[14] In response, the Croat government progressively stripped Serb minorities of their jobs, properties and rights. Fighting was particularly violent in border regions, the Krajina, eastern Slavonia and Vukovar. After eight months of war, ineffective European Community mediation, and a German-led campaign to recognise the secessionist state, the front line stabilised. Roughly one third of Croatia was occupied by Serb forces. In January 1992, a cease-fire held long enough for the international community to prepare to send UN peace-keeping troops.

The Bosnian leader Alija Izetbegovic and his Macedonian counterpart did their utmost to preserve Tito's Yugoslavia.[15] When it came to the crunch however, the former refused to vote in favour of the state of emergency required by the constitution to deploy the JNA in Slovenia and Croatia.[16] Yet, during the war, Izetbegovic attempted to appease his forcible neighbour by letting the JNA use Bosnia to attack Croatia. Studies still debate the president's naiveté and the wisdom of his policy, which included the disarmament of Bosnian territorial defence units and accepting a Portuguese proposal to create "ethnic zones of influence" in Bosnia. Izetbegovic seemed unaware of, or unwilling to face up to, the fact that Tudjman and Milosevic were discussing the partition of Bosnia from March 1991 onwards. [17]

In the early days of the conflict, American and European negotiators constantly tried to avoid an implosion of the federation, thus supporting Belgrade.[18] As the war developed however, Germany put its weight behind Croatia and pushed its reluctant European partners towards recognition. In March 1992, UNPROFOR troops were sent to provide protection for the newly-created United Nations Protected Areas - UNPAs - i.e. zones of Croatia controlled by the Serb military. Working with the UNHCR, the lead agency for humanitarian aid in Former Yugoslavia since November 1991, UN soldiers were to help in stabilising Serb populations whilst encouraging the return of Croat displaced persons.

Thus, issues of forced displacement presided and even preceded the explosion of violence in Bosnia. This was also the case in Rwanda where, since independence and the first mass expulsion of Tutsi populations, refugee issues represented a permanent threat to political stability. Since 1990, the French-backed Habyarimana regime faced a guerrilla war launched by the Rwanda Patriotic Front - RPF - a refugee-based army, itself supported by the government of Uganda. In conjunction with internal opposition parties, the RPF also demanded the democratisation of political institutions. Despite condemning RPF guerrilla, opponents to the Habyarimana regime hoped the war would force the government to the negotiation table.

An RPF offensive in February 1993 led to the displacement of around 800,000 Hutu peasants.[19] The government, although rescued by the French army fighting on its behalf, was pressurised into signing a power sharing agreement in August 1993. The Arusha settlement allowed for the progressive democratisation of the institutions and the return of refugees both in the country and into politics. The UN Department of Humanitarian Affairs - UNDHA -, the World Food Programme - WFP -, the ICRC and NGOs such as Oxfam became involved in the shelter and return of Rwandan IDPs since 1993.[20] A UN peace-keeping contingent - UNAMIR - was sent to Kigali to ensure the necessary security for the RPF, the opposition and the government to implement the power-sharing agreement. Extremist factions of the Habyarimana government, fiercely opposed to the democratisation process, provoked the deadlock of negotiations and promoted instead politics of hatred between Hutus and Tutsis. By the first months of 1994, some government and administration officials openly encouraged militia's violence against rural Tutsis. UNAMIR had no means to investigate pogroms and killings. In this explosive context, UNAMIR's mandate was narrowly renewed on April 5th 1994.[21]

To sum up, the above presentation does not pretend to do justice to the complexity of each conflict. However, it outlines similarities and disparities across cases. First, significant forced migrations were part of the political scenes. Iraqi authorities forcibly displaced rural Kurdish civilians in a move to increase control over them. In Former Yugoslavia, hundreds of thousands of people were "cleansed" during the Croatian war. Finally, Rwandan civilians fled *en masse* the north-east controlled by the RPF. Second, in all three cases population movements occurred during conflicts seriously challenging the state (Yugoslavia) or the nature of government (Iraq, Rwanda). Differences between cases are also noteworthy. Although the international community involved itself in each country's politics, it did so in distinct ways. In Iraq, the US led a war against the invasion of Kuwait. By March 1991, Iraq was a defeated and pariah state. Early 1992, EC negotiators were attempting an exercise in damage limitation whilst reluctantly supervising the dismemberment of Yugoslavia against the will of its main power centre. In Rwanda, the UN, with little financial means, were pushing a dictatorial government towards democratisation. Involvement with displaced persons, although varied, was usually the lot of humanitarian agencies. Only in Croatia did UN peace-keepers have a specific role related to forced migrants.

Initial Reactions to Resumed Mass Flights

In Iraq, the extent to which coalition governments expected uprisings following the military defeat of the Iraqi army is unclear. George Bush had called upon the Iraqi people to "take the matter in their own hands."[22] The US president publicly and repeatedly upheld the idea that Saddam Hussein should be replaced.[23] However, Western governments seemed to expect a military coup against the despot rather than popular revolts which, bringing to the fore the internal weaknesses of Iraq, put the coalition in a difficult situation. The Gulf War had been an exercise in re-establishing a state's borders. The revolts presented the US and its allies with a dilemma. The power rise of the Iran-backed Shi'a people in the south combined with the Kurdish revolt in the north could lead to the disintegration of the Iraqi state.[24] Not only the US but Turkey and Saudi Arabia were openly worried about such a prospect which would open a Pandora's Box of minority, borders and economic quarrels.[25]

Western governments made clear that they would "not interfere," that is, not support the rebels.[26] They thus let the Republican Guard, the Iraqi elite troops, turn their wrath against the insurgents. In the early days of the revolt, the Allies shot down two Iraqi planes over Kurdistan. However, a few days later, the US declared that Iraqi helicopters were not included in the terms of the no-fly zone.[27] Despite acknowledging the use of helicopters to terrorise and uproot populations,[28] the US and their allies upheld their position not to interfere in the internal matters of Iraq. This attitude led most commentators to think that the allies deliberately left Saddam Hussein to crush the revolts.[29] Clearly, protection was not on the international agenda.

Likewise, the protection of Bosnian IDPs was ignored during the first months of the Bosnian war. Early April 1992, Bosnian Serb paramilitary and the JNA orchestrated a violent campaign of ethnic cleansing in northern and eastern Bosnia.[30] Hundreds of thousands of people were thrown on the roads, moving from countryside to towns and towards Croatia. The international community reacted cautiously, not to say slowly. According to Malcolm, "In early May the [UN] Secretary-General Boutros-Ghali ruled out the use of UN peace-keeping forces in Bosnia and, on 16th May most of the UN force already in Sarajevo was withdrawn."[31] Late May 1992 sanctions, excluding oil, were voted against Serbia and Montenegro despite French and Greek oppositions.[32] On 8 June 1992, UNSC voted the establishment of an airlift to Sarajevo.[33]

From April to July 1992, although Western governments kept discussing the Bosnian war, little was said about IDPs.[34] The co-ordination of humanitarian aid was left to the ICRC and the UNHCR.[35] Despite Ogata's dramatic appeal of late April 1992,[36] and Croat complaints about incoming waves of refugees, the only diplomatic event bearing potential consequences for IDPs was an Austrian-sponsored refugee conference. However, most participants limited themselves to offering financial aid and material expertise to the Croat government to enable it to accommodate Bosnian refugees.

Whereas the potential for violence in Bosnia and northern Iraq was recognised, the Rwandan genocide seemed to take the world's most powerful governments by surprise. It was organised by a faction of extremists unwilling to lose or share power. It started as the presidential plane was shot down above Kigali, killing the presidents of Rwanda and Burundi, both Hutu. At once, extremist Hutus and their militias - the Interahamwe - started a systematic killing of all members of the opposition, Hutu and Tutsi alike, in Kigali. Massacres were rapidly extended to the countryside through an efficient administrative chain of command. Within hours of President Habyarimana's death, people's identity cards were checked at roadblocks, Tutsis and political opponents of the extremists were immediately killed. Massacres took on gruesome dimensions as desperate civilians took refuge in communal buildings, schools, churches, hospitals, searching for security in numbers. A detailed account of the genocide is provided by African Rights.[37]

In April 1994, as the Rwandan genocide started, the international community considered protecting only its expatriate community. After the murder of ten Belgian soldiers and the Rwandan Prime Minister whom they were to protect,[38] the French and Belgian governments organised the evacuation of Westerners from Kigali.[39] Two weeks after the beginning of the massacres, a UNSC resolution drastically reduced the number of UNAMIR soldiers in Kigali and changed their mandate.[40] UN troops were to "act as an intermediary ... assist the resumption of humanitarian relief operations to the extent feasible and monitor the development in Rwanda, including the safety and security of civilians who sought refuge with UNAMIR."[41] Although the resolution acknowledged increasing displacements as people were trying to flee killers as well as the resumed civil war, this was not acted upon. To be fair to UNAMIR troops left in Kigali, they did protect civilians who had gathered early enough in the Hôtel des Milles Collines, the Faisal Hospital or the stadium. The ICRC and few MSF doctors, working in Rwanda throughout the crisis, denounced the withdrawal of peace-keepers as irresponsible.[42]

To summarise, as three tense situations turned dramatic, UNSC members chose to disregard both the humanitarian and migratory dramas unfolding. Non-action prevailed, except for the establishment of an airlift to Sarajevo which could not affect the bulk of displaced Bosnians. International action remained limited to declarations or confirmations of arms embargoes (Bosnia, Rwanda), sanctions (Serbia, Iraq) and provision of funds for refugees (Bosnia). International NGOs (ICRC, MSF) warned against humanitarian catastrophes and progressively planned for them. Only the ICRC was constantly present in Rwanda, northern Iraq and Bosnia, although it withdrew from Sarajevo after the death of its field director, François Maurice, on 22 May 1992. MSF was both in Iraq and Bosnia. Despite being caught noticeably unprepared, UNHCR worked in Bosnia from the onset of the crisis on the basis of its humanitarian mandate. In fact, in the first weeks (Iraq) or months (Bosnia, Rwanda) of the conflict dealing with IDPs remained a task left to humanitarian agencies (ICRC, MSF) plus, in the case of Bosnia, the UNHCR.

Declining Involvement: Reflections

Whereas UNSC and Western governments were engaged in peace processes or war-making, they dealt only marginally with displaced persons. Although forced displacement was intrinsic to conflict resolution, it was largely left to humanitarian agencies. As violence and subsequent displacements re-surfaced, the international community stood by or withdrew. The pace of events, lack of information or lack of understanding are often presented as reasons for the international community apathy.

Governments claimed that events happened too quickly. It is undeniable that within a week, Kurdish rebels went from claiming to have conquered Kirkuk to fleeing *en masse*. In Rwanda, killings spread very rapidly and thousands of people instantly fled the front line areas, before the RPF. Yet such an argument cannot withstand the fact that, in response to previous warnings and reports on forced migrations, the international community decided not to act. At various stages in the crises, Western leaders made clear that they were not interested. Even in Bosnia, abuses and forced displacement lasted for months with little more than diplomatic rhetoric as a response.

Can the international community claim it did not know? Never had a war been more broadcast than the Gulf War and its aftermath. The Kurdish revolt was followed closely by state and media analysts and, although rumours were rife, a fairly accurate description of the situation was provided day by day. By mid-March, news media reported appeals and warning by Kurdish leaders, the Iranian government and later MSF.[43] By the end of March, newspapers were filled with Kurdish refugees' testimonies retracing terror, the use of helicopter gunships, and warnings of mass uprooting owing to fears of the use of gas. In Bosnia, news focused first on Sarajevo, the 6 April demonstration, the barricades, the shelling, the Serbian attempt to split the town and to isolate the Bosnian president.[44] However, events east of Sarajevo, in particular the attacks on Zvornick and Bijeljina were reported to international authorities. Returning from Belgrade, Jose Maria Mendiluce, a UNHCR senior officer, witnessed the attack on Zvornick.

> I could see trucks full of dead bodies. I could see militiamen taking more corpses of children, women and old people from their houses and putting them on trucks. I saw at least four or five trucks full of corpses. When I arrived the cleansing had been done. There were no people, no one on the streets. It was all finished, they were looting, cleaning up the city after the massacre. I was convinced they were going to kill me.[45]

Mendiluce also met thousands of people from Zvornick begging for his protection. Both Mendiluce and the Serbian extremist Seselj were explicit that the JNA itself attacked the town.[46] As already mentioned, on 30 April 1992, the UNHCR made public a refugee estimate in order to obtain some funds. In the course of May, international newspapers were filled with articles recounting the ordeal of refugees interviewed on the Dalmatian coast. UNSC resolution 752 of 15 May 1992 denounced ethnic cleansing practices as well as the activities of the JNA and paramilitary gangs on Bosnian territory.[47] In addition, there was evidence that internal UN reports on the Bosnian Serbs detention camps had already circulated amongst UN agencies.[48] Malcolm convincingly argues that the UN had largely enough information available to be in no doubt about the nature of the war.[49]

In Rwanda, there was ample evidence of planned genocide. The existence of "Network Zero," an extremist militia, was made public as early as March 1992.[50] In March 1993, an International Commission on Human Rights composed of several experts denounced numerous extra-judicial killings and the government's open support for militias.[51] In August of the same year, the Commission's findings were confirmed by the UN special rapporteur on extra-judicial, summary and arbitrary executions for the UN Commission on Human Rights who also expressed further fears for the Tutsi community.[52] In March 1994 UNAMIR complained that it could not stop weapons from being openly distributed to the population.[53] UNSC resolutions 893, of 6 January 1994, and 909, of 5 April 1994, both record the deterioration of the situation in Rwanda because of increased violence and non-compliance with the Arusha timetable for government sharing. UNHCR also warned against a blood bath.[54] During the first weeks of the genocide, although journalists focused on massacres, ICRC and MSF records of population displacement were also reported.[55] The ICRC president denounced the "irresponsibility" of the international community's withdrawal[56] and complained that nobody paid attention to the lack of food which was a major cause of internal displacement. Although attention turned towards Ngara (Tanzania) during the first cross border exodus, the establishment of camps and traditional refugee policy that ensued did not attract as much interest as the events within Rwanda. Throughout May, massacres in churches or the battle for Kigali occupied the headlines. In fact, little was said about internal displacement in Rwanda.

Indeed, public information on forced migrants was available in Iraq and Bosnia, far less in Rwanda. The possibility that decision-makers witnessed events without understanding them must be considered. In Iraq, no one doubted the dangers threatening Kurdish populations. Western governments repeatedly acknowledged the use of warplanes, even warned Saddam Hussein against the use of chemical weapons.[57] A foretaste of the Kurdish exodus was given in mid-March when tens of thousands of Shi'a's

55

fled a merciless repression in the area of Bassorah. Diplomatic statements presented repression as the origin of flights. Hence the danger fled by Kurdish refugees was real in the sense that Western institutions acknowledged it as such. In Bosnia, but above all in Rwanda, it was often argued that, although Western journalists, diplomats and governments witnessed the violence against civilians, they did not grasp the extent to which these exactions were planned. In other words, although they saw, they misunderstood. Many newspapers indeed portrayed the outbreak of violence as a spontaneous, uncontrollable resurgence of long lasting ethnic hatreds.[58] Despite evidence that the violence was one-sided, prepared and purposeful, international mediators kept referring to "factions" turning against one another.[59]

In Bosnia however, the international community displayed early signs of understanding. As already mentioned UNSC resolutions denounced Serbian attempts at ethnic recomposition, displaying awareness and fear of a Croat re-play. Although the role of the JNA may have been unclear in the very early days of the fighting,[60] by late April, E.C. ministers asked Serbia to withdraw its army from Bosnia.[61] On 11 and 12 May 1992, US and European countries symbolically withdrew their representation from Belgrade showing where responsibility lay in their eyes. In August 1992, George Kenney resigned from the US State Department, denouncing the hypocrisy of the US government which, according to him, used rhetoric on ethnic wars in order to avoid facing evidence of planned massacres.[62]

The UN special envoy in Rwanda seemed to understand neither the killings nor the civil war. Mr. Booh-Booh insisted on negotiating cease-fires whereas the RPF made clear it would not talk to the interim government that was established a few days after the assassination of President Habyarimana and contained only hard-liners.[63] On 20 April, Boutros-Ghali described the killings as spontaneous and presented the interim government as legitimate, showing little grasp of the events. However, the report also stated that a mass reinforcement of UNAMIR could stop the killings.[64] Although this option was supported by the UN Commander in Kigali, the UNSC refused it. Despite the fact that leading analysts and NGOs denounced the organised character of the killings from May onward,[65] Western governments' understanding of the nature of events is difficult to assess. Still, their denial that genocide was taking place lasted long after serious evidence regarding the nature of the killings was gathered by NGOs and the ICRC. This prolonged official confusion leaves much room to question when exactly governments were aware of the gravity of the situation.[66]

To sum up, in Bosnia, diplomatic acknowledgment of the wrongdoings of one side suggests that UNSC members understood, if only partly, the events. The Rwandan case is less clear. In both cases however, governments reluctant to interfere were keen on confusing the issues and keeping their populations in the dark as to what was happening in order to avoid pressure to act. Indeed, Western governments merely refused to react. As a result, most Kurdish, Bosnian and Rwandan civilians, whether displaced or not, met with indifference. Abandoned by Belgian soldiers nearby whom he sought protection, Jean-Paul, an inhabitant from Kigali, asked:

> We were there, they were there and could see what was happening in Rwanda ... But the UN protects no-one. They had been sent to Kigali to assure the security of Kigali. What about the people of Kigali? How can they protect the security of Kigali when they are doing nothing to protect its people?[67]

From Impassivity to Action

Bearing in mind the initial disregard for people on the move, the rise of concern and action on their behalf needs investigating. This section clarifies correlations between refugee pressure and international protection for IDPs. Three points are made. First, debates on the protection of IDPs appeared in the wake of refugee crises. Second, IDPs' safety was sponsored by protagonists with a vested interest in avoiding refugee outflow. Third, IDPs' backers often simultaneously tried to prevent their escape. Thus, the section closes by suggesting that international protection for IDPs may have been a response to refugee outflow. The immediate problem raised by such reading is examined and ways to explore the matter further are suggested.

Care Followed Refugee Crises

The protection of displaced persons in northern Iraq was debated first on 5 April 1991 after around one million Iraqi Kurds had crossed the Iranian and Turkish borders.[68] Serious discussions on the fate of Bosnian displaced persons took place during a conference on humanitarian aid organised by UNHCR in late July 1992 after more than 500,000 Bosnians had fled towards

Croatia, Serbia, Austria and Hungary. Third, UN circles considered displacement within Rwanda only after some 250,000 people had crossed the Rusomo river towards Tanzania within a week-end. Hence IDPs were of no interest to the international community until masses reached borders.

These coincidences are not limited to the initial involvement of the international community. As conflicts developed, initiatives to increase IDPs' safety often surfaced during or following debates on refugee issues. In Bosnia, safe areas were discussed first in July 1992 as Slovenia proposed a plan to solve the refugee crisis.[69] Dropped from the international agenda, the idea re-surfaced in October, at the initiative of the ICRC. The Swiss institution was unable to close Bosnian detention camps for lack of host countries to admit ex-prisoners. It thus asked the international community to organise "safe areas" for Bosnians.[70] The call echoed appeals by the UN Human Rights commissioner for the Former Yugoslavia Tadeusz Mazowiecki, to welcome expelled persons and create safe areas in Bosnia.[71] Both petitions also followed the fall of Jajce in central Bosnia leaving thousands of Bosnians stranded on a closed Croat border.[72] Discussed in a UN debate, a "safe haven" proposal was watered down and left to the UN Secretary-General to study.[73] The UNHCR was largely opposed to the idea on the grounds that safe areas set up without agreement of the parties would be very difficult to sustain and might indeed encourage ethnic cleansing.[74] The UNSC members favoured increased humanitarian action. Three months later however, as UNHCR planned the evacuation of Srebrenica, the town was declared a safe area.[75] Indeed in Bosnia, the option "safe area" always rose as a potential response to mass flights or evacuation dilemmas.

However, even in the confines of these three cases, not all refugee movements led to the design of protection policies for IDPs. No safe areas were established along the Iran-Iraq border or in eastern Rwanda. Whereas all IDP protection debates are preceded by refugee outflows, not all exoduses lead to debates on forced migrants' safety. This suggests that refugee movements alone are necessary yet insufficient to engender action for IDPs.

One must also search for situations in which protection emerged independently from refugee dilemmas. Srebrenica might be a case in point. In spring 1993, planned evacuations from the besieged pocket were intended towards Tuzla, in northern Bosnia. Hence, no cross-border population movement was on the agenda. In addition, because of high media pressure, most observers saw the safe area announcement as a public gesture intended to appease international outrage. However, studies of the declaration show that for diverse reasons the Bosnian government, UNHCR, UNPROFOR and mediators favoured keeping the population within the city. Vance and Owen, in their attempt to negotiate their plan with Bosnian Serbs, had strong incentives to preserve Srebrenica as a "Muslim canton." The fall of the town would have meant the end of the plan. UNHCR also expressed concern about the fate of male inhabitants of Srebrenica if women and children were to be evacuated.[76] Indeed, safe area building in Srebrenica is not a simple case of media induced pressure. There were strong political incentives for not giving up the town at that stage and this implied limiting evacuations.

"Bad Neighbors, Bad Neighborhoods"[77]

For Myron Weiner, the bad neighbours are refugee-producing countries. A neighbourhood however is made of at least two parties and is thus the product of refugee-receiving as well as refugee-sending states. In the crises reviewed, neighbouring countries all became involved, yet adopted widely different strategies. On 2 April, Turkey and Iran asked for an extraordinary UNSC meeting about northern Iraq. Both governments emphasised the human suffering and their powerlessness to protect people because of the scope of the catastrophe.[78] Yet, from the onset of the crisis, Turkey also highlighted the necessity to stop the exodus. In an address to the UNSC, its delegate drew a stark picture:

> In the chaotic conditions prevailing in northern Iraq, it is conceivable that a million people might be forced to move from that country to Turkey. No country can cope with such a massive influx of destitute people fleeing for their lives. Turkey will not allow its border provinces to be overwhelmed by such a flood of displaced persons.[79]

Turkey made it explicit that its policy was dictated by refugee pressure. The exaggerated figure, the Turkish government itself estimated the number of refugees at around 200,000 at the time, shows the play on fear of mass displacement that took place in UN circles. However successful Turgut Ozal was in framing the issue as a threat to security, after resolution 688 was voted, he proposed and campaigned for a "safe haven."[80] Whereas humanitarian agencies insisted on protecting fleeing civilians wherever they stopped,[81] Turkey was adamant that security should be established within Iraq. Its NATO partners took various positions: John Major, after trying to convince Turkey to open the border[82]

59

became himself an advocate of the safe haven concept which he presented to his European colleagues on 8 April 1991. Major suggested "the establishment of a safe haven in northern Iraq under UN control where refugees, particularly Kurds, would be safe from attacks and able to receive relief supplies in a regular and ordered way."[83] During the same press conference, Major went on: "What we are seeking to do is to provide protection for Kurdish people and other refugees from the treatment that they have faced in the last few weeks."[84] Much campaigning however was necessary to convince the US that the operation was both necessary and feasible. Even after James Baker's visit to the Iraqi-Turkish border, on April 7, the US remained reluctant to get involved. As late as 13 April 1991, George Bush is quoted saying: "I do not want one single soldier or airman shoved into a civil war that's been going on for ages."[85]

In the first months of the Bosnian war, the international community's attention was focused on Sarajevo. Nagging their European partners for help with refugees, Croat and Austrian governments called for a UN intervention in July 1992.[86] Similarly to Turgut Ozal, President Tudjman made clear that he called for action to stop the abuses triggering the exodus.[87] The appeal was ignored by UNSC members and deemed non-realistic by diplomats.[88] Throughout 1992, the government of Austria, itself a major refugee recipient, was a prominent force on behalf of Bosnian displaced persons. Austria supported the creation of safe areas discussed in the UNSC in November 1992.[89] Its foreign minister also toured European capitals to defend the project.[90] The Austrian government publicly expressed concerns regarding the prospect of a "permanent" refugee population.[91] Finally, UNHCR itself in charge of displaced persons and in needs of funds was keen to debate forced displacement. In late July 1992, it organised a one-day debate on humanitarian action which shall be examined later in the chapter.

The protection of Rwandan IDPs surfaced as 250,000 refugees flooded the Tanzanian region of Ngara (29 April-2 May 1994). In his 30 April statement, Boutros-Ghali expressed concerns about displacement within and outside Rwanda, called for the protection of displaced person and stressed "the importance of ensuring that the situation in Rwanda does not affect adversely the security and stability of neighbouring countries."[92] From that time onwards, UN officials became instigators of action on behalf of Rwandans on the move. In the course of May, African states appeared keen on acting. Lacking financial means, they offered troops to become UN peace keepers. UNSC permanent members in contrast dragged their feet in all the debates and postponed providing financial and material backing for UNAMIR II.[93]

In short, neighbouring countries facing refugee outflow and/or refugee organisations, the UNHCR and the ICRC in particular, supported action on behalf of displaced persons. By contrast, Western states, especially the US, were slow in picking up the issue. Second, neighbouring countries clearly related their interests for IDPs to the on-going refugee crises. Third, a common argument used to try and involve reluctant UNSC members into intervention was that of "threat to peace and security in the region." In fact, not only did the "champions of protection" for displaced persons had vested interests in avoiding refugee flows but they explicitly linked internal protection to pre-empting refugee outflow and organising repatriation. Not all neighbouring states pushed for action on behalf of IDPs though. But before we study the positions of Iran or Tanzania, we shall examine how refugee-fearing countries promoted protection verbally as well as wishes to contain.

Closed Versus Open Borders

Turkey shut its borders to Kurdish refugees early April 1991. Despite numerous reports highlighting disastrous humanitarian conditions in the mountains, Turkey remained inflexible concerning its frontier while campaigning for the establishment of a "protected zone" in the Iraqi valley.[94] Clearly, containment had priority over safety and consequently Turkey largely contributed to the creation of a nightmare of a neighbourhood.

Simultaneously with, or sometimes prior to calling for international action, Bosnia's neighbours raised barriers to forestall incoming exoduses. In May 1992, the German government re-introduced visa requirements for Bosnians, in an attempt to limit access to the German territory.[95] It then officially closed its border after failing to convince its European partners to share its burden under "refugee quota policies." [96] Although it supported the quota principle, Sweden also refused newcomers after June 1992.[97] From late June onwards, Hungary refused entry to refugees deported by Serbian authorities.[98] Whilst making an appeal for intervention in Bosnia, President Tudjman also announced that Croatia would no longer welcome Bosnian refugees.[99] Instead, Croatia offered to be a transit station for Bosnian refugees to be re-settled in third countries. This closed border policy was progressively implemented in the summer and autumn of 1992. Thousands of male Bosnian refugees were sent back to Bosnia.[100]

Slovenia, also very active in devising refugee policies, announced its border closure during the course of August 1992.[101] On grounds of national security, Greece rebuffed all asylum seekers from Former Yugoslavia although it offered places for medical evacuations from Sarajevo.[102] Italy kept most refugees in camps at the Slovenian border.[103] Responding to and shaping the above positions, UNHCR set out to design a preventive protection policy to which we shall return. By July 1993, Amnesty International commented: "Most European governments had imposed visa requirements on people from former Yugoslavia, including nationals of Bosnia-Herzegovina which, in practice, make it extremely difficult for most Bosnian Muslim refugees to leave Croatia for other European countries."[104] Since no country answered the Croat request,[105] Bosnian borders were increasingly tightened during the summer 1992.[106]

After the first Rwandan exodus to Tanzania, humanitarian agencies warned and prepared against further mass displacement. While Boutros-Ghali tried to re-activate UNAMIR in New York, both the WFP and the ICRC organised food convoys to be sent to people on the move. There is little doubt that the ICRC sought to meet the needs of IDPs wherever they were.[107] The food however, was also to act as a barrier in the hope that people would settle rather than flee to Zaire.[108] The UNHCR also participated in cross-border relief supplies. Again, institutions appealing for international intervention on behalf of civilians involved themselves in devising policies averting cross-border exoduses.

The contradiction of calling for action on behalf of people to whom one refuses the basics of asylum requires more work. However, before doing so, we must outline the positions of potential "good neighbours," countries which did not obstruct refugee entry, namely Iran and Tanzania.

Both the Iranian population and the government mobilised immense resources to meet the needs of the one million refugees that crossed the border. The international aid received by Iran was but a drop in the ocean in comparison with the provision met by local and national organisations.[109] The Iranian government's response was remarkable in humanitarian terms, especially compared with the deadlock created at the Turkish border. Similarly, Tanzania was congratulated by Ogata for its generosity towards Rwandan refugees.[110] Such an openness directly challenges the hypothesis. Two potential reasons may explain open borders: neighbouring states may have genuinely chosen to accept the refugees or they may have been unable to stop the inflow.

For John Fawcett, IRC director for Iraq in Spring 1991, both the Iranian and Turkish governments knew that their borders were ill-defined, and that refugees came and usually returned.[111]   Hence the relaxed position of Iran and its early support for the repatriation programme. In late April, the Iranian government emphasised:

> the magnitude of the disaster requires immediate action by the UN without further delay both in order to address the basic needs of the refugees and also to arrange for their repatriation.[112]

In fact, despite their claims to have always kept the border opened,[113] Iranian authorities tried to close it. As refugee numbers increased dramatically, the government decided to close its border "temporarily" on 7 April 1991 but reversed the decision the following day.[114] These moves may indicate a technical problem at the border. Alternatively Iran may have tried to close its border but gave up because of the sheer pressure of people forcing their way in. In those hectic days, journalists claimed that the line of cars waiting on the Piranshar road to enter Iran was 70 km long.[115] Moreover, the Iranian border is much longer and more difficult to patrol than the Turkish one. The Iranian call for repatriation quoted above was addressed to the UNSC just after the short-lived attempt to close the border.

Tanzania's position may have been similar to that of Iran, given that African understandings of refugees are more flexible than the 1951 convention definition. Tanzania however forced mass repatriation in 1996. It is therefore possible that it "welcomed" refugees out of sheer weakness and inability to control borders and did not plan or want them to settle. None of the African states surrounding Rwanda had the military means to stop people from coming through. The first exodus towards Ngara was at such short notice that Tanzania did not try to close its borders but instead appealed for international aid. Zaire hardly tried to control the inflow towards Goma. Yet in August, it did try to close its border to forestall an exodus following the withdrawal of French troops. Burundi did announce that its borders were closed in July 1994 but seemed to have little means of control. Burundi received some Rwandans but it was shielded partly by Zone Turquoise, partly by Hutu refugees' legitimate terror of Burundi's heavy handed Tutsi military regime. Although there are grounds to suggest that, at least in the case of Iran and Tanzania, borders could not be closed to refugees, time and space do not allow one to explore this claim thoroughly. Still, whether temporary asylum was granted by or forcefully taken from the above states, their emphasis on repatriation makes clear their wish not to keep the refugees.

The author is aware that she has outlined only potential causes of open-border policies. However, in doing so, the importance of repatriation and the fact that open state concerns for civilian protection are enshrined in discussions on returns emerged. This in fact strengthens the hypothesis. First, it confirms open states' concerns about refugees, suggesting that the neighbouring countries policies vary in means rather than ends. Second, the fact that states keeping open borders are less concerned with initial debates on IDPs' safety suggests a connection between taking a stand on containment and promoting IDPs safety. The Iranian government, for instance, entered the debate on safe havens later than Turkey. In addition, its main contribution to it was that safe areas should be run by the UN not the US.[116] This may enlighten a problem previously raised, namely that the existence of refugee movement alone does not necessarily promote IDPs' protection. An active containment policy may be necessary. Consider for instance the flight of Iraqi Kurds towards the Iranian border in the Autumn of 1995 and that of 24,000 persons who followed the mercenary warlord Fidrec Addic into temporary exile in the Croat Serb Krajina in 1994. None of these cross-border movements promoted significant responses. Yet, neither Iran nor the Serb Republic of Krajina closed their border to the exiled. Overall, it might have been the position of the neighbouring countries regarding the exoduses which, to a great extent, determined the policy implemented.

Protection Pledges in lieu of Hospitality

Promoting international protection of people on the move occurred only after, or in the course of, refugee crises on the Iraqi/Turk, Bosnian/Croat or Rwandan/Tanzanian borders. Both in Iraq and Bosnia, the protection of IDPs was raised by neighbours of the troubled state when facing mass arrivals. In Rwanda however, it was not Tanzania but the UN Secretary-General, as well as the UNHCR and the ICRC, who rang the alarm bell. In all cases permanent members of the Security Council, the US in particular, were slow in becoming involved in Rwanda, Bosnia but also in Iraq, something which is usually overlooked. In addition, states that called for international action on behalf of IDPs, in particular Turkey, Croatia and Slovenia, did so while closing their borders. Humanitarian organisations also tried and averted outflows using food as incentive. In effect, policies of containment and protection appeared correlatively. From the perspective of the displaced persons, protection was enhanced if, and only if, they were on their way out of the country. Some states however remained open to refugees. Iran and Tanzania were involved in debates on protection while defining repatriation procedures.

Although the above coincidences make the hypothesis plausible, correlation does not necessarily imply causality. The emergence of protection for IDPs could be an aim in itself, possibly a direct response to media rather than refugee pressure. The plight of Iraqi Kurds stranded above Cukurka was main news, eclipsing the allied Gulf War victory and the "New World Order" campaign. In Rwanda, journalists only progressively discovered the genocide. In Bosnia, pictures of detention camps stirred public emotions in August 1992 and weighed on Western leaders during the London Conference. Before addressing this issue in conclusion, we shall take a closer look at diplomatic debates connected with policy design hoping to obtain further insight into the nature of the protection pledged.

International Presence, for what Purpose?

Concern for IDPs seems to appear as a response to refugee flow. Still, an enquiry into decision-making processes checked against the implementation of resolves on the ground is needed to decide on the intentions of international actors.

Diplomacy: the Quest for Stability

On 5 April 1991, UNSC members voted for resolution 688, which demanded immediate access to northern Iraq for aid agencies and which insisted that repression be stopped. International humanitarian action was justified on the ground that the "exodus threatens peace and security in the area" which led Frelick and Adelman to argue that migratory pressures grounded international reaction.[117] Resolution 688 was not passed in order to set up a safe haven. It neither mentions the term nor even suggests the idea. When they started air-drops, the US were adamant that these operations were strictly humanitarian and did not constitute a violation of Iraq sovereignty. However, neither the air-drops nor the reinforcement of the no-fly zone, announced on 10 April, defused the crisis. By mid-April, the US government spokesperson acknowledged that hundreds of persons were dying daily on the Turkish border.[118]

Whereas the US believed in the mitigation of the problem with humanitarian aid, its partners came to terms earlier with the idea of a safe haven. Beyond the plethora of declarations on the need to save,[119] the concept was depicted as a way to hold people within the Iraqi territory and a justification to repatriate those who had managed to escape. The fact that it was originally proposed by President Ozal is itself enlightening. As the first sponsor of the idea, Turkey insisted that a "protected zone" was to be temporary and that important matters were "the conditions under which these populations can return home."[120] Likewise, for the British government, the issue was ultimately that of repatriation. John Major pictured the safe haven as a two-stage process: "Get the Kurds and the other refugees down from the mountains and into the safe areas and then back home."[121] Douglas Hurd claimed that he wanted first to keep refugees alive, second to return them home.[122] For him safe havens represented "way stations" towards home. Jacques Santer presiding over the EC meeting during which the British proposal was accepted, declared to *Le Monde*: "Our policy is to prevent an exodus that would be irreversible. We do not want to let the Palestinian problem repeat itself."[123] George Bush, asked whether Kurdish refugees would remain so, answered: "I hope not. We've got enough - what looks like permanent refugees, and we are trying to do something about that in various areas."[124]

Furthermore, all governments involved shared the concerns for Iraq's sovereignty that were initially expressed by the US and the UN Secretary-General Perez de Cuellar. John Major made his position clear: "We are not dividing the country ... we are not in the business of altering the borders of Iraq."[125] Virtually every government's statement contained reassurances to Iraq.[126] A UN Memorandum of Understanding (MOU) was signed with Baghdad on 18 April 1991 allowing the establishment of camps in northern Iraq. Despite Iraqi diplomatic protests regarding the presence of foreign soldiers on its national territory, a working co-operation was quickly established.

In short, the allies wished to defuse the border crisis in ways that would neither increase refugee numbers nor dismantle Iraq. Coalition governments remained faithful to their position held throughout the Gulf War: to preserve borders. Turkey's refusal to provide asylum was hardly challenged, and it took a border deadlock to convince the US to encroach temporarily on Iraq's sovereignty "not in its principle but in its exercise" as Mitterrant indeed said.[127] Contrary to conventional wisdom,[128] this intervention was little about overriding Iraq's sovereignty for media induced humanitarian reasons. It was primarily designed to protect borders and

66

regional order. Brent Scowcroft, President Bush's national security adviser, claimed that the US responded to Turkey's anxieties rather than to any form of media pressure:

> Without Turkey factored in, with just television pictures, I don't know what our response would have been. We were very sensitive to Turkey's anxiety about allowing the Kurds to stay. That was fundamentally what motivated us.[129]

The initial reluctance of the US to interfere militarily and their emphasis on air-drops shows a divergence in policy means rather than ends. Answering a journalist's question in the press conference during which he announced the intervention, President Bush declared: "How do you talk scared people into coming down? [from the mountains] you talk to them about security."[130] Bush made clear that security (protection) was the answer to the problem, i.e. "getting those scared people down from the mountain." The emphasis was on "how." Providing security was to be a means.

As the war broke out in April 1992, the UNHCR lead agency for Former Yugoslavia extended its work to Bosnia. Anxieties about ethnic cleansing,[131] increasing difficulties in resettling refugees and the necessity to secure funds for the winter urged the institution to organise a conference on Bosnia on July 29 1992. In search of immediate and long term solutions, the UNHCR sought to offer the following approach:

> ... a comprehensive approach which serves to: i) enhance respect for human rights and humanitarian law; ii) strengthen efforts to prevent or contain displacement; iii) provide temporary refuge and material assistance for those in need of international protection; iv) initiate action to create conditions, including the socio-economic rehabilitation of affected areas, in order to encourage refugees and displaced persons to return home.[132]

UNHCR promoted two approaches towards displaced persons: preventive and temporary protections.[133] Two responses emerged. The German government suggested a quota policy whereby EU countries would temporarily accept refugees in percentage of their populations and resources.[134] The speakers for Britain and France led the charge against the idea. Both argued that refugees should be protected as close as possible to their homes to oppose ethnic cleansing and encourage early return.[135]

Thus, both states approved only of the "preventive" part of the UNHCR proposals. During the conference, France and Britain supported a Slovenian proposal to create security zones in Bosnia under the protection of international peace-keepers.[136] The Slovenian representative suggested that, in such zones ethnic cleansing should "be prevented by all means and refugees who would otherwise flood Europe could be accommodated there. This would also meet the requirement that refugees should remain as close to their homes as possible."[137] Note the difference in emphasis: remaining close to home is no longer "better" for war victims, it is simply "a requirement." In the weeks following this meeting, Sadako Ogata held discussions with the UN Secretary-General on the possibility of creating such protected zones. Indeed, Germany remained isolated, whereas preventive protection was adopted as the framework for action.

Forced displacement issues seemed less prominent during the London Conference held in the wake of the outrage caused by news on detention camps. They were nonetheless underlying many discussions as this comment by acting US Secretary of State Lawrence Eagleburger makes clear:

> We must also funnel humanitarian assistance to hundreds of thousands more who are besieged inside Bosnia, so that they do not become the next wave of refugees. It will require the opening of safe corridors to accomplish this goal.[138]

By September 1992, a comprehensive strategy designed to prevent further exodus was being set up and the approach was confirmed in a "note on international protection" submitted to the UNHCR executive committee in October 1992.[139] It involved all "people of concern" as it was feared that many civilians would be displaced shortly by hunger if not military action. Interestingly enough, UNHCR itself spoke of "preventing or containing" flights: Prevention was intended for those who had not yet moved, containment for those who had. IDPs were the latter.[140]

In Rwanda, after his first call for action, Boutros-Ghali was required to co-ordinate and improve humanitarian aid deliveries. In the following weeks, the UN General Secretary made various appeals for action. On 17 May, the UNSC met again to re-assess its position on Rwanda. The US, led by Madeleine Albright, argued against the reinforcement of UNAMIR.[141] Under pressure from others, the US finally voted UNAMIR's expansion "in principle." UNAMIR II was to be given 5,500 troops able, among other things, to "contribute to the security and protection of displaced persons, refugees and civilians at risk in Rwanda, including through the establishment and maintenance, where feasible, of secure humanitarian areas."[142] In the debate on safe areas, the US argued that blue helmets should be deployed along Rwanda's borders, although within the country, to protect refugees and act as a buffer zone.[143] By contrast, Boutros-Ghali and France wanted to intervene in Kigali itself. The former argued that displaced persons in the interior of the country outnumbered those in border areas and in neighbouring countries by a factor of five.[144] According to him, "If humanitarian efforts were concentrated on border areas, the protected sites could act like a magnet to people in need in the interior of the country and increase the number of displaced persons."[145] The idea of intervening in Kigali rather than at the borders was not only because of fierce fighting but also because the capital city, at the centre of the country, could be made an island of security and prevent or re-direct displacement.

As the international community procrastinated over involvement, France obtained UNSC clearance to intervene on its own terms, in late June 1994.[146] As hundreds of thousands of people were fleeing the advance of the RPF and between 1.5 and 2 million people were on the move, the French government presented a new safe zone project to the UNSC. In a letter to Boutros-Ghali, Jean-François Mérimée, the French ambassador to the UN, pointed out the necessity to prevent the exodus so as to avoid a humanitarian crisis and the creation of intractable refugee problems. France offered two alternatives to the Security Council: the creation of a "safe area" in the three southern districts of Rwanda, Cyangugu, Gikorongo and one third of Kibuye, or the withdrawal of French troops.[147] The safe area was immediately legalised. Whatever France's motives were, and however suspicious other members of the Security Council were, the ways in which Mérimée presented the case for Zone Turquoise and its immediate endorsement is evidence of UN anxieties about mass population movements.

In all cases, action on behalf of IDPs was not only introduced but also discussed and justified in terms of its efficiency in stopping cross-border population movements. The questions debated were technical: "How do we keep them in Iraq?" "Where do we provide security in Rwanda so as to minimise outflow?" "Where do we accommodate Bosnian displaced persons?" "Which protection measures are necessary and sufficient to prevent further exodus?" Participants did not discuss which measures would improve people's safety best but which forms of protection would forestall the outflow best. This indicates that the provision of protection was constructed to solve the refugee problem therefore upholds reading protection for IDPs as an instrument of containment policies. We shall now turn to examine the initial measures affecting IDPs.

In the Field: from Air Drops to Safety Zones

In their flight from the Iraqi Republican Guards, the first Kurds to reach Turkey met local border guards and populations who allowed them in. Quickly however, the former were replaced by the Turkish army under strict instructions to prevent the displaced persons from crossing the border. Turkish soldiers erected barriers but also entered Iraq to distribute food.[148] Since the camps were hardly accessible by road, air-drops delivered most of the aid received during the first weeks of April. A few days after the MOU was signed, American troops entered Iraq to build the camps. Whereas US authorities were keen, not to say anxious, to see international NGOs and the UN involved in the project, UNHCR was very reluctant to enter Iraq. Only in June did it take over running Zakho.[149] The US military also had to persuade people that returning to the valley was safe. An "information campaign" was set up in late April, with helicopters flying the leaders of the exiled communities to the camps so as to show them that Americans, not Iraqi, were in charge.

Despite diplomatic allusions to the creation of "corridors," the allies did not mean to allow movement of people both ways. In mid-April, Douglas Hurd opposed the idea of resettling refugees further inland in Turkey:

> Some refugees are now being admitted to places in Turkey and Iran where they can be better cared for. That is welcome, but it is not the right answer except temporarily. We should not aim to add new permanent refugee problems to the others that already disfigure the world.[150]

In fact, Operation Provide Comfort aimed at the early repatriation of the refugees and the return of the displaced persons stranded in the mountains. George Bush, when joining the consensus on the safe haven, declared himself hopeful that the concept of "way station" would convince people to leave their refuge. Camps in the safe haven were transit camps. The MOU signed with Baghdad established "routes of return."[151] Iran provided free transport and food packages for people returning until the end of May. The rest of the transport was organised by the IOM.[152] Evacuations had no part in Provide Comfort's wording.

70

Similarly in Bosnia, presence and reassurance were the key features of the international approach to forced displacement. During the summer of 1992, the UNHCR tried "boosting its moral presence and visibility around Banja Luka in the hope of stabilising the situation and stemming the systematic campaign of terror that is the usual precursor of ethnic cleansing"[153] However, deploying staff in regions conquered by the BSA was insufficient to slow the campaigns of terror. Early August, the UNHCR was forced to "evacuate" 8,000 expelled persons from Bosanski Novi. After the operation, Ogata denounced the operation as a "cynical manipulation" of the humanitarian mandate. "UNHCR was caught in a scandalous blackmail, which left us with no choice but to accept expulsion in order to prevent more killing and terrorising of people."[154] After this event, UNHCR warned against further mass displacements, because of exactions but also because of the lack of means to survive the winter.[155] In September 1992, resolution 776 expanded UNPROFOR and mandated UN peace-keepers to escort humanitarian convoys.[156] Thus technically, UNPROFOR was not in charge of the protection of civilians but dispatched to assist UNHCR. By December 1992, the Preventive Protection approach adopted in the summer had failed to curtail ethnic cleansing but achieved the containment of people on the move. According to Ogata herself:

> We have been able to protect and assist people as close to their homes as possible, either in Bosnia and Herzegovina itself or in the neighbouring countries. We are assisting over 1.7 million displaced and other affected people in Bosnia and Herzegovina, and almost 1.3 million refugees and displaced persons in the other republics of former Yugoslavia. In comparison, around 600,000 persons have found refuge in other European countries. Therefore, with the help of the countries in the region and the international community, *the refugee problem has been contained, but it has hardly been reduced, and certainly not prevented.*[157]

Despite the recognition that the number and plight of IDPs was worsening by the day, the preventive protection approach remained the framework for action in Bosnia.[158] Evacuations in particular were not encouraged. In the first months of the war, UNPROFOR troops based in Sarajevo did evacuate some wounded to Zagreb and Belgrade.[159] However, except for rare cases,[160] evacuation remained restricted to the Former Yugoslavia. In August 1992, UNHCR and Unicef issued a joint statement concerning the evacuation of children warning that well-meant attempts could "not be the most appropriate solution" and could exacerbate ethnic cleansing. The text reminded the international community that:

The primary mission of the airlift is to bring desperately needed food and relief into Sarajevo for the besieged population. Furthermore sufficient security between the city and the airport and in the airport does not exist for the use of the airlift for evacuation. In light of this security situation and in an effort to maintain the fragile airlift operation, UNPROFOR and UNHCR have delineated a policy that only those persons whose medical situation is life threatening and also cannot be treated with the facilities available in Sarajevo should be considered for evacuation by the airlift.[161]

Given that not many wounded in a life-threatening condition are fit enough for an airlift, this policy amounted to limiting evacuation to a minimum. In the autumn, UNHCR and UNPROFOR opposed evacuation from Sarajevo to prevent further ethnic cleansing.[162] Their opposition was reiterated in December 1992.[163] UNPROFOR also ignored demands by authorities under BSA attack to move displaced persons crowded in Central Bosnia.[164] In short, international organisations largely opposed evacuation.

Lawrence Eagleburger talked about opening "humanitarian corridors." Nevertheless, the corridors negotiated in Sarajevo for instance were for food delivery only.[165] The French contingent in the Autumn 1992 came closer to promoting free circulation with its commander insisting that humanitarian corridors also meant "trade corridors": "We are in Bosnia to feed the refugees [IDPs] and help local populations to set up economic network."[166] However, real circulation became increasingly difficult for Bosnians because of the war, the winter and UNPROFOR repairing only the roads necessary to deliver supplies.[167]

In Rwanda, action was hampered from the start by a stark lack of commitment and thus resources. Despite numerous appeals by Kofi Annan, then the head of the UN Department of Peace-Keeping Operations, the ICRC or MSF, Western states, especially the US, delayed providing resources for UNAMIR II.[168] Consequently UN troops were not operational before August 1994. Meanwhile, the French army rescued thousands of people, mainly Tutsi, who were in hiding or trapped in south-west Rwanda: 8,000 in Cyangugu, a couple of hundred hiding around Ruhengeri, in the rain forest of Nyumba and Bugaramsa, some groups of nuns. Their number however, was much lower than expected, not only by the French but also by the international community.[169] In addition, only a minority of the rescued were indeed evacuated. 8,000 persons in Cyangugu, for instance, were to take care of themselves. The French army claimed that its presence deterred killings.[170] Turquoise troops also distributed food amongst displaced persons. After the fall of Butare and

Kigali, France fortified its military positions around Gikorongo and renewed its appeals to cautious humanitarian agencies to work within Zone Turquoise.[171] However, until the end of July 1994, displaced persons in Rwanda, first Tutsi and then Hutus, were largely left to struggle on their own. As Vassal Adams notes, numbers will probably never be known,[172] but this remark from Nick Wilson, an Oxfam engineer in Goma, encapsulates well what happened in Rwanda. "It took me a week or two to realise that there were no old people in Mugunga refugee camp. They didn't make it."[173]

In addition, France kept emphasising its concerns for civilians' safety implying that the RPF was a threat to them.[174] Yet, there was, at the time, no evidence that the advance of the RPF was endangering civilian lives.[175] A Pan African Movement fact finding mission team visited the areas under RPF control on 5-8 June 1994 and interviewed prisoners, including Interahamwe prisoners in Gahini. They reported no mistreatment. On the contrary, many, having escaped the killings, seemed relieved to be on the "right side" of the war. In Byumba, surviving ministers of the late government gave accounts of their flight. They emphasised their "initial fears about the RPF and said that their rescue to RPF controlled area was changing their perception."[176] Care and other NGOs, working in RPF Zones throughout the crisis, reported a secure situation.[177] Both the RPF radio and international press broadcasted the killing of 13 clergymen suspected of complicity in murders in the Kabgayi seminary. Later however, Amnesty International accused the RPF of large-scale reprisals in the areas most affected by the genocide.[178] Despite the refusal of UNAMIR to endorse Amnesty's thesis, reprisals appear fairly plausible. Still, in July, there was no evidence of systematic and organised murders by the RPA. On the contrary, the Front insisted on reconciliation and, more important, had consistently invited all international organisations to visit and work in the zones under its control.[179] In particular it urged the UN to send relief workers to the part of Kigali it controlled.[180] It also welcomed all UN observers from the early days of the war - although it later became less keen on them. Indeed, by July 1994, despite acts of violence, observers agreed that the RPF stopped the massacres rather than advocated them. Accordingly, the French argument that a safe zone from the RPF was the only way to safeguard displaced and local civilians was unconvincing.[181] Further, reports show that the French did not protect all people seeking help.[182] There was daily violence in displaced persons camps. The FAR were not disarmed[183] but worked with French soldiers fortifying French positions around Gikorongo. French commanders also

73

refused to arrest people accused of leading the genocide. Radio Mille Collines itself kept broadcasting appeals to violence until late July. Indeed, the French behaviour brought little safety to displaced Hutus. Instead, it confirmed their hysterical fears of the RPF, a collective paranoia created and sustained by the authors of the genocide. Lastly, French indifference to the exodus towards Goma suggests that IDP containment was, for France, merely a way to get UN approval.

This sketch of the first measures taken on behalf of people on the move shows that the international community involved itself first through the provision of food. France provided a very limited protection for Rwandan genocide victims and food for IDPs. In Bosnia, the UNPROFOR mission was undertaken to pre-empt further displacement by ensuring efficient relief deliveries. Frelick argues that "humanitarian assistance" (i.e. the delivery of aid) was not only justified in terms of forestalling refugee outflow but also considered to be enough to achieve this aim.[184] Beneath the deployment of staff and peace keepers, also lies the assumption that their presence both deters abuses and re-assures civilians against flying. This implicit message may yield difficult situations when troops are unable or unwilling to fulfil such expectations or when they leave. The implications of this aspect of preventive protection will be assessed in Chapter III. Finally, evacuations were always kept to a minimum and humanitarian corridors, when constructed, were to allow movement only one way. Escaping was never encouraged.

Finally, moves increasing IDP protection were discussed in terms of their efficiency, itself understood as stopping or reversing movements of populations. In addition, the international community focus on food distribution and its reluctance to evacuate also upholds the hypothesis. Attention to the timing of events also shows that policy building followed a pattern. International action on behalf of IDPs started with the provision of aid in all three cases. If circumstances allowed, as in Bosnia, international human rights observers were deployed. Observers and negotiators were followed in the case of Bosnia and Iraq by the establishment of no-fly zones, and, finally, safe areas. International involvement was thus incremental. Even in Iraq where the whole crisis took place in less than a month, the steps are clearly delineated. In Bosnia, interestingly enough, this pattern of involvement exists not only for the country as a whole but also for Srebrenica as a town. Under siege, the city was completely cut from supplies during winter 1993. A newly-elected Bill Clinton started air-drops to relieve the suffering of populations most of them displaced persons. As the situation worsened, the UN issued a reinforcement of the no-fly zone, on March 31st 1993,[185] and, two weeks later, declared the town to be a safe area. In Rwanda however, whereas UN discussions suggest a similar course of engagement, the French intervention complicates the picture. On the one hand, the establishment of a safe area was quickly implemented. On the other hand, the French military ignored the exodus to Goma showing that displacement was not their prime concern. Still, the international community committed itself step by step as early, and relatively cheap, measures reached their limits. In Rwanda, aid deliveries came only after the ICRC and UNHCR cried out that the quest for food was a crucial factor of displacement.[186] In Iraq, many Kurds tried to cross the Turkish border also in search of food, initially to buy it, then to beg for it. Air-drops were usually promoted by the US who saw them as a way around issues of intervention and sovereignty, for instance in Iraq, or to by-pass, yet not oppose, the BSA in Bosnia. Neither air-drops nor the deployment of aid workers in Bosnia reduced refugee pressure. In fact, the humanitarian living conditions of displaced persons worsened: Kurdish refugees camped and died in front of Turkish border guards. An increasing number of Bosnian civilians were thrown on the roads and it became clear that no humanitarian effort could cover the winter needs of these starving individuals. In Rwanda, food aid was far from sufficient and powerless to stop the uprooting of Hutu civilians under total control of authorities determined to terrify the population into exile. In all cases, the response to failure of initial plans was to step up protection activities yet maintain the same approach. In the UNHCR' words "bring safety to people rather than people to safety." This incremental construction of IDP policies resembles a trial and error strategy starting with aid policies and providing more extensive forms of protection when cheaper ones fail. This not only suggests that the international community consistently underestimated efforts needed to contain people, but it also confirms that protection is provided in proportion to the estimated urgency, the refugee pressure and the will not to open borders.

Unraveling the Threads: Why Protection was Promised

Bringing Crowds to a Standstill

Prior to refugee crises and despite evidence that international authorities knew about internal displacement and about some of the suffering associated with it, no policies for displaced persons were considered. This is taken as evidence that the protection of civilians in itself was not the aim of international action. Second, institutions affected by refugee flow, neighbouring countries or UN institutions, played an instrumental role in bringing to the fore the issue of displacement, sometimes while trying to contain IDPs within the confines of their home states by force and/or persuasion. Third, international actions were partly justified by their sponsors as a means of halting the exodus. Fourth, they were discussed primarily in terms of their efficiency in doing so. In addition, the first measures taken on the ground confirm that the international community tried primarily to defuse border crises. Since the rhetorical emphasis on care and suffering is contradicted by the indifference displayed in the early days of the crises, containment remains as the main objective spelt out for the international community's action. The study indicates not only that protective measures emerged as responses to refugee crises but also that stepping-up protection was considered an efficient mean to anticipate or reverse refugee outflow.

Although many of the points outlined above will not be new to area specialists, some details from primary sources are revealing. For instance, attention to the speeches of President Bush on northern Iraq, of European leaders regarding Bosnia or of Boutros-Ghali concerning Rwanda, brought to light the fact that Western leaders clearly spelt out their desire to contain forced displacement. Linked to this is the fact that, in all three cases, protection measures were discussed in terms of their migration potential. These points are very rarely acknowledged. More often, journalists and academics placed the emphasis on the humanitarian rhetoric only, and then taxed Western institutions with hypocrisy or failing to achieve their aims for lack of will. Indeed, the above discussion shows the necessity to pay attention to initial objectives. Comparisons across cases are also rarely attempted and yet yield interesting findings. Contemplate the fact that, both in Iraq and Bosnia, safe areas issues were raised by neighbouring refugee-receiver countries and that most institutions championing IDP safety sought at the same time to contain displacement. Similarities between the Iraqi case and subsequent interventions in the 1990s are usually overlooked. Action in Iraq is often presented in a different light from that in Bosnia and Rwanda. Whereas international procrastination in the latter two cases is widely acknowledged, Operation Provide Comfort is still perceived as a timely pro-active, humanitarian minded intervention that raised hopes for an increased international engagement in favour of the defence of human rights in the 1990s. Hopes that were later disappointed.[187] By contrast, the author argued that, even in Iraq, protection declarations and sometimes actions were stepped up incrementally as previous measures failed to forestall the exodus crisis. This, as part of the overall proposition that protection for IDPs should be understood as a tool of containment, could be rightly challenged on the ground that the potential direct influence of news media has not been considered. Before coming to this point, the author must re-state why her approach differs from most writers on IDPs.

As argued in Chapter I, IDP policies are not examined as part of humanitarian or security studies. The author chose to focus on IDP policies as such because the topic is under-researched. Moreover, in the context of IDP policies, she works on the links between containment and protection objectives, an issue very rarely tackled. Thus focus on the diplomatic processes signalling the passage from indifference to action is to yield suggestions regarding policy objectives and outcomes specifically for IDPs.

Consequently, the approach differs from that of Adelman, Loescher, or Drüke. For instance, it implicitly suggests that one should study actions regarding IDPs as a continuum where various measures should be understood not only in their context of emergence but also in relation to one another, to previous experiences and to alternatives. As a result, the present writer tends to differentiate between safe area construction in Srebrenica and Sarajevo whereas most studies see the Srebrenica experiment as a forerunner for the other safe areas set up in May 1993. Using different lenses can be enough, in itself, to yield different conclusions, all of which may enrich our understanding of IDP policies.

About Media-Induced Humanitarianism

Even though the study does not seek to explain humanitarian action in general but only policy affecting IDPs, one needs to address the issue underlying most approaches to international interventions: "Is protection, at least partly, due to media pressure?" The conclusion of the book deals comprehensively with this issue. The purpose of this section is to clarify why the chapter's findings already suggest that the impact of news media on IDPs policies was limited.

Proponents of media influence highlight that pressure to act increased as humanitarian catastrophes worsened or were highlighted in the news: the plight of the Kurds, the Bosnian Serbs detention camps, the Rwandan genocide. This however, fails to explain why the home country of CNN, the Western state most subject to outraged opinions, in other words the US, was always the one least amenable to interfere on behalf of IDPs. Ozal convinced Bush, not the other way round.[188] Whereas there is ground to the argument that the Sarajevo airlift was a response to the widely broadcasted shelling of the city, policies concerning Bosnian IDPs were not discussed in May or June 1992. They came on the agenda in the heat of July, usually not a prime time for audience mobilisation in Europe. More importantly, the "preventive protection" approaches were designed and settled upon before Gutman published his heart-breaking prisoners' photographs, on 2 August 1992. In Rwanda, pressure to act came from within the UN in early May. As mentioned above, at that time, journalists were busy reporting "tribal massacres" in churches. Operation Turquoise may have been partly motivated by French public opinion. It was strongly opposed from everywhere else. Nevertheless, France's strategic incentives to interfere do not allow for simple explanations. In summary, initial action concerning IDPs as responses to media pressure is a view supported neither by the timing of events nor by the enrolment of actors.

A second problem with media-based explanations for the study of IDP policies is that emphasis on the media leads to analyses that predict whether or not action takes place, but says little regarding the nature of the measures taken. In Rwanda, the outrage caused by the unfolding genocide in the course of May 1994 was irrelevant to the type of discussions held in New York. For discussions were not about stopping the genocide but about stopping the mass displacements resulting from the advance of the RPF. Likewise, French public opinion pressure does not explain why France refused to support UNAMIR II, why protection meant the establishment of Zone Turquoise, stopping the RPF's advance but not arresting the genocide leaders or disarming the militias. Although it makes sense to see UN Bosnian resolution 771 voted on 13 August 1992 as a response to international outrage on detention camps, why did UN instances respond to what they termed "life-threatening" situations by securing aid deliveries?[189] Safe areas discussed the previous week were no longer an item for discussion. In 1993, why wasn't violently besieged Mostar declared a safe area?

In addition, media-focused studies tend to assume that states are ruthless entities which protect only in front of cameras. As already mentioned, this can be misleading. Although neighbouring states and international organisations always emphasised protection, they also made plain their wishes to stop exoduses. UNHCR made clear that the aim of its action in Former Yugoslavia was to stabilise population.[190] Ogata was publicly explicit about it.[191] Presidents Ozal, Tudjman and Bush made numerous statements on the necessity to stop refugee outflow. Baker, when interviewed by Steven Livingston, said: "Once they [the Iraqi Kurdish refugees] all went into Turkey, it was important to get them back into Iraq."[192] States do not always hide their containment policies under protection foliage. Furthermore, the assumption that media presence constrains states into promoting protection is too simplistic. Turkey chose to leave thousands of people to die at its borders possibly to put pressure on the US via CNN. Similarly Croatia closed its border in the hope of internationalising the refugee issues after it failed to receive adequate support. In both cases, neighbouring countries addressed and threatened Western powers using news media. The presence of journalists might have even led to the increase of people's hardship so as to force issues on the international agenda. The Bosnian government was often torn between asking for evacuation and refusing it. Although Bosnian authorities were concerned for desperate IDPs, media proximity did offer opportunities to use people's suffering. Lastly, attention to media presence does not clarify either why, despite the continued presence of journalists, the situation of Bosnian displaced persons was arguably worse than that of Kurds in northern Iraq under Operation Provide Comfort II, that is once American troops and journalists had left.

These issues highlight the difficulties of applying studies designed to understand humanitarian intervention in general to IDPs. Thus it is necessary to conduct further, and better focused, research on the influence of the media on policies for people on the move. The hypothesis proposed can already offer perspectives on variations in shielding vulnerable displaced persons.

New Perspectives

In the policy construction described above, protection came to mean safety from hunger, sometimes from shelling, but rarely from the persecution of one's own kind. At a time when UNHCR leads committee work on "International Protection," where peace-keepers in charge of food deliveries can be called "United Nation Protection Force," we need analytical tools to make sense of the variety in international protection. "Protection qua instrument of containment policy" allows one to explore both the quality and intensity of international responses to displacement dilemmas. The above study suggests that the vulnerability of borders, the ability and/or willingness to contain the uprooted seem key criteria to grasp policies towards IDPs. The place and role of the media is not to be ignored but still to be worked out.

Frelick and Barutciski rightly argued that borders rather than people were protected in Bosnia. Borders were also created. Turkish troops had to determine where the Iraqi frontier line was, and to build barbed wire barriers in order to direct and control the populations towards the few practicable roads. Later, American authorities were keen on maintaining fictions of Iraqi sovereignty. A Baghdad official, flown to Zakho to negotiate with Kurdish rebels, was required to sign aid workers' visas so as to legalise their presence in Iraq.[193] Whereas aid workers had entered and left that country freely from the early days of the crisis onwards, it mattered to Americans taking leave of Iraq that Baghdad controlled the border crossings, if only on paper. This example illustrates what the study of borders under refugee pressure could bring to our understanding of state sovereignty. This, however, is another book.

Whereas most readings acknowledge and accept the ambiguities of interventions seeking to contain and care, the idea that the international community protected in order to contain raises interesting questions: what happens, for instance, when people's safety requires their immediate evacuation? Can the absence of protection be used as an incentive to depart? In other words, can the lack of safety be deliberately maintained, even enhanced so as to induce IDPs to leave? Would protection measures ever be increased beyond the stage at which people do not flee? These are the issues faced in the coming chapter addressing implementation policies.

Notes

1   Maass, *Love Thy Neighbour*, 4-5. The interview took place in Split, Croatia, early summer 1992.

2   Chaliand, Gérard, *The Kurdish Tragedy* (London: Zed Books Ltd, 1994). Studies by Van Bruinessen and MacDowall can be found in Kroyenbroek, Philip and Sperl, Stepan, eds., *The Kurds, A Contemporary Overview* (London: Routledge, London, 1992). See also MacDowall, *The Kurds*, A Minority Rights Group Report, published by Minority Rights Group, London, September 1991.

3   Malcolm, Noel, *Bosnia, a Short History*, 2nd edition (London: Papumac, 1996); Bennet, Christopher, *Yugoslavia's Bloody Collapse: Causes, Course and Consequences* (London: Hurst and Company, 1995); Cigar, Norman, *Genocide in Bosnia: the Policy of "Ethnic Cleansing"* (College Station (USA): Texas A&M University Press, 1995); Little, Alan and Silber, Laura, *The Death of Yugoslavia* (London: Penguin Book, 1995).

4   Lemarchand, René, *Rwanda and Burundi* (London: Pall Mall Press, 1970);

Newbury, Catharine, "Rwanda: Recent Debates Over Governance and Rural Development," in Hyden, G. and Brattan, M., eds., *Governance and Politics in Africa* (London: Lynne Rienner Publisher, 1992); Waal, Alex de, *Rwanda Death Despair Defiance*, 2nd edition (London: African Rights 1995); Prunier, Gérard, *The Rwanda Crisis, History of a Genocide, 1959-1994* (London: Hurst and Company, 1995); Franche, Dominique, *Rwanda, Généalogie d'un Génocide* (Paris, éditions des mille et une nuits, 1997); Heusch, Luc de, "Anthropologie d'un Génocide: Le Rwanda," No. 579 (December 1994), *Les Temps Modernes*, 1-19.

5   MacDowall estimates the number of displaced persons in Turkey between 1925 and 1938 to be a million. MacDowall, *The Kurds*, A Minority Rights Group Report, 17.

6   Chaliand, *The Kurdish Tragedy*, 116.

7   The Iraqi Kurdish minority represents around 25% of Iraq's population, a higher percentage than either in Turkey or Iran (respectively around 20 and 15%). Those figures however should be treated with caution since there never was a census of the Kurdish populations. Chaliand, *The Kurdish Tragedy*, 69.

8   Baghdad unilaterally attributed the status of autonomy to the region in 1974 in the middle of a war against the Kurdish Democratic Party, KDP.

9   *Background Paper on Refugees and Asylum Seekers from Iraq*, UNHCR Centre for Documentation and Research, Geneva, September 1996 (On-line: http://www.unhcr.ch/refworld/country/cdr/cdrirq2.htm, no pagination).

10   Chaliand, *The Kurdish Tragedy*, 69.

11   Foreign and Commonwealth Background Brief: *The Kurdish Problem in Iraq*, May 1992 (not official document), in Weller, ed., *Iraq and Kuwait*, 547. See also Chaliand, *The Kurdish Tragedy*, 70.

12   Chomsky, Noam, "The Middle East in the New World Order, A Post War Teach in" May 1991, Z Magazine, The Chomsky Archives (on-line: http://wwwdsp.ucd.ie/~daragh/articles/a_z_saygoes.html, no pagination). See also Campbell, David, *Politics Without Principles, Sovereignty, Ethics, and The Narratives of the Gulf War* (London: Lynne Rienner Publishers, Inc., 1993).

13   Stromseth, Jane, "Iraq's Repression of its Civilian Population: Collective Responses and Continuing Challenges," in Fisler Damrosh, Lori, ed., *Enforcing Restraint, Collective Interventions in Internal Conflicts* (New York: Council on Foreign Relations Press, 1993), 77-118, 82.

14   Gutman, Roy, *A Witness to Genocide* (London: Element Books, 1993), 3. Bennet provides a milder account of the JNA cleansing tactics which, according to him, counted few victims. Bennet, *Yugoslavia's Bloody Collapse*, 167.

15   Bosnian authorities feared for the cohesion of the republic because of the structure of its population. Figures on the pre-war Bosnian population come from a general census carried out in April 1991. The mixed republic recorded 4.354.911 persons, 43.6% Muslim, 31.1% Serb, 17.3% Croat and 5.2% Yugoslav, quoted from Bennet, *Yugoslavia's Bloody Collapse*, 180.

16   A chronological account of these events can be found in Little and Silber, *The Death of Yugoslavia*, 129-145.

17   Malcolm, *Bosnia*, 231-233. According to Gutman, Haris Silajdzic, the Bosnian foreign minister, made public his concerns as early as December 1991. Gutman, *A Witness to Genocide*, 7.

18   Accounts of Western position to the break up of Yugoslavia can be found in

Bennet, *Yugoslavia's Bloody Collapse*, 173-179. Little and Silber also discuss James Baker's visit to Yugoslavia a few days before the outbreak of the hostilities and before the E.C. decision not to recognise the declarations of independence. Little and Silber, *The Death of Yugoslavia*, 164-166.

19 Prunier, *The Rwanda Crisis*, 175.

20 Ibid., 84. See also *The United Nations and the Situation in Rwanda*, reference paper, UN Department of Public Information, April 1995, 5-6, and an interview with Philippe Gaillard, then head of ICRC Rwanda, "La saison en enfer du délégué de la Croix Rouge," *Le Monde*, 5 July 1994, 3.

21 UNSC S/RES/909 (1994), 5 April 1994.

22 Quoted in Nye, Joseph and Smith, Roger, eds., *After the Storm, Lessons from the Gulf War*, (Lanham, Maryland: The Aspen Institute, 1992), 338.

23 US President's News Conference, 16 April 1991, Weekly Compilation of Presidential Documents, Vol. 27 No. 16, in Weller, ed., *Iraq and Kuwait*, 718.

24 "Alors que les Américains parlent de 'libanisation' de l'Irak, les rebelles kurdes s'attendent à une contre-offensive imminente des forces de Bagdad, "*Le Monde*, 23 March 1991, 6; "Un peuple naufragé", *Le Monde*, 6 April 1991, 1; "'Safe haven' is not enough," *The Financial Times*, 10 April 1991, 19.

25 For national security advisor Brent Scowcroft's position see "L'obsession de Georges Bush: Réfugiés kurdes en Turquie," *Le Monde*, 16 April 1991, 1.

26 In the early days of the Shi'a revolt the US even told them that they were bound to fail, while at the same time warning Baghdad not to use chemical weapons in its internal war. Nye and Smith, eds., *After the Storm*, 344.

27 "D'après le Général Schwarzkopf, les pilotes américains ont reçu pour instruction de ne pas abattre les hélicoptères irakiens," *Le Monde*, 26 March 1991, 5; "Bien que prenant acte de l'échec de la révolte en Irak, les Etats Unis se disent prêts à rencontrer les leaders de l'opposition kurde," *Le Monde*, 3 April 1991, 3. See also Stromseth, "Iraq's Repression of its Civilian Population," in Fisler Damrosh, *Enforcing Restraint*, 105 note 32.

28 "La rébellion kurde annonce la reconquête de l'important centre pétrolier de Kirkouk 28 mars 1991," *Le Monde*, 30 March 1991, 3; "L'armée irakienne affirme avoir repris les villes kurdes de Dohouk et Irbil," *Le Monde*, 2 April 1991, 5; "Kirkuk 'retaken' in Kurd counter attack," *The Financial Times*, 30 March 1991, 2.

29 Livingston, Steven, *Clarifying the CNN Effect: An Examination of Media Effects According to Type of Military Intervention*, Research Paper R-18, June 1997, The Joan Shorenstein Center on the Press, Politics and Public Policy, Harvard University, Cambridge MA, 18 pages, 10.

30 Although Bosnian Serbs Nationalists pre-emptively declared a secession of their Serbian republic from Bosnia - December 1991 - and engaged in violence in Sarajevo following the referendum on secession - 29 February and 1 March 1992 -, full-scale war did not start before April 1992. Gutman, *A Witness to Genocide*, 12-14.

31 Malcolm, *Bosnia*, 242. See also UNSC S/RES/758 (1992), 8 June 1992. For comments regarding UN action in these early months of the conflict see Helsinki Watch (a Division of Human Rights Watch), *War Crimes in Bosnia-Hercegovina*, a Helsinki Watch report, August 1992, 145-171.

32 UNSC S/RES/757 (1992), 30 May 1992.

33   UNSC S/RES/758 (1992), 8 June 1992. See also subsequent related resolutions UNSC S/RES/761 (1992), 29 June 1992, and S/RES/ 764 (1992), 13 July 1992.

34   For news on the various European negotiations regarding Bosnia, in addition to UN debates, see "Bosnie: les Douze tentent de relancer leur politique de paix," *Le Monde*, 5 May 1992, 3; "En dépit des réticences françaises et grecques: Les douze pourraient arrêter des sanctions," *Le Monde*, 26 May 1992, 4.

35   Mercier, *Crimes without Punishment*, 52.

36   On 30 April 1992, Sadako Ogata declared that 1.2 million persons were displaced in Former Yugoslavia, a number "increasing hourly" and appealed for funds. "L'ex Yougoslavie: Plus d'un million de réfugiés," *Le Monde*, 4 May 1992, 5.

37   Waal, *Rwanda, Death, Despair, Defiance*.

38   Prunier, *The Rwanda Crisis*, 230.

39   The abandonment of civilians who had taken refuge with Belgian soldiers or tried to board planes for expatriates is retraced in Waal, *Rwanda*, 1112-1113 and Prunier, *The Rwanda Crisis*, 235.

40   UNSC S/RES/912 (1994), 21 April 1994.

41   *The UN and the Situation in Rwanda*, UNDPI, 8.

42   "Le président du CICR dénonce les responsabilités majeures de la communité internationale," *Le Monde*, 9 May 1994, 22. Except for the ICRC and MSF, all humanitarian agencies withdrew their workers in the first weeks of the genocide. See also "Rwanda: des parachutistes français prennent position sur l'aéroport de Kigali," *Le Monde*, 11 April 1994, 3; "Des dizaines de collaborateurs locaux de l'ONU et de la Croix-Rouge ont été victimes de massacres," *Le Monde*, 16 April 1994, 4. For an account of the ICRC's activities during the genocide, see ICRC, *Annual Report 1994 on Rwanda*, 30 May 1995, and ICRC, *Public Statements Issued by the ICRC on its Activities in Rwanda* - April-August 1994, 10 August 1994.

43   Bernard Kouchner, the French state secretary for humanitarian action but also a founding member of MSF, denounced inaction on 28 March 1991, "Confusion au Kurdistan Irakien. Les insurgés annoncent avoir perdu puis repris Kirkouk," *Le Monde*, 1 April 1991, 3.

44   Little and Silber, *The Death of Yugoslavia*, 245-268.

45   Quoted in Little and Silber, *The Death of Yugoslavia*, 246. Early May, Bosnian Serbs also displayed an agreement signed with Croats concerning the establishment of a corridor linking Serbs holdings in Bosnia, "La situation en Bosnie-Herzégovine; Les combats ont repris à Sarajevo," *Le Monde*, 15 May 1992, 3.

46   Little and Silber, *The Death of Yugoslavia*, 247. UNHCR was aware of the risks for displaced persons. According to Michelle Mercier, herself an ICRC member, "On April 11, Mendiluce persuaded the three presidents of the parties comprising the Bosnia-Hercegovina government coalition to sign a declaration on the 'humanitarian treatment of displaced persons' within the republic." Mercier, *Crimes without Punishment*, 51.

47   UNSC S/RES/752 (1992), 15 May 1992.

48   The first documents were gathered by Bosnian authorities. Later UN peace-keepers reports confirmed Serbian practices but were not investigated by higher UN authorities according to *Le Monde*. "Camps Serbes en Bosnie: L'ONU disposait depuis juin de rapports sur les camps." *Le Monde*, 8 August 1992, 4. See also Malcolm, *Bosnia*, 244-245. On 27 July 1992, UNHCR published details

about human rights abuses including a report on the treatment of prisoners in Omarska, UNHRC, *The State of the World's Refugees* (New York: Penguin Book, 1993), 53.

49   Malcolm, *Bosnia*, 244-245.

50   Prunier, *The Rwanda Crisis*, 168.

51   Vassal-Adams, Guy, *Rwanda: An Agenda for International Action* (Oxford: Oxfam Publication, 1994), 25.

52   Ibid., 26.

53   Prunier, *The Rwanda Crisis*, 205-206.

54   Ibid., 207.

55   ICRC, *Public Statements Issued by the ICRC on its Activities in Rwanda - April-August 1994*, 10 August 1994, in particular Public Releases of 28 April, 4 May and 20 May 1994, 10-15.

56   "Le président du CICR dénonce les responsabilités majeures de la communité internationale," *Le Monde*, 9 May 1994, 22. See also Prunier, *The Rwanda Crisis*, 273.

57   "Les Etats Unis mettent en garde Bagdad contre toute utilisation d'armes chimiques," *Le Monde*, 12 March 1991, 4.

58   Malcolm, *Bosnia*, 239; Waal, *Rwanda*, 250-251.

59   It took three months in Rwanda before genocide (i.e. organised and systematic killing of a specified part of the population) was recognised in a UN Report published on 30 June 1994. The report also denounced the role of Radio des Milles Collines and the interference of states selling weapons to the regime, "La situation au Rwanda: un rapport de l'ONU conclut à la perpétration d'un génocide," *Le Monde*, 2 July 1994, 3. As for Bosnia, coverage was often pro-Bosnian, as they suffered most. However, there was a pervasive assumption that all "factions" were similar in aims and methods and therefore that, given the weapons, the Bosnian government would act as violently as Serb and Croat nationalists. Hence the maintenance of the arms embargo throughout the war. For a deconstruction of this doctrine of moral equivalence, see Malcolm, Noel, "Bosnia and the West, A Study in Failure," Spring 1995, *The National Interest*, 3-14.

60   In particular since President Izetbegovic asked the JNA for help. Both and Honig, *Srebrenica*, 73.

61   UNSC S/RES/752 (1992) of 15 May 1992 and most subsequent resolutions in 1992 ask for the withdrawal of the JNA from Bosnia.

62   Maass, *Love Thy Neighbour*, 57-58.

63   Waal, *Rwanda*, 1120-1122.

64   UNSG S/1994/470.

65   OMAAR and Waal, *Rwanda: Who is Killing, Who is Dying, What is to be Done; a Discussion Paper*, May 1994, Refugee Studies Programme Documentation Centre, Oxford. See also NIEDRUM, Susanne (coordinator for the inter-agency information sharing effort), University of Leeds Department of Civil Engineering, *Rwanda Situation Update* (faxed summary of information compiled from information from Oxfam, MSF, Human Rights Watch, Accord, CARE and Amnesty International over the 3 and 4 May 1994), 5 May 1994. This document is listed under "Oxfam" in the bibliography.

66   US spokespersons were given orders not to use the term "genocide" and France refused to refer to genocide until well after the fall of the interim government.

Waal, *Rwanda*, 1128 and Prunier, *The Rwanda Crisis*, 275.

67   Quoted in Waal, *Rwanda*, 1115.

68   S/PV.2982, 5 April 1991, *Proceedings of the UNSC Regarding the Situation in Northern Iraq*, in Weller, ed., *Iraq and Kuwait*, 123-137.

69   Barutciski, Michael, "EU States and the Refugee Crisis in the Former Yugoslavia," Vol. 14, No. 3 (1994), *Refuge*, 32-35, 33. See also Frelick, "Preventive Protection," 443.

70   Mercier, *Crimes without Punishment*, 64-65. See also "La situation en Bosnie Herzégovine; Faute d'asile en occident, la libération de cinq mille détenus des camps a été repoussée au 3 novembre," *Le Monde*, 26 October 1992, 3; "Les détenus libérés des camps de Bosnie attendent des pays d'accueil," *Le Monde*, 28 October 1992, 4; "Le CICR appelle à la création de 'zones protégées'," *Le Monde*, 3 November 1992, 3.

71   Quoted in "La protection des convois humanitaires: L'ONU interdit aux Serbes l'espace aérien bosniaque," *Le Monde*, 12 October 1992, 1. See also interviews of Tadeusz Mazowiecki in the following articles: "Des réfugiés de l'ex-Yugoslavie 'en danger de mort'," *Le Monde*, 28 October 1992, 1; "A l'issue d'une deuxième mission dans l'ex-Yougoslavie, le Rapporteur de l'ONU M. Mazowiecki, estime que la 'purification éthnique a déjà largement atteint ses objectifs'," *Le Monde*, 30 November 1992, 3.

72   "Bosnie-Herzégovine: des réfugiés sont la cible des bombardements," *Le Monde*, 2 November 1992, 3; "L'épreuve de force à Belgrade entre M. Milosevic et M. Panic et la situation en Bosnie-Herzégovine: des réfugiés de Jajce bloqués à la frontière croate,"*Le Monde*, 4 November 1992, 3.

73   UNSC S/RES/787 (1992), 16 November 1992. For comments on these issues see "La Suisse accueille 1500 ex-prisoniers de Bosnie," *Le Monde*, 14 November 1992, 6.

74   Mercier, *Crimes without Punishment*, Appendix, Document VIIIb, 14 December 1992, "Safe areas for humanitarian assistance." (SC resolution 787), position of UNHCR, 211-213. See also *Humanitarian Issues Working Group of the International Conference on the Former Yugoslavia*, UNHCR, working document, prepared for the meeting of 4 December 1992, 30 November 1992, 3-4.

75   UNSC S/RES/816 (1993), 16 April 1993.

76   Interview with Louis Gentile, UNHCR, 11 September 1998.

77   Borrowed from Weiner, "Bad Neighbors, Bad Neighborhoods."

78   Letters from the Permanent Representative of the Islamic Republic of Iran to the United Nations: 22 March (S/22379) and 4 April (S/22447), letter from the permanent Representant of Turkey to the UN dated of 3 April 1991 (S/22435), in Weller, ed., *Iraq and Kuwait*, 604.

79   Declaration of Turkey, proceedings of the UN Security Council S/PV.2982, 5 April 1991, in Weller, ed., *Iraq and Kuwait*, 123-124.

80   S/RES/688 (1991), 5 April 1991. See also "L'exode des réfugiés aux frontières irakiennes. Washington et Ankara suggèrent la création en Irak de zones de sécurité placées sous le contrôle de l'ONU," *Le Monde*, 9 April 1991, 4; "La morale contre l'étatisme, à propos des zones de sécurité en Irak," *Le Monde*, 10 April 1991, 1.

81   Only the ICRC was working within Iraq at the time, for all institutions needed

Baghdad's approval. "Irak: Paris envoie une aide humanitaire au Kurdistan, les Français donneurs de leçons," *Le Monde*, 5 April 1991, 4.

82   Ibid., 4.

83   Statement of John Major at a press conference 8 April 1991, HMSO, in Weller, ed., *Iraq and Kuwait*, 714.

84   Ibid., 714.

85   Remark made at Maxwell Air Force Base War College in Montgomery Alabama 13 April 1991, Weekly compilation of Presidential Document 22 April 1991 Vol. 27, No 16, 433, quoted in STROMSETH, "Iraq's Repression of its Civilian Population," in Fisler Damrosh, ed., *Enforcing Restraint*, 105-106. Regarding the US reluctance to be involved, see also the above quoted work page 84 and "La marche arrière de M. Major à propos du projet de créer des zones de protection pour les réfugiés kurdes d'Irak," *Le Monde*, 11 April 1991, 3.

86   "Les combats en Bosnie-Herzégovine: Les dirigeants bosniaques, croates et slovènes réclament une intervention militaire 'rapide et énergétique' de l'ONU," *Le Monde*, 15 July 1992, 4.

87   Ibid., 4.

88   Ibid., 4.

89   Gutman, *A Witness to Genocide*, 129-130. "La Suisse accueille 1500 ex-prisoniers de Bosnie," *Le Monde*, 14 November 1991, 6.

90   Both and Honig, *Srebrenica*, 100-101.

91   "La visite du président autrichien à Paris M. Thomas Klestil plaide pour l'admission rapide de l'Autriche dans la CEE," *Le Monde*, 15 October 1992, 4.

92   *The United Nations and the Situation in Rwanda*, UNDPI, 9.

93   S/1994/728, 20 June 1994, letter dated 19 June 1994 from the Secretary-General addressed to the President of the Security Council.

94   "Ils doivent pouvoir rentrer chez eux, reportage l'exode des réfugiés kurdes irakiens," *Le Monde*, 12 April 1991, 1.

95   "Lors d'une conférence à Vienne, l'Europe tente de se mobiliser en faveur des réfugiés de Bosnie et de Croatie," *Le Monde*, 23 May 1992, 5.

96   "La Slovénie ferme ses frontières aux réfugiés de Bosnie", *Le Monde*, 24 August 1992, 4. This article also reports that Rudolph Seiter, the German interior minister, announced the border closure on 17 August 1992.

97   "La Suède est favorable à une répartition par quotas des réfugiés yougoslaves," *Le Monde*, 4 July 1992, 3.

98   "Yugoslavs try to deport 1800 Muslims to Hungary," 3 July 1992, Gutman, *A Witness to Genocide*, 20-23. See also "La Hongrie veut fermer ses frontières aux personnes expulsées de Bosnie," *Le Monde*, 11 July 1992, 3.

99   Croatia announced its border closure on 14 July, "A l'initiative du HCR, cent soixante-dix pays au chevet des réfugiés de l'ex-Yugoslavie," *Le Monde*, 29 July 1992, 3.

100   "La Croatie contraint des réfugiés musulmans à repartir pour le front," *Le Monde*, 20 August 1992, 3. According to Amnesty International, large-scale deportations of men of military age took place in September and October 1992 pursuant on an agreement between the governments of Croatia and Bosnia. EUR/48/05/93, *Bosnian Refugees: A Continuing Need for Protection in European Countries*, London, July 1993, 5.

101   "La Slovénie ferme ses frontières aux réfugiés de Bosnie," *Le Monde*, 24 August

1992, 4. According to the article, the decision was announced on 21 August.

102   UNHCR, *Report on Former Yugoslavia*, September 1993. "A l'initiative du HCR," *Le Monde*, 29 July 1992, 3.

103   Ibid., 3.

104   Amnesty International, EUR/48/05/93, *Bosnian Refugees*, 1-2.

105   Britain in particular kept deporting Bosnian asylum seekers to the countries they had travelled through under the E.C. rule of "first country of asylum" i.e. that asylum applications should be entered in the first country of refuge. "Polémique en Grande Bretagne après le refoulement de réfugiés," *Le Monde*, 14 August 1992, 4.

106   In the course of the autumn, UNHCR also interfered to oppose a local decree and prevent the eviction of unregistered Muslim displaced persons in Tomislavgrad. Along the same line, the Croat office of displaced persons cancelled the refugee status of persons from Western Hercegovina which was declared a safe place to return to. Again, UNHCR intervened and negotiated the non-expulsion of Bosnian Muslims. *Information Notes on Former Yugoslvia*, UNHCR office of the Special Envoy for Former Yugoslavia, External Relation Unit, No. 11, November 1993.

107   ICRC, *Annual Report on Rwanda 1994*, 30 May 1995.

108   "Projet Français d'intervention au Rwanda: Un Zaire providentiel et inquiet," *Le Monde*, 23 June 1994, 3.

109   United Nation Regional Humanitarian Plan of Action to the Crisis between Iraq and Kuwait, Second Update 9 April 1991, mentions that what Iran was spending to cope with the crisis was way beyond any help brought by the international community, in Weller, ed., *Iraq and Kuwait*, 611-612. See also *Mass Exodus, Iraqi Refugees in Iran*, Issue Brief, US Committee for Refugees, Washington, July 1991, 1-2.

110   "Le président du CICR dénonce les responsabilités majeures de la communité internationale," *Le Monde*, 9 May 1994, 22.

111   Interview with John Fawcett, February 1997.

112   United Nation Regional Humanitarian Plan of Action to the Crisis between Iraq and Kuwait, Second Update 9 April 1991, in Weller, ed., *Iraq and Kuwait*, 613.

113   S/22463, 8 April 1991, letter from the Permanent Representative of the Islamic Republic of Iran to the United Nations addressed to the Secretary General, in Weller, ed., *Iraq and Kuwait*, 608.

114   "Children perish on the road to Iran," *The Financial Times*, 9 April 1991, 1. See also "L'exode aux frontières de l'Irak et l'organisation des premiers secours," *Le Monde*, 9 April 1991, 3.

115   "Children perish on the road to Iran," *The Financial Times*, 9 April 1991, 1.

116   "Une 'zone de protection' est instaurée de facto dans le nord de l'Irak," *Le Monde*, 12 April 1991, 3.

117   See the already quoted article of Frelick, "Preventive Protection," and Adelman, "The Ethics of Humanitarian Intervention."

118   "La tragédie kurde, chronologie mensuelle encadrée," *Le Monde*, 14 May 1991, 24. Humanitarian organisations claimed that between 400 and 1,000 persons died daily on the border. These figures, although inflated according to John Fawcett, were nonetheless publicly referred to by US officials. Interview with John Fawcett, February 1993.

119   Proceedings of the UN Security Council S/PV.2982, 5 April 1991, in Weller, ed.,

Iraq and Kuwait, 123-137.
120   "Une 'zone de protection' est instaurée de facto dans le nord de l'Irak," *Le Monde*, 12 April 1991, 3.
121   UK F& C Office, Press Office 8 April 1991, in Weller, ed., *Iraq and Kuwait*, 715.
122   Ibid., 715.
123   "Au conseil européen de Luxembourg les Douze se mobilisent en faveur des kurdes irakiens," *Le Monde*, 10 April 1991, 4. On precluding a "Palestinian style exodus" see " 'Safe haven' is not enough," *The Financial Times*, 10 April 1991, 19, "Equal in misery- Belatedly, the West is doing something for Kurds and Palestinians. But not enough," *The Financial Times*, 11 December 1991, 19.
124   US The President's News Conference, 16 April 1991, in Weekly Compilation of Presidential Documents, Vol. 27 No 16, in Weller, ed., *Iraq and Kuwait*, 718.
125   UK F& C Office, Press Office 8 April 1991, in Weller, ed., *Iraq and Kuwait*, 715.
126   Adelman, "The Ethics of Humanitarian Intervention," 74-75.
127   François Mitterrant, author's translation, quoted in "La morale contre l'étatisme, à propos des zones de securité en Iraq," *Le Monde*, 10 April 1991, 1. On this issue, see also Adelman, "The Ethics of Humanitarian Intervention," 74-75.
128   As developed for instance by Pellicer, Olga, "Successes and Weaknesses of Recent UN Operations in the Field of International Security," Vol. 47, No. 2 (1995), *International Social Science Journal*, 305-314, 310.
129   Interview with Steven Livingston quoted in Livingston, *Clarifying the CNN Effect*, 10.
130   US The President's News Conference, 16 April 1991, in Weekly Compilation of Presidential Documents, Vol. 27 No 16, in Weller, ed., *Iraq and Kuwait*, 718.
131   See the contribution of Soren Jessen Petersen (UNHCR) in Domestici-Met, Marie-José, ed., *Aide Humanitaire Internationale: un concensus conflictuel* (Paris: Economica, 1996), 117-118.
132   UNHCR, HCR/IMFY/1992/2 24 July 1992, 2.
133   "An important objective of humanitarian action in the Former Yugoslavia has been, and should continue to be, to prevent and contain displacement, to the extent possible, by providing protection and assistance to victims of the conflict who might otherwise feel compelled to move." HCR/IMFY/1992/2 24 July 1992, 3.
134   Statement by Rudolf Seiter, German Federal Minister of the Interior, International Meeting on Humanitarian Aid for Victims of the Conflict on the Former Yugoslvia, Geneva, 29 July 1992.
135   Statements by Bernard Kouchner, France, Ministre de la Santé et de l'Action Humanitaire and by the Right Honorable the Baroness Chalker of Wallasey, Minister for Overseas Development, International Meeting on Humanitarian Aid for Victims of the Conflict on the Former Yugoslvia, Geneva, 29 July 1992.
136   Statement by Joze Pucnik, Vice-President of the Government of the Republic of Slovenia, International Meeting on Humanitarian Aid for Victims of the Conflict on the Former Yugoslvia, Geneva, 29 July 1992.
137   Ibid.
138   Quoted in Frelick, "Preventive Protection," 451.
139   Jaeger, Gilbert, "The Recent Concept and Policy of Preventive Protection," Vol. 14 (January 1994), *Refugee Participation Network*, 20-21, 20.
140   UNHCR, HCR/CRHC/FC/2, 31 August 1992, *Comprehensive Response to the Humanitarian Crisis in Former Yugoslavia*, Working Document for the Second

Meeting of the CRHC follow-up Committee, Geneva, 4 September 1992, 10 pages, 4-5.

141   Waal, *Rwanda*, 1126-1132.

142   UNSC S/RES/918 (1994), 17 May 1994. This mandate is reiterated in UNSC S/RES/925 (1994), 8 June 1994.

143   "Surmontant les réticences américaines, le conseil de sécurité de l'ONU préconise le déploiement de 5,500 'casques bleus' au Rwanda," *Le Monde*, 18 May 1994, 4.

144   At the time around one million persons were estimated to be displaced.

145   *The United Nations and the Situation in Rwanda*, UNDPI, 10.

146   UNSC S/RES/929 (1994), 22 June 1994. The resolution does not even mention France as the operation leader. Humanitarian concerns put forward by the French to justify Operation Turquoise are riddled with contradictions. By the end of June, the genocide was mostly over. France, among others, had stood by motionless: it voted the withdrawal of all UN significant forces on 22 April at the height of the killings; it ignored the opportunity to offer soldiers and logistic for the UNAMIR II Mission voted for on 17 May, a couple of weeks before Operation Turquoise. This ignored alternative alone challenges the view that the operation was mainly, or even partly, about saving lives. Moreover, as the USCR pointed out, by June 1994, the only Tutsi left in government-controlled Rwanda were in hiding. Thus the threat of an international intervention to rescue them could simply accelerate the "nettoyage" (i.e. search and kill) strategies. US Committee for Refugees, *The Rwanda Crisis Advocacy Action* Alert 2, 27 June 1994, 1.

147   S/1994/798 (6 July 1994) Jean-François Mérimée, French ambassador to the UN, letter to the UN Secretary General, dated 2 July 1994.

148   "Ils doivent pouvoir rentrer chez eux, reportage l'exode des réfugiés kurdes irakiens," *Le Monde*, 12 April 1991, 1.

149   In late April, US Command asked the IRC (International Rescue Committee) to run the camps. Interview with John Fawcett, February 1997.

150   UK House of Commons parliamentary debate, 15 April 1991, in Weller, ed., *Iraq and Kuwait*, 717.

151   "Bagdad and UN sign accord to aid Kurd refugees," *The Financial Times*, 19 April 1991, 4.

152   In Weller, ed., *Iraq and Kuwait*, 629 and 630. The IOM transported 262,000 persons from Turkey and was also in charge of repatriation from Iran.

153   *Update on Ex Yugoslavia*, UNHCR, 13 August 1992.

154   Frelick, "Preventive Protection," 447.

155   "200,000 personnes pourraient être touchées par le 'nettoyage ethnique' dans le nord de la Bosnie," *Le Monde*, 21 August 1992, 3. "Le HCR assure faire tout son possible pour enrayer l'exode en envoyant vivres et personnel sur place mais reconnaît qu'il est peut-être trop tard. La pénurie des produits de première nécéssité et les rigueurs de l'hiver pourrait avoir raison de ceux qui hésitent encore à partir."

156   UNSC S/RES/776 (1992), 14 September 1992.

157   *Statement by the United Nations High Commissioner for Refugees at the Meeting of the Humanitarian Issues Working Group of the International Conference on Former Yugoslavia*, Geneva, 4 December 1992, 5 pages, 1 (author's italics).

158   *Summing-up of the Chairman, Meeting of the Humanitarian Issues Working Group of the International Conference on the Former Yugoslavia*, 4 December

1992, 2 pages, 1.

159   "Bosnie. Les Douze tentent de relancer leur politique de paix," *Le Monde*, 5 May 1992, 3.

160   For instance when 68 severely wounded persons were evacuated to Britain by airlift. "Le HCR confirme que l'avion humanitaire italien a été abattu par un missile," *Le Monde*, 18 September 1992, 13.

161   HCR/CRHC/FC/2/Annexe I, *UNHCR/UNICEF Joint Statement on the Evacuation of Children from Former Yugoslavia*, 1.

162   Petrovic, Drazen, "International Humanitarian Aid and the Civilian Population of Sarajevo," in Bisersko, Sonja, ed., *Yugoslavia's Collapse War Crimes*, (Belgrade: Centre for Anti-war Action, 1993), 267-274, 272. A controversy over a NGO sponsored evacuation of a thousand children to be sheltered in France for the winter 92-93 developed in autumn 1992. "Elaboré par l'association Equilibre, le projet de faire venir en France un millier d'enfants bosniaques suscite une polémique." *Le Monde*, 24 October 1992, 20.

163   Humanitarian Issues Working Group of the International Conference on the Former Yugoslavia, working document, prepared for the meeting of 4 December 1992, 30 November 1992, 8 pages, 6. See also the annex entitled *Note on the Deployment of UNPROFOR and its Incidence on UNHCR Operations in Bosnia and Herzegovina*, 3 pages.

164   "La nasse bosniaque: L'étau serbe se resserre autour de Zenica qui regorge de réfugiés musulmans," *Le Monde*, 17 November 1992, 1.

165   "Pour assurer la sécurité de l'acheminement des vivres vers la capitale, l'ONU tente de mettre en place des couloirs humanitaires entre l'aéroport de Sarajevo et le centre-ville," *Le Monde*, 8 July 1992, 5.

166   "Un bataillon français en Bosnie," *Le Monde*, 30 October 1992, 1.

167   "Bosnie la bataille des routes," *Le Monde*, 18 November 1992, 3; UNHCR also complained that UNPROFOR was deployed too slowly. "La lenteur du déploiement des forces de l'ONU bloque l'acheminement des secours," *Le Monde*, 7 November 1992, 4.

168   ICRC, *Public Statements Issued by the ICRC on its Activities in Rwanda - April-August 1994*, 10 August 1994, 10-15.

169   In August, the ICRC re-evaluated the number of victims of the genocide because many people, believed to be hiding, were dead. USAID *Rwanda Report* 5-8 August 1994, 21. This can be due to the systematic "nettoyage" (cleaning) of the places from all possible survivors. Since May 1994, militias were asked by radio to check systematically every area of the country so as to extinguish the Tutsi people. *Human Rights World Report 1995* (London: Human Rights Watch, 1995), 40.

170   "Rwanda, une mission au fil du rasoir." *Le Monde*, 5 July 1994, 3.

171   Alain Juppé, French Minister for Foreign Affairs, "Point de vue: l'intervention de la France au Rwanda" in *Le Monde*, 2 July 1994, 4.

172   Vassal-Adams, *Rwanda*, 39.

173   *The Rwandan Crisis*, "Information from Oxfam" leaflet, Oxfam, Oxford, 1994.

174   S/1994/798 (6 July 1994). See also Juppé, French Minister for Foreign Affairs, "Point de vue: l'intervention de la France au Rwanda" in *Le Monde*, 2 July 1994, 4.

175   "Un jour comme les autres à Kigali," *Le Monde*, 1 July 1994, 1. This article

includes evidence of Hutus seeking refuge in RPF controlled zones.

176 *Fact Finding Mission Report*, Pan African Movement, 5-8 June 1994, 13.

177 Niedrum, *Rwanda Situation Update*, (faxed summary of information compiled from information from Oxfam, MSF, Human Rights Watch, Accord, CARE and Amnesty International over the 3 and 4 May 1994), 5 May 1994, 1, document listed under "Oxfam" in the bibliography. Wallace, Steve, Care Rwanda in Kenya, *Draft Comments on the Rwanda Disaster and Care's Response to it*, 14 June 1994, 10 pages, 1.

178 According to Amnesty International and UNHCR reports, the reprisals could have made around 30,000 victims. Economist Intelligence Unit Country Report, Uganda Rwanda Burundi, London 4th quarter 1994, 25.

179 *Circular to all NGOs, UN and International Organisations*, Republic of Rwanda, Ministry of Rehabilitation and Social Integration, Kigali, 25 July 1994. Rwandese Patriotic Front - RPF - Letter of the First Vice Chairman RPF, Patrick Mazimhaka, Mulindi, 7 May 1994, and *Rwanda Victims Humanitarian Appeal to International Community*, Patrick Mazimhaka (First Vice Chairman -RPF), Brussels, 8 May 1994, 2 pages.

180 Ibid.

181 In fact, the decision to create a zone forbidden to RPF protected members of the Interim-Government, prevented its army from being completely disbanded and gave time to organise at least a co-ordinated retreat, and possibly to prepare for a long-term resistance to the RPF. The French kept insisting on the necessity of a cease-fire between parties and on negotiations on the terms of the Arusha agreements, even when the Interim-Government had lost both credibility and war.

182 Prunier, *The Rwanda Crisis*, 293.

183 *Rwanda Update*, Report from the Jesuit Refugee Service, Fr. Mark Raper, Rome, 28 July 1994.

184 Frelick, "Preventive Protection," 451.

185 UNSC S/RES/816 (1993), 31 March 1993. A no-fly zone above Bosnia was proclaimed in the autumn of 1992 in UNSC S/RES/781 (1992), 9 October 1992 and S/RES/786 (1992), 10 November 1992. However, it was regularly violated.

186 UNHCR appeals May 1994. See also ICRC News No. 26, 29 June 1994, and No. 27, 6 July 1994, in ICRC, *Public Statements Issued by the ICRC on its Activities in Rwanda*, April-August 1994, 10 August 1994, 21-22.

187 On this issue see Barnett, Michael, "The Politics of Indifference at the United Nations and Genocide in Rwanda and Bosnia," in Cushman, Thomas and Mestrovic, Stjepan, eds., *This Time We Knew, Western Response to Genocide in Bosnia*, (New York: New York University Press, 1996), 128-162.

188 Kirisci, "Provide Comfort and Turkey," and Kirisci, Kemal, "Refugee Movements and Turkey," Vol. 29, No. 4 (1991), *International Migration Review*, 545-560, 551.

189 UNSC S/RES/771 (1992), 13 August 1992.

190 Mercier, *Crimes Without Punishment*, 51.

191 For instance in her 1992 Elberg Lecture in International Studies, *Refugees, a Multilateral Response to Humanitarian Crises*.

192 Livingston, *Clarifying the CNN Effect*, 10.

193 Interview with John Fawcett, February 1997.

3 Humanitarian Spaces without Exit

If, as argued in the previous chapter, the protection granted to people on the move is constructed so as to forestall exodus, implementing such safety promises must exhibit particular features. As a policy device, "providing protection" should be flexible, vary according to migration pressures rather than to humanitarian considerations and always be subordinated to containment objectives. Consider the following postulates:

1. "Irrelevance of need." Safety provision does not vary according to displaced populations needs.
2. "Controllability." Protection varies according to states' political and technical ability to control cross-border displacements.
3. "Containment first." Containment objectives always take priority over protection.
4. "Protection withdrawal." The international community may use threats, the refusal to provide safety or its withdrawal to preempt exoduses, to promote departures or returns.
5. "Stabilisation only." Protection never extends beyond the stage at which populations settle.

In this chapter, two salient features of action regarding IDPs, relief delivery and military protection, are assessed against the above postulates. Concluding remarks tie the threads of aid and safety policies together in a *prima facie* assessment of protection for displaced civilians. It is suggested that the range and variety of policies surveyed confirm an instrumental migration-driven use of protection.

Aid, Need and the Control of Migration Flows

What were we doing in Banja Luka? We were welcomed by the Serbs for whatever aid we could bring in. We were welcomed by the minorities for whatever protection we could give them. But were we doing enough of either? Should we be bussing people out and not bringing aid in? No.

93

There were in the region about three hundred thousand displaced and vulnerable people, a third of whom were Serbs. Aid had to come through. Should we be bringing aid and bussing people out? Definitely. What was the core problem? The abuse of minorities. How can you stop that? Appeal to the better nature of the perpetrators? They have got none. So what next? Bring in enough troops to prevent their action? Serbs will not let you, the International Community will not produce them. Take all the minorities out? To where? No one will take them.[1]

This section ponders on some of the intractable problems UNHCR veteran Larry Hollingworth had to solve: aid in war zones, early repatriations and reconstruction programmes. A short overview of the relief supplies programmes suggests that, despite a swelling number of IDPs - many of whom relied increasingly on aid - responses to increased hardship varied greatly across cases. Overall, discrepancies in aid distribution are as well understood by reference to fear of mass out-migration as by focusing on need and the media. Furthermore, aid was constructed from the start as a way to stabilise populations in specific locations and to encourage early returns. A study of early repatriation procedures makes clear the "compellence" mechanisms at work in aid distributions. Last, the author looks briefly at reconstruction in so far as it applies to IDPs. Indeed, examples of aid programmes extending beyond population stabilisation give a measure of the bounds of the hypothesis.

Relief under Strain: Blockades, Winters and Time

The Iraqi blockade of Kurdistan and that of central Bosnia by Croatia left displaced persons in precarious situations at the onset of rigorous winters. From September 1991 onwards the Iraqi government engaged in economic warfare with the areas of Kurdistan outside its control. Civil service incomes were blocked and all food supplies stopped. This, in addition to more fighting, led to increased need for humanitarian aid throughout the region, as waves of people fled anew towards Iran. The UNHCR appealed for international funds and organised a camp and aid delivery system that preempted cross-border movements. When asking for funds after fighting threw Kurdish communities on the roads for the second time in six months, UN agencies warned stingy donor states of potential "reversed movements of populations."[2] The threat of mass exodus was considered to be most effective to encourage Western generosity. Although UNHCR secured adequate funding, its shelter programme was criticised as late and not adapted to the needs of the population for reasons that shall be detailed later.

In April 1993, while the UN Security Council declared Srebrenica a safe area, the humanitarian food pipeline broke down. The WFP had warned against this disruption since January 1993.[3] Agencies slowed down already insufficient deliveries, not only because of fighting in central Bosnia, but also because of a lack of gifts.[4] However, according to the WFP, immediate media coverage of the situation led to further government pledges.[5] As war developed in the summer,[6] humanitarian agencies made provision for the expected increase of needs. They organised the pre-positioning of food stocks throughout Bosnia.[7] The project's purpose was to avoid situations in which civilians would starve following another breakdown of the flow of aid, either for lack of international funding, or because the war made deliveries impossible. Indeed, the aim of the scheme was to avoid the creation of new "Srebrenica March 1993" scenarios. Nevertheless, throughout the war, the UNHCR remained far from meeting its own targets. Tuzla airport for instance remained unused until February 1994 because of its exposure to Serbian artillery.[8] In Srebrenica itself:

> During 1994, a total of 5,858 tons were delivered by 122 convoys. This was less than the 8,916 tons of the year before and by the end of 1994 there were increasing shortages which led to growing tensions not only with the Muslims but also with the Serbs because the knock-on effect was that Muslims began to mount more raids.[9]

Although the food situation in that particular enclave improved in 1995, trends overall varied tremendously depending on places and times. By May 1995 for instance, the pocket of Bihac had been blockaded for a year with hardly any UNHCR aid allowed in.[10] It is also noteworthy that humanitarian agencies not only anticipated the needs but also gave ample warnings to donors using media relays when necessary. UNHCR convoy organisers became specialists in keeping journalists alerted about their delivering efforts so as to maintain pressure both on obstructors on the ground and governments abroad.[11] So did the ICRC.[12]

The situation in Rwanda differed markedly from the above two. Once the Rwandan population was considered stabilised in the autumn of 1994, aid dwindled. Early in 1995, deliveries of aid were drastically reduced.[13] The WFP claimed that food shortages were due to the reluctance of donor countries to provide the funds necessary for the purchase of commodities.[14] However, as humanitarian agencies appealed for help and warned that "food shortages may destabilise the camp" in Zaire,[15] they had themselves started to reduce food rations in Rwanda, in the context of Operation Retour. In agreement with the RPF's decision that people should return to their villages, agencies had decided to close the camps progressively. These operations will be detailed below.

This overview does not seek to picture precisely the work of humanitarian agencies over the years. Rather, it aspires to highlight the variety in the management of food pipelines and in responses to appeals for funds. Analyses emphasising the role of the media make sense of the overall patterns of events: in northern Iraq and Bosnia the tragic plight of displaced persons, their increased and anticipated needs tended to be broadcast and provision was made to avoid a complete breakdown of the deliveries during winters. By contrast, in Rwanda and Zaire, trends towards decreased help were less publicised. Still, when food went short in January 1995, the WFP appeals did not create much international interest. In Western consciousness, Rwandan displaced persons were often associated with the 1994 genocide. Thus, they were often perceived as guilty, somewhat responsible for their fate. In contrast, Kurds and ethnically cleansed Bosnians were considered mere victims. It is plausible therefore that public pressure to come to the rescue of persons perceived to be innocent victims was greater. However, migration based explanations are also consistent with the variations outlined. In Bosnia and northern Iraq, the international community wanted displaced people to stay where they were, whereas it was decided that Rwandan IDPs should return to their villages. In the first two cases, overall aid supplies were maintained or increased whereas in the latter they progressively shrank. This represents a prima facie case for a potential link between relief and migration policies.[16] It requires further investigation regarding the extent to which relief was conditional on compliance with Western designed plans for IDPs.

The Creation of "Safe" Roads of Return

Relief policies in northern Iraq and Rwanda were implemented from the start so as to discourage exodus and encourage early return. The situation in Bosnia differed as the constant worsening of the war made it impossible to plan meaningfully the early return of displaced persons.

In August 1994, French troops were to leave south-west Rwanda, handing political control of the area to the RPF and UNAMIR in a swap much feared by the displaced persons. This exchange created large and realistic fears of a second Goma-like exodus, this time towards south

Kivu.[17] Whereas previous ICRC appeals for displaced persons in south-west Rwanda had been ignored, the threat of another catastrophic exodus had a definite impact on the international community.[18] In his 3 August report to the Security Council, Boutros-Ghali emphasised that risk:

> Although the flight of people seems to have slowed, the situation remains volatile and extremely fluid. Of particular concern is the possibility of another massive outflow from the humanitarian protected zone in south-west Rwanda when the French forces withdraw.[19]

Anticipating such movements, humanitarian agencies organised a vast operation designed to retain, in Rwanda, most IDPs ready to leave their country. USAID described the sudden care for people left in Zone Turquoise:

> The WFP and the ICRC have asked the US military in Entebbe to airlift their food stocks in Daar el Salam and Monbasa to Bujumbura. They have also asked that water bladders currently stored in Entebbe be flown to Bujumbura to meet critical food and water shortfalls in Gikorongo prefecture.[20]

UNHCR concentrated its relief assistance in the Kibuye and Gikorongo areas "in order to discourage further movements south" towards Zaire.[21] According to a USAID report, it also planned to use "the forest between Gikorongo and Cyangugu as a natural boundary."[22] In a second phase of the emergency plan, agencies were to follow the population on the move, providing services and simultaneously using "means of persuasion to discourage the movement, and deter by not supplying assistance ahead of the movement."[23] Finally some camps were opened south of Cyangugu so as to channel the population in the direction of the Uvira valley rather than Bukavu. Purposefully placed near the border, the camps were designed to reassure people on the move while still containing them within Rwanda.[24] All humanitarian agencies, including MSF, participated in this "strategy of containment of the displaced through offers of assistance and opening of camps."[25] Interestingly enough, evaluations of the operation differ. MSF claimed that it failed as around 120,000 persons left for Zaire in the course of August 1994.[26] By contrast, late August 1994, the United Nation Department of Humanitarian Affairs, the UNDHA, asserted confidently: "The international strategy to place people into camps within Rwanda rather than allowing them to move to Zaire appears to be working."[27] The extent of the operation's success is uncertain. Besides, it is unclear whether a mass exodus was averted because of the humanitarian strategy or because the RPF had accepted not to take immediate control of the area. In any case, the design of the response to the threat of exodus reveals that containment was at the heart of UN concerns.

In parallel to the above described endeavour, the international community sought to encourage the early return of IDPs to their villages by offering transport and aid packages. In the context of Operation Homeward which started in September 1994, trucks were placed at the disposal of Rwandan candidates to return.[28] In January 1995, the operation was renamed Operation Retour and its rhythm stepped up. The UNHCR claimed it would try to organise the "military escorts for all [Rwandan] returnee convoys during the initial phase of repatriation and on an *ad hoc* basis as the situation stabilise[d]."[29] Although most returns took place on foot, the UNHCR did provide some trucks after the Kibeho massacre.

Besides transport, "way stations" or "transit centres" were set up in Iraq and Rwanda to grant both refugees and displaced persons medical and humanitarian support, as well as a safe rest. According to UNHCR, the relief effort in northern Iraq "employed numerous aircraft to deliver food, drugs and medical supplies to refugees along their [Kurdish IDPs'] paths of descent from the Turkish mountains."[30] People were then expected to stay for a few weeks in the Zakho transit centres. Likewise, during August 1994 in Rwanda, way stations were set up on the roads from Gysengi to Ruhengeri and Kigali. The distance between each station was approximately a day's walk. This was deemed to encourage people to make their way home as soon as possible.[31] Care International claimed that "Approximately 1,000 people a day stop at the stations, where they can pick up their rations, receive medical care and camp overnight in a safe area."[32] Later, the Rwandan and neighbouring governments also promised to establish "safe corridors" both outside and within Rwanda to speed up returns.[33]

Finally, in addition to transport and way stations, attraction poles were created by sending food ahead of return movements in particular directions. To encourage people to go back to Dohuk, technically outside the original protected haven, a UNHCR food convoy was sent to the town to attract daring returnees. Sadruddin Aga Khan, the UN special envoy, justified the decision in the following terms:

> The key to the solution of the bulk of the remaining caseload in Turkey, as well as the massing of displaced persons near Zakho (where 25,000

people are in the US built transit centre awaiting a chance to return) is the creation of confidence in the greater Dohuk area. In this context I decided that a convoy be sent to Dohuk ... The Dohuk sub-office will distribute these essential supplies and maintain the UN flag that could provide a stimulus to refugees returning home.[34]

In Rwanda, numerous reasons lay beneath the reluctance of displaced persons to return to their villages.[35] UNHCR responded to such fears with the creation of Open Relief Centres (ORCs), designed to welcome returnees and shelter people in case of increased tension. The UNHCR claimed that:

> The combined presence of a civilian administration, of international military contingents, of humanitarian personnel and of human rights monitors, offers the best available substitute to the formal creation, within Rwanda of "security zones." Such zones might raise questions of national sovereignty and might induce returnees to stay and to continue to rely on humanitarian assistance, instead of returning home. Moreover, the Open Relief Centres in home communes, while essentially serving assistance and short term shelter purposes, are envisaged as an additional tool for protection, to which returnees and other civilians, can turn in case of inter-communal tension, or when they feel threatened otherwise.[36]

Thus ORCs were constructed first to encourage return, second to stabilise people in their villages. As in Zakho, safety appears available primarily on a temporary basis. It is also noteworthy that UNHCR itself reflected on issues of "security zones," "national sovereignty" and describes the ORC project in strategic, migration-related terms. Overall, to create incentives for people to go home, agencies provided forms of safety that were spatially allocated to designated roads of return. Thus, security became finite as the displaced persons were then expected to leave the safe environment of way stations, transit centres and ORCs to make their final journey home.

From Incentives to Threats

The difference between encouraging a certain behaviour and attempting to compel is a fine line indeed. This holds especially for displaced persons as surrounding institutions possess much leverage on their material life conditions. When coalition troops prepared to depart from northern Iraq, many Kurdish displaced decided to return to their ancestral villages rather than to the collective towns from which they had fled. According to the UNHCR, "between 30% and 60% of the population refused, at one time or another, to return to their place of origin; in government-controlled collective towns or ... cities."[37] In Suleymaniyah for instance,

> Although the majority of the Kurds had returned to the governorate by the end of June 1991, nearly half refused to move onwards into government controlled areas; in August, at the peak of uncertainty, about 500,000 persons were living under makeshift shelters in the northern and western regions of the province.[38]

In fact, many Kurdish displaced persons wanted to rebuild their homes in mountain villages destroyed by the various eradication campaigns prior to the Gulf War, the infamous Anfal campaigns. The UNHCR was initially opposed to this solution. For John Fawcett, then working with the IRC, the UNHCR workers "assumed that people could not survive a winter back in their original homes ... they could not see how people would do it."[39] In the dispute, the organisation forbade people to take their tents and move back where they wanted to. Only in September, when it became clear that people would not return to "Saddam cities" nor to unprotected camps, did the UNHCR launch its "winterisation programme."[40] According to the UNHCR, the project's "basic idea was to provide shelter against the winter for this group [an estimated 640,000 returnees/displaced persons without adequate housing] and thereby forestall any further large movements of population in the area."[41] Further fighting and population movements in the autumn revealed the extent to which the UNHCR was unprepared. Thus, the organisation's plan was criticised for coming late and being inadequate.[42] Furthermore, UN agencies also used aid to deter unwanted population movements.

> In October, reports surfaced of a dispute over strategy between the UNHCR and NGOs operating in northern Iraq. The UNHCR stationed food distribution points only in the lower areas in an attempt to lure returning refugees into the lowlands and to discourage the newly displaced Kurds from fleeing back into the mountains in response to violence. The UNHCR was concerned about the onset of winter and the availability of permanent shelter for returning Kurds. NGOs had warned that priority should be placed on rebuilding homes in the destroyed villages in the mountains because Kurds would be better protected there than in the lowlands from attacks by the Iraqi army.[43]

In Rwanda, humanitarian agencies also phased out food distributions to "encourage" people to leave the camps. In agreement with the RPF's decision that Rwandan displaced should go home,[44] humanitarian agencies decided to close the camps progressively.[45] An Integrated Operation Centre - IOC - was created for this purpose. However, the policy of incentives to return that was launched in January 1995 failed because of insecurity in areas of return. According to Randolph Kent, the director of the IOC, "by February 1995 ... insecurity in the communes was reversing the returnee flow ... Even worse were clear indications that more people who had never been IDPs were swelling the camp numbers."[46] Despite increasing pressure and progressive camp closure, some displaced persons managed to avoid returning to their villages for months. Oxfam reported that people repatriated in the context of Operation Retour "re-appeared" a few days later in their camps.[47] As one report noted, some displaced persons even switched camps in an attempt to evade closures.

> With the closure of Rukondo, the last of the major camps to the north of the Gikorongo-Cyangugu road, all the displaced people camps administered by WFP are now closed. However, it is estimated that up to 50% of the population in these camps has moved to the southern camps which are supplied by ICRC.[48]

Indeed, the closure strategy was counter-productive as the population of Rukondo, Cyanika and Kibeho increased.[49] Kent honestly details how it was then decided to reduce and stop the distribution of food rations in the remaining camps to persuade Rwandan IDPs to take the roads towards their villages.[50]

> Camps populations were to be separated into their home communes and, based upon an agreed sequence, each of these communes-targeted groups would be informed that they would receive three weeks of food rations and then they would only receive food assistance in their home areas. Services would not be cut off, but rather shifted to the communes. To that extent, it was clear that the aid agencies had accepted that the camps would be closed, and that the IDPs had no choice but to move.[51]

The language used here is interesting as relief is still presented as an attraction pole and its "displacement" a way of achieving return objectives. This strategy however also failed as camps were forcefully and violently closed by the RPA.

Repatriation problems in Bosnia were of a different nature. In contrast to Rwanda most displaced Bosnians expressed their wish to go home after the war.[52] Nevertheless, repatriation remained a slow and incomplete process. Many Bosnian refugees were sent back to their country on the ground that the war was over and that they had been granted only "temporary protection."[53] Officially, the UNHCR resisted an all-out expulsion of refugees from European countries. However, its durable solution programme suggested an "initial voluntary relocation of refugees, to new geographical areas in Bosnia and Herzegovina." [54] In other words, refugees could be returned to Bosnia, although not to their area of origin, thus transforming them into displaced returnees. This, as Amnesty International pointed out, is not entailed in the Dayton Agreement.[55] Displaced persons and new returnees, on the other hand, hardly ventured into areas controlled by opponents. Initially, whereas the international community insisted that refugees return to Bosnia, attempts of people to return to their homes were hardly backed. In the years following the peace settlement, the proponents of Dayton were very cautious not to upset the existing political order, hence to limit instances of spontaneous, uncontrolled returns that added to the risk of ethnic confrontation.[56] International bodies, for instance, avoided making any statement that "might imply promises of financial assistance to returnees rebuilding their homes."[57] Indeed, half-hearted support of return translated into financial and economic non-provision. In the September 1996 elections, a year after the signature of the Agreement, Western fears of clashes were such that the OSCE tried to discourage IDPs from returning to vote in their villages of origin and NATO severely limited the freedom of movement on election day. As a result, only a fraction of the IDPs who had registered to vote at home made the journey.[58] By September 1996, of the two million persons displaced by the war, refugees and IDPs, UNHCR claimed that "only some 250,000 have been able to return, almost exclusively to areas where they are members of the majority ethnic group."[59] Positions regarding return changed with time and the realisation that "the threat to stability and peace comes not from a reintegration of the three ethnic groups but from continued large-scale internal displacement."[60] However, to assess whether the international community really gave Bosnian IDPs the choice would require more resources than the author can spare. For the purposes of the argument it is enough to point out that, initially, Western fears for stability took priority over the wishes of individuals.

These examples underline some instrumental aspects of aid deliveries. Clearly, the politics of return implemented in Bosnia differed from the other two countries. Not only were international objectives concerning IDPs unclear, but also food was less of an issue. "Compellence" policies in northern Iraq and Rwanda were crude. The provision of basic relief items such as food, water, tents was used to control movements of populations. Nevertheless, in all cases, though in different ways, the international community made life difficult for displaced persons where they did not want them to stay or go. Alternatively, agencies attempted to improve the quality of life in locations where people were deemed to go. It is not claimed that all humanitarian action was instrumental. Still, the very existence of the above strategies raises queries regarding policy objectives at the core of humanitarian action. In fact, many aid workers readily admitted their confusion on the purpose of their efforts, as this comment on Srebrenica testifies.

> What about education? Or electricity? And what about trying to restore these things in a situation where fighting and ethnic cleansing and rape are still going on all around? Again the question comes down as it has from the beginning, to what we are in fact trying to accomplish here. We have to decide, and even after two years we haven't done that yet.[61]

Scant Aid beyond Stabilisation

The extent to which the international community involved itself in post-crisis reconstruction matters. Extensive support of the return and reintegration of displaced persons, in other words, the re-creation of normal life conditions[62] would challenge the idea that aid is an instrument of migration policies.

Although initially reluctant to enter Iraqi Kurdistan, UNHCR took responsibility for the return of refugees and initial relief assistance in their homes. However, the institution made clear that it wanted its work to "stop short of rehabilitation of infrastructure."[63] As already mentioned, it emerged that Kurdish communities would not comply and return to major Iraqi cities. Because of the UNHCR/Kurdish struggle, reconstruction started late. International efforts to de-mine, or identify mine fields were also inadequate. Locals did most of the work, progressively helped by NGOs. Mine fields were an enormous hazard and continue to be so.[64] Nevertheless, from 1991 onwards, a form of political autonomy was developed in northern Iraq, the hallmark of which were the independently held elections of 1992. This development however was not wholeheartedly supported by coalition governments.[65] Since April 1991, they had encouraged the Kurdish leaders to negotiate with the regime in place. When Saddam Hussein's regime organised its internal blockade of Kurdistan, the Security Council members refused to exempt Kurdistan from the general sanctions against Iraq.[66] For fear of encouraging separatist tendencies, the international community also refused to open special bank accounts on behalf of Kurdistan. Whereas humanitarian aid was available, local authorities were kept under harsh financial pressures, impeding any new development. Gunter contends that two years after the election of May 1992, the area was lurching towards economic disaster. "While the US and its allies spent millions of dollars for humanitarian aid to alleviate the suffering of the Kurds, it at the same time denies them the very economic trade they could use to help themselves become economically self-sustaining."[67] The lack of international investment in infrastructure, de-mining and agriculture promoted short term profit from smuggling to the detriment of productive investment and led to what David Keen called "the decay of the economy rather than its development."[68] Finally Western aid, when available, was concentrated along the Turkish border, thus created inequalities between regions that contributed to the feuds under which the short-lived Kurdish unity crumbled in the course of the 1990s.

The Rwandan government's sincere efforts to prevent revenges and exactions against returnees[69] were hampered, from the start, by a drastic lack of funds. The country had been completely looted by the retreating FAR. Even outside assets, such as bank accounts and embassies were not made available to the new government until they had themselves been plundered. Drumtra, a policy analyst for the USCR estimated that the new Rwandan government was placed before a set of unachievable demands. More precisely it was:

> ... caught in a political trap by the policies of the international community, including the United States. The new government has been signalled that it must induce millions of Hutu refugees and internally Displaced Persons to return to their homes so as to boost the new government's credibility among international donors. Yet the new government, deprived of bilateral aid, has virtually no administrative capacity to create conditions for repatriation or to cope with the tensions and disputes certain to occur when millions of uprooted Hutu return home.[70]

The new authorities were starved of funds in different ways.[71] France blocked funds as soon as news of human rights abuses emerged.[72]

The EU was hardly more supportive and limited its help to humanitarian aid.[73] One year after the genocide, the IMF and the World Bank refused to release new funds on the grounds that Kigali did not pay its arrears.[74] Moreover, despite the fact that the international war crimes tribunal for the Former Yugoslavia was extended so as to try the authors of the genocide, the main presumed leaders of the killings lived freely in African and European capital cities as late as May 1995.[75] The Rwandan justice system had been decimated during the genocide.[76] Returning from a visit to the country in February 1995, Dr. Joseph Mucumbitse of the Association des Droits de l'Homme in Brussels described the new structure meant to investigate the genocide in a vivid picture: "One magistrate, four helpers, one typewriter and one car."[77] On the one hand, Rwanda received little help to deal with the tens of thousand of persons accused of participation in the killings and for the rebuilding of a wrecked country. On the other hand, the country remained under scrutiny for the disastrous conditions in its over-crowded prisons.[78] Human Rights Watch and ICRC's repeated appeals not only to the Rwandan Government but also to the international community for the improvement of prison conditions and support of the justice system fell on deaf ears.[79] The money pledged after the genocide did not arrive and all funds were blocked after the attack on Kibeho to which the author shall return.[80] The absence of justice for the 1994 martyrs keeps poisoning social relations in Rwanda. Some people have taken justice into their own hands. This has maintained a climate of fear, distrust and personal revenge particularly dangerous for displaced persons.[81] A detailed account of the lack of support for the rebuilding of Rwanda can be found in the fourth study of the Steering Committee of the Joint Evaluation of Emergency Assistance to Rwanda.[82] This situation led to a radicalisation of the Rwandan government and its contempt for the international community, both dramatic for displaced persons and refugees. As late as January 1997, Amnesty International claimed that persons forced to return were not safe from persecution.[83]

In Bosnia, despite the signature of the Dayton Peace Agreement, the freedom of indicted war criminals initially preserved a political climate polarised around ethnic and nationalist claims detrimental to displaced persons' hopes of returning home.[84] The well-known case of seven survivors of Srebrenica who were handed over to the Serbian authorities by IFOR and unfairly tried in Republica Srpska illustrated how little displaced persons could trust the Bosnian Serb legal system.[85] Although more interest and reconstruction money were invested in Bosnia than in either northern Iraq or Rwanda, the extent to which this benefited displaced persons remains questionable. Despite reassuring reports from the UNHCR, the OSCE and NATO, several observers questioned the treatment received by displaced persons.[86] During travels in Mostar, Vlasenica and Tuzla in the years following the peace settlement, the author felt that IDPs were no more than second class citizens, often the poorest, despised and used by their own leaders as political pawns. However, a serious investigation of the extent to which reconstruction funds trickled down to IDPs would require more time and space than one can devote here. The matter shall therefore remain unanswered. It will be borne in mind that reconstruction in Bosnia could contradict the idea that only the strict minimum to stabilise populations is done.

Safety on the Roads of Return, Dwindling Care Elsewhere

That aid is part of political deals is not new. It became obvious during years of interventions in Bosnia when, for instance, Western political negotiators treated aid as a bargaining asset.

> Lord Owen, for example, threatened in no uncertain terms in November, 1993, that unless the Bosnian Government signed the peace plan then on the table, humanitarian aid might end and the sanctions against Serbia lifted.[87]

Senior UNHCR officer Mendiluce used to remind staff new to Bosnia to forget whatever they might know on refugees and to consider aid an integral part of the war.[88] UNHCR sometimes threatened to and stopped aid deliveries to try and secure better working conditions. It did so in September 1992 after the shooting down of an Italian aeroplane above Sarajevo and after the death of some of its personnel in Vitez in November 1993.[89] At the same time, Gentile also suggested to withhold UNHCR plans of expansion in Banja Luka to put pressure on the Bosnian Serb authorities and make them stop the harassment of minorities.[90] However, given Western pressure on UNHCR, none of these attempts lasted for long.

Although some acknowledge that humanitarian actors have their own objectives, most observers stress "the web of interests" in which aid workers are unwillingly caught. [91] The ICRC or the head of UNHCR throughout the 1990s, Mrs. Ogata, regularly denounce the politicisation of aid.[92] These public stances suggest that humanitarian work is compromised solely because of the political manipulations of relief. Governments and warring parties are naturally blamed. Frelick, himself involved in humanitarian work, wrote:

> Governments are bound ... to use the term coined by the UNHCR Sadako Ogata "preventive protection" differently than humanitarian agencies. For them this concept implies the promotion of an important self-interest, which often includes keeping refugees out, especially those who come in large numbers, destitute and unlikely to leave soon.[93]

Here lies the commonly held assumption that humanitarian missions, though properly designed, become distorted at operational level. This, added to the mainstream view that agencies only focus on life-saving activities in catastrophic situations, sustains the picture of humanitarian agencies as reactive in essence. Nevertheless, as the above discussion showed, there is plenty of evidence that agencies are pro-active. They gather and use their resources for explicit strategic purposes. At first sight, it seems that both media coverage and out-migration pressures affect relief provision. However, a closer look at some emergency operations showed that food and aid were available where displaced persons were encouraged to go or to remain. In contrast humanitarian support was not provided or progressively dwindled in locations deemed unfit or undesirable. Humanitarian agencies created discourses that delineated the options available to IDPs. Thus, humanitarian agencies tried to shape and control population movements, although such policies sometimes failed. In addition, reconstruction efforts in Rwanda and Iraq were insufficient to significantly improve displaced persons' fate.

From Unsafe Heavens to Nowhere

Western powers entered northern Iraq, Rwanda and Bosnia with unclear protection mandates. Furthermore, nobody really knew what declaring certain areas safe implied on the ground. In northern Iraq, it was the first time that NATO had used the concept of safe haven since the end of the Cold War. In Bosnia, Western powers did not want to be seen to take sides, thus used this concept only reluctantly. In Rwanda, the French army had already been involved alongside the defeated genocidal regime and therefore its offer to create a safe zone was received with caution. For the purposes of this work, the ways in which troops were committed, responded to renewed violence and organised evacuations expose the priorities of the institutions that intervened. In the following paragraphs, it is argued that despite growing numbers of IDPs in the aftermath of the Kurdish and Rwandan safe area declarations, the troops committed to their security were speedily withdrawn. In Bosnia, most of the troops initially considered were not made available. Very weak reactions to further violence against people on the move also suggest that, overall, no effective protection was achieved unless people threatened to overrun valued borders or existing political orders. It is further argued that evacuations were constructed as "last resort" options. Rarely were they used for the benefit of the persons who needed them most. The section closes with a summary of the international commitment to IDPs' safety and outlines various interpretations of it.

The Morning After: Supplying Troops to Enhance Security "in Situ"

Despite an increase in IDPs because of early, yet incomplete, repatriations, American troops entered northern Iraq, established camps and left less than three months later.[94] Humanitarian agencies, encouraged by military officials to settle in Zakho, were surprised when the withdrawal was announced for June.[95] The move though was postponed to July after joint Kurdish, NGOs and allies pressures. Under the Memorandum of Understanding signed between Iraq and the UN, the allied troops were to be replaced by 500 UN "lightly armed" guards.[96] By June however, only a token force could be deployed for lack of funding.[97] Later, the programme was implemented, albeit with enormous financial difficulties. UN guards were neither mandated nor in a position to protect displaced civilians against military violence. Indeed, they were reported to be the first fleeing the fighting of late 1991 and July 1992.[98] Nor were they equipped to deal with worsening social conflicts emerging in the wake of Baghdad's internal blockade against Kurdistan. US ambassador Perkins claimed that "these guards perform an essential job." Yet this was in "providing a measure of protection for United Nation personnel and equipment."[99] As far as IDPs were concerned, UN guards' functions were symbolic, limited to patrolling and reporting. The UN mission however was backed by Operation Provide Comfort II - initially named Poised Hammer - whereby American jets patrolled Iraqi skies, north of the 36th parallel. This distant shield was valued by Kurdish populations. As one KDP spokesperson put it: "If Poised Hammer is withdrawn, Saddam's units will again reign in this region and we will lose everything."[100] Still, as will be described below, American planes made little impact on the daily hardship faced by displaced persons.

Rwandan IDPs received no more support than their Iraqi counterparts. By late July 1994, UN and humanitarian agencies started to fear that a second mass exodus towards Zaire, this time the south Kivu, would follow the departure of French troops from Zone Turquoise. However, despite UN requests, French authorities refused to delay their departure from south-west Rwanda. Turquoise troops were replaced by UN blue berets, this time African peace-keepers. Although 5,50 in number, UNAMIR II soldiers were neither equipped nor trained to deal with displaced civilian security. Furthermore, because they were English native speakers, Ghanaian and Ethiopian blue berets found it especially difficult to inspire confidence among French-speaking Hutus stranded in Zone Turquoise. After several attempts at repatriation coordinated with UNHCR, UNAMIR drew up a confidential plan for the closure of 20 camps and the trucking of 350,000 IDPs back to their villages. Named Opération Rondaval, it was designed with little or no involvement of humanitarian agencies but reflected Rwandan officials anxiety to rid themselves of the IDP issue.[101] The humanitarian community convinced the Rwandan government to let them try through incentives and took over the planning of returns until programmes collapsed in violence in April 1995. More will be said about this later. So far, it is enough to mention that, overall, UNAMIR II proved unable to tackle problems of law and order both suffered and inflicted by Rwandan displaced persons. In addition, very few UN personnel, human rights observers and humanitarian staff were deployed to cope with the intense social problems linked to mass return movements of people such as property claims, genocide denunciations, revenges, balancing humanitarian aid etc. The UN human right observer field director resigned in September 1994 to protest against lack of material and human resources. Indeed, after the August 1994 bid to reassure displaced persons so as to prevent further exodus, the functions of UN troops, apart from reporting to the UN Security Council, remained unclear.

Bosnia is a case of unfulfilled promises. Contrary to the two above examples, and despite renewed ethnic cleansing in central Bosnia, safe area declarations were not followed by a significant influx of troops mandated to protect people on the move, if only temporarily.[102] Rather, UNPROFOR was left in charge, with a protection mandate which it chose to interpret to its bare minimum.[103] For fear of alienating Bosnian Serb nationalists or Croatian nationalists, whose co-operation was deemed necessary for the diplomatic peace process, UNPROFOR limited its use of force to a minimum of self-defence.[104] Muhamed Sacirbey, the Bosnian ambassador to the UN was quoted as saying: "UNPROFOR offers neither protection nor force."[105] At grass root level, UNHCR remained solely responsible for the protection of civilians. However, for lack of means and bargaining power, its so-called "protection officers" had to keep negotiating with the very local authorities organising the cleansing.[106] Both Gentile and Hollingworth described numerous lost battles against the Bosnian Serbs of Banja Luka who violently bullied displaced and minorities into fulfilling their pre-drawn, ethnically homogenised, maps of Bosnia.[107] As a result, forced displacement carried on unabated throughout the war. In 1994, according to Human Rights Watch:

> The most savage and institutionalised "ethnic cleansing" today is taking place in areas where there is no fighting ... conditions in the Bosanska Krajina and Bijeljina areas (where Bosnian Serbs have power) provide a powerful counterweight to the claims of high ranking officials and other international leaders that Human Rights abuses will decrease after an overall peace accord is signed.[108]

Despite numerous Bosnian appeals,[109] international procrastination lasted until the events following the fall of Srebrenica in July 1995. The Serb offensive on safe areas was counteracted in August by a large Croatian reconquest of the Krajina, eastern Slavonia and parts of Bosnia. After the US operation Deliberate Force, during which Serb Nationalist military facilities in Bosnia were bombed, the Bosnian and Croatian armies swept through western Bosnia.[110] The Dayton Peace Accord represented a renewal of international promises to Bosnians. They were followed by the deployment of 53,000 NATO soldiers. However, armed troops did not directly ensure the safety of civilians. According to ICG, "IFOR insisted all along that although it would provide 'area security' that is, prevent the outreach of hostilities, it would not be responsible for guaranteeing the security of individuals."[111] As for SFOR, which replaced IFOR after one year, its mission was "to deter a resumption of hostilities and to stabilise the peace in Bosnia and Herzegovina." The operation was dubbed "joint guard."[112] IFOR, then SFOR, hardly tackled forced displacement related issues. Nor did they oppose residual ethnic cleansing from being carried through. Aliosha, the young Bosniac translator who helped the author supervise the municipal elections in Mostar in September 1997, had been cleansed from the Croat-controlled part of that town only the previous year.[113] In fact, displaced persons security was to be dealt with by the Bosnian police, itself monitored by the International Police Task Force (IPTF). The latter was to observe, record local police activities and report abuses in the hope that, with the appropriate political pressures, these could be punished via the Bosnian police hierarchies.[114] According to the ICG again, this was inadequate protection for displaced persons.

> The reluctance of NATO led implementation force for Bosnia (IFOR) to help the unarmed International Police Task Force (IPTF) exert control over the local Bosnian Serb Ministry of Interior police led to continued ethnic cleansing, the inability of refugees to return to their homes, and the further ethnic partition of Bosnia.[115]

Besides, debates on the departure of Nato troops also showed that withdrawal was an option closely linked to fears of the resumption of fighting rather than safe repatriation. For instance, in November 1996, two options were discussed by the international community:

> IFOR reduced by about half with a substantial elite force based locally to prevent and deter any renewed conflict. The second, preferred by politicians, calls for a similar reduction with a rapid reaction force based outside Bosnia. Troops in the country would instead concentrate their efforts on stabilisation and reconstruction.[116]

Interestingly enough, the debate, especially the rapid reaction force alternative, although it was not opted for in the end, resembled that in Iraq. The countries involved sought to stabilise the situation rapidly, then depart progressively, leaving behind early warning and rapid reaction mechanisms.

To sum up, in two of three cases, military troops trusted by the displaced populations were quickly withdrawn. They were replaced by UN forces and human rights observers little equipped to ensure protection. In the third case, Bosnia, the troops required to stop displacement did not arrive for years.

Evacuation: out of the Question

As mentioned in Chapter II, evacuation signals priority given to people's physical safety. Hence the need to study its occurrence during crises so as to complete the security picture for IDPs. In theory, the international community planned to respond to intensified threats with stepped-up protection measures. Nevertheless, when the latter proved insufficient, agencies still had the option to remove vulnerable people from exposed sites. However, notwithstanding worsening living conditions in the months following international intervention, evacuation was not considered an option in northern Iraq or Rwanda. In Bosnia, constructed as a "last resort" option, evacuation applied differently to Bosnian Serbs, Croats and Bosniaks.

In northern Iraq, humanitarian agencies did not evacuate people, except in rare medical circumstances and usually towards the medical facilities in camps. As a rule, people who sought refuge across borders had to use their cars or their feet to flee. Humanitarian and military actors would provide transport only in the repatriation direction. Likewise, little or no evacuation took place in Rwanda. The international community's efforts were focused on preventing people from fleeing to Zaire, Burundi or Tanzania from the early days of the genocide onwards. In Bosnia, too, evacuation was rare. A few spectacular and well covered airlifts of children[117] cannot obscure the fact that these were the exceptions. International organisations opposed international evacuations.[118] After Allan Little of the BBC had broadcast the plight of little Irma and thousands of hospital beds were offered for her all over the world, he tried to establish which international organisation was in charge of finding places for the casualties of Sarajevo. "It turned out that none of them was."[119] In particular, nobody wanted to evacuate wounded soldiers.[120] By September 1993, only 142 persons had been evacuated from Sarajevo on medical grounds.[121]

Evacuation, it was argued, would make the international community accomplice to the politics of ethnic partition. In Ogata's words:

> Evacuation is the last resort in that is acquiesces in the very displacement that preventive efforts aim to avoid. But in some circumstances, it is the only way to save lives. There is a very thin line between refusing to facilitate ethnic cleansing and failing to prevent needless deaths.[122]

Indeed, the Bosnian Serb leaders asked the international community to evacuate Bosniaks from the towns they besieged as well as Bosnian Serbs from the places under Bosniak government control. International authorities' responses however varied. Bosnian Serbs who wanted to leave were left, sometimes helped, to do so. In one particular instance, General Morillon, at the time the head UNPROFOR, accused the local authorities of Tuzla of impeding humanitarian action by refusing to organise the departure from Tuzla of at least 500 Serbs from the 10,000 living there. Their departure was required by General Mladic in exchange for allowing UNHCR to bring relief to Srebrenica.[123] In contrast, the international community did not ask that IDPs in Srebrenica be allowed to leave the besieged pocket, in spite of desperate living conditions as pictured below by MSF:

> Although safer from shelling than it has been in over a year, the social situation [in Srebrenica] is worsening daily as basic survival needs are not met. Violence, black-market activities, prostitution, theft are becoming the only activities of the population. Tensions are mounting between the majority refugee population and minority local population. As always, the women, children and elderly are most at risk. The enclave must now be recognised for what it is, namely a closed refugee camp of 50,000 persons without adequate facilities for more than 15,000.[124]

Tony Land from UNHCR was also quoted as saying: "Everyone wants to get the hell out of Srebrenica. They know there is no future there."[125] Still, only occasional civilian evacuations were allowed before the tragic fall of the town. Since the signature of the DPA and the arrival of NATO troops in Bosnia, evacuations of Bosniaks are out of question. Still, the mass departure of Serbs from Sarajevo, organised - sometimes enforced - by Republica Srpska authorities in January 1996 was hardly opposed. In fact, the extent to which the international community stood against forced displacements when abuses were conducted or condoned by the IDPs' own leaders is questionable. Likewise the fact that only Bosniaks would not be evacuated from besieged cities raises questions about the international strategy to oppose ethnic cleansing. This issue will be further discussed in the book's conclusion. So far it is enough to highlight that because of their reluctance to evacuate, international authorities sometimes found themselves cornered into overseeing deportations in catastrophic circumstances.

Monitoring Duress?

Escalating conflicts combined with the withdrawal or the non-commitment of troops and the reluctance to evacuate led to a drastic deterioration of the situation of IDPs in the year following Western main promises. UN troops faced two scenarios regarding IDPs: open fighting leading to further displacement and attacks against particular sets of displaced persons besieged or re-grouped in camps.

The international community responded weakly to attacks against IDPs. In October 1991, 200,000 persons fled to the mountains of northern

Iraq in the Suleymaniyah area and towards Iran because of renewed fighting.[126] Little was done on their behalf. Allied governments justified inaction by arguing that "fighting took place outside the protective security zone" and "did not appear to violate allied prohibitions on Iraqi fixed-wing aircraft north of the 36th parallel."[127] Indeed, helicopters do not have fixed wings. Indeed, the 36th parallel is north of some important areas of Kurdistan such as Kirkuk, considered by most Kurds as belonging to Kurdistan, although this claim is disputed, Suleymaniyah and the area around the ghost town of Halabja. In these regions, only the armed Peshmerghas opposed Baghdad. When the UNHCR withdrew from northern Iraq in April 1992, an estimated 450,000 persons were still displaced and 200,000 returnees had been displaced again in ongoing violence.[128] Forced migration was a constant feature of daily life.

> As recently as March 1992, UNHCR officials reported a "quite dramatic increase" in Iraqi shelling along the front line in northern Iraq. The "shelling and shooting" caused 40,000 people - reportedly the entire population of the Kurdish Great Zab River region - to flee.[129]

In addition to the fighting between the Peshmerghas and Baghdad, Kurdish displaced faced Turkey's attempts at recreating the no man's land established by Saddam Hussein along the Iraqi-Turk border. Allegedly seeking to destroy support for the PKK, the Ankara government repeatedly attacked refugees in the protected zone. On 8 August 1991 however, relief workers claimed "that the raids targeted villages not PKK bases, and that the casualties were [Kurdish] Iraqi civilians."[130] During Turkish raids in 1992, one of which destroyed a resettled village,[131] the Ankara government received the clear support of US diplomats.[132] In March and April 1993, the Iranian army also launched attacks against Kurdish villages on the Iraqi side of the border, north of Suleymaniyah, and wrecked one village without attracting much protest.[133] The no-fly zone maintained after the Allies departure was of limited use as it only applied to Iraqi aeroplanes. In addition, it did not prevent assaults by ground troops, whether Turkish, Iranian or Iraqi. In March 1995, Turkey sent another 35,000 troops inside northern Iraq.

> Thousands of refugees were displaced anew, according to UNHCR and the head of the UN contingent in northern Iraq said that Turkish Troops

had stopped UN guards from visiting Kurdish villages and carrying out normal patrols.[134]

No international reaction occurred. Detailed records of the numerous breaches of the UN resolutions aimed at protecting the Kurds, most of which remained without international reaction, can be found in David Keen's study.[135] The Allies answer to further fighting within the No-fly Zone also reveals their absence of concern for displaced persons: In September 1996, in-fighting between Kurdish separatist parties, one of which, the KDP, was allied with Baghdad led to thousands of people taking the roads of exile towards Iran. This was met not with the re-establishment of a safe zone but with air strikes against Iraqi military targets. Again, the protection of displaced persons mattered less than balancing the overall power of Iraq and its neighbouring countries.

While taking a stand on Bosnian besieged cities in the spring of 1993, Western leaders ignored thousands of persons thrown on the roads in some of the worse ethnic cleansing episodes of the war.[136] The battle between Bosnian Croats and Bosniaks raged from spring 1993 to the Washington agreement signed in March 1994. Villages were wiped off the map and scores of Bosniaks chased towards a diminishing central area left under Bosnian government control. Although, the first two could have fallen to Croat attacks, neither Travnick, Mostar nor Zenica ever became safe areas. Zenica progressively turned into the ultimate shelter for multiple displaced persons. As in north-east Iraq, only humanitarian agencies dealt with the IDPs in central Bosnia. Likewise, in its 1994 attack of the Gorazde safe area, the BSA came as near as three kilometres from the city centre. With villagers seeking refuge in the town, the pocket size was drastically reduced. UNPROFOR's response did not enhance the safety of the people newly exiled.[137] After two weeks of negotiations and a UN security council ultimatum, Ukrainian troops took position on the new front lines and froze the territorial gains of the Bosnian Serbs. In any case, the intervention reduced to void any hope of autonomy and return to normal life that displaced villagers may have entertained. MSF wrote after the 1994 BSA attack: "The people of Gorazde may have escaped a massacre by the skin of their teeth but they now have no choice but to continue living in what has effectively become a large open air camp."[138] By contrast, the 1995 Croat-led attack in Western Bosnia leading to thousands of Bosnian and Krajina Serb fleeing towards Banja Luka and beyond towards Serbia met with intense political and military Western involvement. Only in the latter case did the international community show determination to act.

In northern Iraq and Bosnia, world authorities attempted for months to stop or limit forced displacements. By contrast, from August 1994 onwards, they sought to encourage the early return home of Rwandan displaced persons. The latter though preferred to stay in the camps no matter how dubious the security provided by their peers was. Nonetheless, mass population movements took place in Rwanda during the second half of 1994: the return of hundreds of thousands of Tutsi "old caseload" refugees from Uganda,[139] the much smaller and partial repatriation of Hutu refugees from Tanzania and Goma, the return of IDPs, but more often their displacement from one camp to another within zone Turquoise. As already explained by spring 1995, the situation with regard to the return of IDPs was in a deadlock. After humanitarian agencies had tried and failed to convince displaced persons to leave their settlements and return to their villages, the RPA attacked and emptied the camp of Kibeho. By July 1995, there were officially no more displaced persons in Rwanda. At the same time Srebrenica and Zepa fell to the repeated attacks of the BSA.

International answers to the assaults on Srebrenica and Kibeho are worth exploring a little further. For they present similarities, despite the fact that the world had taken a verbal stand on behalf of Bosnian civilians, whereas the presence of hard-line genocide proponents amongst Rwandan IDPs lessened sympathy towards the latter. In both cases, UN troops claimed not to have foreseen the assaults in spite of reporting themselves on the military preparations. Although both offensives lasted for four to five days, UN observers claim to have misunderstood the assailants' aims until it was too late to prevent the fall. In effect, UN troops witnessed the events first hand, oversaw the deportations, and played down official death toll figures.[140] In the wake of these attacks both the BSA and the RPA repeated similar assaults.

The fall of Srebrenica in July 1995 is well documented. Honig and Both convincingly argue that the UN did not defend Srebrenica and Zepa simply because they were perceived to be lost causes. By 1995, most political parties were ready to organise the territory swaps required for a political settlement.[141] According to Both and Honig the attack was designed as an exercise in ethnic cleansing. It lasted four days, with the artillery giving occasional respite for civilians to re-group towards Potocari - the UN base.[142] In addition, fuel and buses were prepared for mass and rapid deportation.[143] UN troops did not seriously oppose the attack and left the population be regrouped at Potocari. Dutch soldiers did not oppose the separation of men and women that took place in the compound.[144] This was a particularly ominous choice given that fears for male prisoners had been

116

regularly expressed by humanitarian bodies since 1993. In fact, one important reason why the UNHCR had been reluctant to evacuate in mass the most vulnerable in the spring of 1993 was their concern for the fate of the male population of the town once "women and children" would have gone.[145] In 1995, the UN acquiesced to the mass "evacuation" towards central Bosnia -Tuzla and Kladanj. Several thousand men were taken away and executed. The UN took weeks to acknowledge that the Serb-ordered "evacuation" left thousands of men missing. Not all people took refuge in Potocari though. A group of men and their families, not trusting in the protection offered by the UN, tried to flee by their own means towards Tuzla. They were expected by the BSA and massacred.[146] For a set of reasons ranging from personal revenge to planned ethnic killing - so as to pre-empt any attempt of return - the BSA had coldly decided to massacre the men of Srebrenica.[147] However, the international community's refusal to evacuate the city, to give it up publicly, as the Serbs demanded and diplomats, in private, had already conceded, may have contributed to the violence of the second fall. Bosnian Serbs also attacked and took Zepa in the wake of the fall of Srebrenica. Late July, they also mounted an offensive against Bihac but failed this last attempt.

A few months before the fall of Srebrenica, the Kibeho camp in Rwanda had fallen to an offensive by the RPA. Although largely covered by the media, the case is less documented than that of Srebrenica. Still, as for Srebrenica, it shows more cooperation between international bodies and the assailants than would be expected from a "protection force." The report of the international commission of inquiry on Kibeho clearly outlines the cooperation that took place between UNAMIR and the RPA and the fact that the forceful closure of the camp had been planned by the Integrated Operation Centre, the international cell in charge of overall IDPs issues.[148] As the RPA surrounded the camp, panic-stricken people sought shelter towards the headquarters of the UN Zambian company. The RPA Chief of Staff and the UNAMIR Deputy Force Commander visited the camp together "to explain the situation."[149] At the height of the violence, international announcements were contradictory and confusing.[150] Whereas UN headquarters protested against the attack and said that the UN "would not transport refugees like cattle," the UNHCR, the IOM and UNAMIR provided transport for those Rwandans who had "agreed" to return to their villages.[151] In practice, UN troops and humanitarian agencies moved swiftly to organise the deportation in efficient ways. For Randolph Kent, "Operationally, the emergency response of the humanitarian community was extremely impressive."[152] In effect, once the

RPA had chased 70,000 persons out of the camp,[153] the international community channelled them towards Butare and further afield towards their villages.[154] Agencies put to use displaced persons' terror of the RPA and the chaos following the attack during which Hutu leaders opposed to the return had lost control of IDPs. Where persuasion and humanitarian coercion had failed, violence succeeded. Some human rights agencies warned against increased insecurity in Rwanda both for the displaced and the international community.[155] Overall, however, a certain leniency regarding the attack prevailed. UN authorities kept referring to the regrettable incidents of Kibeho. Human Rights Watch/Africa commended the RPA for its restraint in the siege of the last thousand of resisters in Kibeho who, besieged by the RPA, "deprived of food and clean water and surrounded by human waste," capitulated over a two week period.[156] The fact is that the RPA managed through force where international efforts had been fruitless. The widespread conviction that the camps should be closed, that the final resisters were guilty, plausibly enhanced the tolerance shown towards the attack. An international commission of enquiry only regretted that "UN agencies and NGOs were not able to contribute more efficiently to the speedy evacuation of IDPs from the camp."[157] In other words, only the implementation of the "well planned closure"[158] fell short of expectations. Issues relating to the expelled persons' safety were not addressed despite consistent reports about their insecurity.[159] In October 1996, the RPA attacked and dispersed the Mugunga camp in Goma, Zaire. This assault alone suggests that international reaction to the fall of Kibeho did not prove a deterrent against further aggression. In fact, according to Nicholas Stockton of Oxfam, not long before the attack on Mugunga, the United States had proposed the withdrawal of humanitarian aid to the refugee camps as an "incentive" to return to Rwanda.[160] After unsuccessfully using positive incentives, the UNHCR had also accepted to make life difficult in the camps.[161] To sum up, in Rwanda, not only was daily insecurity tolerated, but assaults to provoke specific displacements were readily endorsed by the international community. Moreover, the international commission report made plain that, as the crisis unfolded "the limited delivery of food, water and general facilities were used as an incentive for IDPs to leave the camp."[162] This remark, presenting the dearth of humanitarian assistance as an additional tool to convince fearful crowds that departure was the only option, suggests a continuum in coercion policies. Humanitarian incentives, deprivation and standing by violence were indeed incremental steps in the same return policies.

Overall, the above examples show little commitment to ensuring safety for displaced persons. Still, treatment does vary across cases. In Bosnia, expulsions towards central Bosnia from Herzegovina or Banja Luka, towards central Gorazde, and later from Srebrenica and Zepa towards Kladanj and Tuzla were not significantly opposed by the international community. By contrast, the expulsion of thousands of Bosnian and Croat Serbs towards Serbia brought about a consequential response. The fact that, in the latter case, mass cross-border migrations were taking place raises, once more, the issue dealt with in the previous chapter: a *prima facie* case for a link between intervention and cross-border forced migration. Again, none of the cases where people were left most vulnerable (Srebrenica, Zepa, Kibeho, Suleymaniyah, the Livno Valley, Banja Luka) implied great cross-border migration risks. Indeed, the pattern of response to violence in so far as it affected people on the move renders plausible the idea that unless many people threatened borders, their safety was ignored.

Violence, Indifference and Surveillance

Across cases and over time, a wide range of policies affecting IDPs' safety emerged: withdrawal of military troops, transfer of responsibility to UN guards, maintenance of an active No-fly zone with planes patrolling the skies, reliance on humanitarian agencies to fulfil security tasks, refusal to interfere against abuses and attacks etc. Both, similarities in policies and differences across cases bring about issues to explore. Overall, however, the international community accepted a high level of danger for displaced persons even when world attention converged towards them. The persistent reluctance to evacuate shows that world leaders were able to resist public pressure when it suited them. Not only was high insecurity tolerated, but assaults to provoke specific displacements were easily endorsed. Given that world leaders had written Srebrenica and Kibeho off the maps but failed to solve the issue by negotiations, it is plausible therefore that the international community somehow acquiesced in the violence used to disperse the populations. In other words, although the international community did not explicitly threaten or attack displaced persons to enforce repatriation or deportation, it did let local forces do it, then helped out in the "evacuations."

Furthermore, military protection did not extend beyond the stage at which IDPs stabilised in a geographical location satisfactory to international actors. In particular, internally displaced persons were never protected against their own thugs. Military troops did not attempt to regulate the behaviour of local police, military and political leaders, for instance to tackle Kurdish rackets, Bosnian smuggling or control Hutu paramilitary gangs. Human Rights missions were and remain chronically underfunded. Even Tadeusz Mazowiecki, the special UN human rights rapporteur had major problems in obtaining adequate funding for a mission designated to explore abuse in Former Yugoslavia.[163] The head of the human rights investigation team in Rwanda resigned in September 1994 in protest against the lack of means available. Insecurity, rapes murders and racket were rife in the Rwandan camps. The international community's support for the emergence of an autonomous more democratic regime in northern Iraq's Kurdistan was dim. Initially, coalition governments did not even wait for the signature of an agreement between Kurd leaders and Baghdad before withdrawing.[164] Thus they put increased pressure on the former to accept any settlement. Within a few years, the social violence and conflicts engendered by economic and political tensions led to a country where, according to Gunter, "thieves steal food stocks and vehicles; corrupt Kurdish officials carry anything they can over the frontier to sell in Iran. Local militias commanders run their areas as personal fiefs."[165] Overall, Western leaders never pressurised Kurdish leaders nor the Iraqi government into greater respect for civilians' rights. Nor did they try and convince Turkey, Syria and Iran, all actively opposing the emergence of a Kurdish state, to soften their positions.[166] Post-Dayton Bosnia was and remain plagued by corruption.[167] The repatriation of Bosnian Refugees went on despite warnings by Amnesty International, that forced returns of people even in their majority area could lead to abuses linked to perceived evasion of military duties.[168] In the same vein, apart from the postponement of the municipal elections until September 1997, international authorities little tackled the manipulation of the Serbian displaced persons, some of whom were threatened with the withdrawal of their humanitarian aid rations unless they accepted to register to vote where told to by the authorities of Republica Srpska.[169] The question raised here is that of emancipation from the reign of terror and corruption that local warlords sometimes inflict on their own people. This never was part of protection mandates. Whether it should be is a complex question that extends beyond the scope of this book. The latter can only highlight that, in the course of the interventions reviewed, the international community never challenged oppressive leaders so long as they controlled the whereabouts of their people. It was because their authority was needed to control masses of displaced persons that the Rwandan genocide organisers remained in charge.

Finally, trends in troop commitment show no long term guarantees for the safety of IDPs *per se* but a pattern of search for disengagement. In all cases, mass intervention (1991 Iraq, 1994 Rwanda, 1995 Bosnia) was followed by the setting up of structures to replace the military (no-fly zones, UN guards, monitoring of local police, peace-keepers, some human rights monitors, election observers etc.). Although unable to protect displaced persons effectively, these personnel share common functions. They personify symbolic concern for destitute populations. Their very presence is also to encourage return. Beyond the symbolic, observers can also witness and report abuses. This characterises the establishment of early warning systems designed to alert the international community of abuses, of potential mass migrations, of political destabilisation. The UNHCR fulfilled this function in Iraq in Autumn 1991. However, when no reaction is associated to early warning, the extent to which the above personnel can indeed improve human rights records, thus go beyond symbolic or surveillance functions, remains limited.

Safe Environments at Strategic Locations

The threads of relief and protection policies remain to be tied. Matching observations to the inferences outlined in introduction, the author shall first expose her claims, second outline the limits of the hypothesis and, finally, discuss perspectives opened by the argument.

A Limited and Tactical Protection

Findings can be summarised in a few points. To start with, international procrastination in Bosnia between 1993 and 1995 is comparable to that in Rwanda in the period May to June 1994. Bearing in mind that the international community steadily refused to provide troops and ensure safety against military violence is a prerequisite to comprehend Bosnian IDP policies. Sadly, this is consistent with the "control ability" idea which suggests that when governments do not manage to control cross-border movements, substantial military involvement on behalf of displaced persons takes place. This emphasis on border protection is also supported by the fact that protected areas appeared spatially located in relation to borders rather than to displaced persons. The Kurdish safe haven had little to do with Kurdish populations' settlements, but followed closely the Turkish

Border. Similarly the no-fly zone cut across Iraqi Kurd-populated areas hence they were isolated from each other. Indeed, long term reconstruction issues were also secondary to border stabilisation concerns. Furthermore, variations in policies surveyed are consistent with an instrumental migration-driven view of protection. Both military safety and relief were delivered at strategic locations and times of high volatility of populations. In other words, safe havens were created in places where the international community wanted displaced to either stay or go (Zakho then Dohuk May 1991, Srebrenica Spring 1993, Kigali Summer 1994). Alternatively, protection was low and aid provision tended to drop despite continuous needs when international authorities decided that people should move on (Northern Iraq Summer 1991, Zone Turquoise Autumn 1994 onwards, Srebrenica 1995 although in the latter case safety standards rather than relief provision deteriorated). This is consistent with the idea that migration objectives came first and always took priority over needs. Overall, safety provision or the lack of it were means to enforce Western objectives. Humanitarian discourses obscured both the instrumentality of protection mandates and the priority given to containment over safety.

Discussing "Enforced" Return

Several criticisms can be levelled against the argument developed in this chapter. One may point out that the practices described are marginal. Humanitarian agencies not only fed displaced persons for months in Zakho or Kibeho but also overcame many obstacles to achieve this. Overall, the bulk of the aid was distributed where people stood. This fact seems to suggest that humanitarian considerations had priority over containment or return. However, what this chapter argued is that efforts to bring aid to IDPs were sustained when both migration objectives and humanitarian needs converged. For example, humanitarian assistance was boosted in northern Iraq (in April and Autumn 1991) and south-west Rwanda during the Summer 1994 and during most of the Bosnian war because agencies wanted to retain the displaced persons who were preparing for further flights. By contrast, whenever international protagonists decided that return movements should take place, relief was progressively displaced so as to induce return. Subsequently, safety prospects for IDPs evolved depending on their compliance with international plans drawn up for them. Hence, a focus on migration aims can make sense of IDP policy choices that would otherwise be unexplained. In other words, it provides a clue as to why the UNHCR can decide to put people's lives at risk. It gives a key to understand Sadako Ogata's dilemma: "to what extent do we persuade people to remain where they are, when that could well jeopardise their lives and liberties?"[170]

A second criticism of the argument lies in the fact that some IDPs embraced the return programmes. Besides, the very failure of the UNHCR voluntary return agenda in Rwanda suggests that the "compellence" narrative presented is exaggerated. In this case, a discussion on the issue of "informed choice" is required. The argument so far presented suggests that the international community participated in the manufacture of circumstances where an absence of choice was enforced. The circumstances under which displaced persons took decisions were bleak. Whether in northern Iraq or Rwanda, the displaced had the choice between squalid, sometimes deteriorating, camp lives and return to unsafe homes.[171] A few months before the attack on Kibeho, a survey run by Oxfam revealed that 86% of the Rwandan displaced population had no intention of returning home "in the near future."[172] Frelick also denounced the absence of information and ensuing absence of dignity that characterised the internationally sponsored return of some Bosnians to Croat controlled areas in 1997.[173] The fact that IDPs have their own will and that agencies fell short of achieving some objectives is a lesson on the limits of the manipulation of humanitarian assistance. Still, a failed enforced return policy remains coercive in essence. Failure itself should not prevent analysis of the compellence mechanisms at work. On the contrary, such a study may help to understand failure.

The reader may also argue - although this is still debated - that reconstruction in Bosnia extends beyond the stage at which people are stabilised. This is accepted. However, although it goes beyond this book, may the author suggest that such reconstruction efforts can be understood by an extension of the hypothesis from IDPs to refugees. Rebuilding was presented as a project able to dissuade local populations from fighting. It is, however, financed mainly by European states with an openly vested interest in repatriation. Rebuilding may be linked to the on-going European effort to convince Bosnian refugees that life is worth living back home. This proposal is yet another issue that warrants further studies. Finally, looking at reconstruction programmes in parallel highlights an interesting point. Across cases, there were no agreements regarding the level of safety that is required for people on the move. The fact that international community rebuilding efforts were far more extensive in Bosnia than in either Iraq or Rwanda might be irrelevant. What counted was to work out for each case the level of safety and economic prospects required to stop flights and induce returns.

This study, however, presents only a *prima facie* case for the hypothesis. It is an initial attempt to investigate humanitarian action for IDPs thematically and comparatively. As the issue of the Bosnian reconstruction makes clear, the framework for comparisons established is still very rough. It was easy to dismiss quickly so-called reconstruction efforts in northern Iraq or Rwanda because there was so little of it. Post-war Bosnia was too complex a case of reconstruction for this study to tackle adequately. Much more time should also be devoted to the cases of the assaults over Zakho, Srebrenica and Kibeho. Besides, the author did not expand on the current debates over withdrawal from Bosnia, nor compare them precisely to the discourses held by Americans in northern Iraq or French in Rwanda. Finally, she did not explore financial constraints on the international community nor legal constraints on UN peace keepers. No doubt that specialists of any of the above-mentioned fields would highlight differences or similarities of which she is unaware. However, the comparison established yields results worth the try, and worth exploring. One such suggestion is developed in the following section.

Humanitarian Spaces without Exit

Much has been written about states' preference for order over chaos[174] and about aid becoming the fig leaf concealing international indifference towards war victims.[175] Both ideas - states' predilection for order and aid as a form of substitute for political action - are the pillars of the assumption that the humanitarian mission is being hijacked and corrupted by governments. Indeed, agencies cry out that while they are given extra responsibilities, they are hampered in their protective missions by a lack of support as well as abuses of humanitarian law. Médecins Sans Frontières, for instance, claimed that however neutral it wanted to remain vis-à-vis Rwandan IDPs return, the aid provided was perceived by other agencies, the RPA and UNAMIR as an encouragement to stay.[176] In effect NGOs, large or small, became involved in security matters. In February 1995, Oxfam granted a loan to a Human Rights Watch team to monitor the situation in Rwanda.[177] Frelick observed that the UNHCR had "changed from an organisation that had a strictly palliative role to the one that is focusing on fixing the problem."[178] This shift brought with it particular dilemmas.[179] According to David Rieff, many UNHCR officers, including Ogata and Mendiluce, felt used in their work in Bosnia.[180] Still, the

UNHCR itself designed the policy of containment in which its workers were trapped. That agencies could threaten to stop feeding populations so as to obtain their compliance hardly fits the picture of humanitarian protagonists responding to a need. It also challenges the belief that aid workers could not do their jobs because other participants, or the recipients of the care themselves, did not respect the neutrality of humanitarian action. Consider how Care International summarised its action in Rwanda:

> Care was a key player in the three major humanitarian initiatives in southern Rwanda: first to establish relief operations in the context of the French security zone to prevent a further massive exodus of refugees in July August; then stepping up relief assistance to encourage the displaced people to stay when the RPA assumed control in September; then in establishing Operation Homeward (later Operation Retour) to encourage them to return home from September onwards (although this had limited success until January).[181]

The emphasis on containment remains puzzling for an NGO. In the same vein the Jesuit Refugee Service emphasised late July 1994 that "Food should be distributed in a way that promotes the refugees' return to their own land."[182] Bearing in mind that UN agencies held the displaced in Rwanda during the summer 1994 with aid and promises of safety, their helplessness to prevent forceful closures a few months later shows either a lack of foresight or a deliberate decision to enforce containment, then return. In northern Iraq the UNHCR was criticised both for not providing assistance in insecure areas and sometimes for doing so in order to attract and stabilise displaced populations[183] Thus the dilemmas in which humanitarian workers were entangled with regards to IDPs might stem from the fact that agencies initially partook in the design of containment policies. From the outset, UNHCR described Rwandan Open Relief Centres in migration-related terms displaying both anxieties about "national sovereignty" and the priority given to the return and stabilisation of displaced populations.[184] For UNHCR Director of External Relations

> The aim of any operation set up by a refugee organisation must be to prevent a refugee from really becoming a refugee and, if s/he became one, to find very quickly a solution to this problem.[185]

Given that IDPs are people in refugee-like situations and often are on their way to crossing borders, this remark begs questions regarding the institution's strategies and their implications for people on the move. However justified the UNHCR is in denouncing governments that evade their asylum duties, some introspection is also necessary.

Although aid deliveries often seemed to vary with public pressure, it remains difficult to distinguish between causal factors since times of complex emergencies combined migration and public pressures for action. Media and migration-driven explanations, though, are not necessarily mutually exclusive. In crisis times, public pressure provided humanitarian agencies with the necessary funds for action. Still, the agencies could decide to use the aid strategically so as to create, shape or control specific population movements. In other words, whereas public outrage occasionally created the possibility of action, agencies determined what was to be done. Sadly, the humanitarian choices made are little investigated by the media-focused analysts despite the fact that some decision defy common sense and first aid principles. One such example is the sustained refusal to evacuate civilians from dangerous sites when they want it. Likewise, withdrawing aid to create and control movements of population is a puzzle for media-based analysis of humanitarian action. Making sense of aid withdrawal from such a viewpoint requires reference to the "donor fatigue" syndrome. The problem remains that some examples of strategic use of aid provision cannot be explained by reference to compassion fatigue. As described above, in January 1995, humanitarian agencies were simultaneously calling for more help for refugees in Zaire and stopping food rations to close the camps in Zone Turquoise. Furthermore, media-induced humanitarianism hardly accounts for weak responses to such a publicised event as the attack on Kibeho. The book's argument also challenges the humanitarian triage postulate. Triage, the difficult choices that aid workers must make, is often assumed to be a particular equation between means and ends in emergency conditions.[186] Means are provided by the international community, hence the implications of the media. The end is assumed to be saving lives. Nevertheless, the range of policies outlined above extends to the use of threats, aid withdrawal that cannot be understood without reference to a containment or return agenda.

The above study suggests that protection can be understood as a tool to control IDPs' movements. Such a viewpoint might shed interesting perspectives on new thinking in forced migration studies. It enlightens the current focus on designing *efficient* response tools to complex emergencies as well as the emphasis on speed and space. Concepts such as early warning systems, humanitarian space, open relief centres, the right to stay and quick impact projects, to name a few, have become essential key words of an emergent forced migration terminology that needs scrutiny. This chapter will close with an illustration. "Humanitarian space" is a concept ascribed with spatial, social and political dimensions:

> Humanitarian space is a dynamic concept with multiple dimensions. The spatial metaphor suggests not a walled room with fixed dimensions but something more akin to an accordion. That is, available access to vulnerable populations may shrink or expand in accordance with the policies or actions of local political and military authorities. Rather than simply filling existing space, outside humanitarian institutions may expand this space through their presence and the international attention they attract.[187]

Startlingly enough, most studies of humanitarian action ignore spatial considerations. By contrast, the author argued that the location of assistance and safety was crucial to the drafting of IDP policies. She also challenged the assumption that international actors only expanded humanitarian space. The accordion metaphor used by Minear and Weiss rightly depicts the flexibility of humanitarian spaces. Still, the authors presume that outside institutions may only enlarge the space and opportunities available to vulnerable persons. Even Ramsbotham and Woodhouse's excellent study, which acknowledges the possibility of reducing humanitarian space, postulates, "The role of military forces in humanitarian intervention, both forcible and non-forcible, is to create humanitarian space for non military relief."[188] This chapter shows that governments and international agencies can choose to contract protected spaces so as to develop a return impetus. Thus, the international community's impact on the size and evolution of humanitarian spaces is greater than accounted for so far. Indeed, in the return, containment and bargaining processes, places such as Kibeho, the front line areas in northern Iraq or Srebrenica turned into snares for their unfortunate residents. They became traps because they were initially created to discourage flights and thus had no escape routes: they were and remained humanitarian spaces without exit.

Notes

1   Hollingworth, Larry, *Merry Christmas Mr. Larry* (London: Heinemann, 1996), 245.

2   Office of the Executive Delegate of the Secretary General for a UN Inter-agency Programme for Iraq, Kuwait and the Iraq/Turkey and Iraq/Iran Border Areas, 15 May 1991, Updated Appeal 12 June 1991, quoted in Weller, ed., *Iraq and Kuwait*, 629.

3   *Assistance to Refugees, Displaced Persons and Other War-affected Populations*, WFP in Former Yugoslavia, Situation Report, January 1993, 6.

4   Ibid., Situation Report No. 2, March 1993, 4 and Situation Report No. 3, May 1993, 9.

5   Ibid., Situation Report No. 3, May 1993, 9.

6   For details on the Croat blockade of central Bosnia, see *Assistance to Refugees, Displaced Persons and Other War-affected Populations*, WFP in Former Yugoslavia, Situation Report No. 4, July 1993, 5; Situation Report No. 5, September 1993, 5 and Situation Report No. 6, November 1993, 4-5, both indicate that, although stocks were sufficient, fighting severely curtailed deliveries in Bosnia.

7   *Winter Programme for Bosnia-Herzegovina, WFP Proposal for the Pre-positioning of Contingency Food Stocks*, World Food Programme in Former Yugoslavia, June 1993.

8   Tiso, "Safe Haven Refugee Programs," 585.

9   Both and Honig, *Srebrenica*, 132.

10   *Information Notes on Former Yugoslavia*, No. 6/95, UNHCR Office of the Special Envoy for Former Yugoslavia, Zagreb, Croatia, June 1995.

11   Hollingworth, *Merry Christmas Mr. Larry*, 39, 57, 162.

12   *ICRC Activities in the Region of Former Yugoslavia*, Fact Sheet, ICRC, Geneva, July 1994.

13   *Oxfam Programme Update 20, Great Lakes Region - Rwanda Crisis*, 17 February 1995, 2.

14   "Hunger stalks forgotten Rwanda refugee camps," *The Independent*, 23 March 1995.

15   *Oxfam Programme Update 20, Great Lakes Region - Rwanda Crisis*, 17 February 1995, 2 and *Programme Update 24*, March 1995, 2.

16   Srebrenica remains a hard case as the food situation improved slightly in 1995, although most political mediators had tacitly given up on the town. This suggests that media induced humanitarianism can take priority over strategic decisions. However, the increase in food deliveries in the besieged town masked a deteriorating security situation. Thus a fair assessment of the situation would require a study of security issues and possibly of the extent to which aid was a substitute for military protection.

17   *UNHCR warns of impeding Bukavu Crisis*, UNHCR Update on Rwanda, UNHCR, Geneva, 12 August 1994, 2 pages.

18   ICRC News No. 30, 27 July 1994 and ICRC News No. 32, 10 August 1994, in ICRC, *Public Statements Issued by the ICRC* -April-August 1994, 10 August 1994, 24 and 26.

19   S/1994/924, 3 August 1994, Report of the UN Secretary-General on the Situation in Rwanda.

20   *Rwanda Report*, USAID, 5-8 August 1994, 7-13.

21   *Rwanda Report*, USAID, 16-18 August 1994, 6-8.

22   Ibid., 6-8.

23   Ibid., 6-8.

128

24   Ibid., 6-8.
25   Torrenté, Nicolas de, *L'action de MSF dans la crise rwandaise, un historique critique*, MSF report, avril-décembre 1994, Version définitive, juillet 1995, 47. Author's translation.
26   Ibid., 9 and 47.
27   94/0279, *Rwanda Civil Disturbance*, DHA-Geneva Daily Information Report No. 32, 26 August 1994 (information provided by UNREO -United Nations Rwanda Emergency Office).
28   Torrenté, *L'action de MSF dans la crise rwandaise*, 48.
29   *Burundi-Rwanda Voluntary Repatriation of Refugees*, Note on Voluntary Repatriation of Refugees, UNHCR, January 1995, 10.
30   *Global Report on UNCHR's Activities in Iraq since April 1991*, UNHCR, Geneva, 1 September 1992, 5.
31   *Rwanda Report*, USAID, 5-8 August 1994, 5.
32   *Rwanda Emergency Update*, Care Britain, 16 January 1995.
33   *Communiqué of the Regional Summit on Rwanda*, Nairobi, 7 January, 1995, 3.
34   Foreword by Sadruddin Aga Khan, United Nations Inter-agency Programme for Iraq, Kuwait and the Iraq/Turkey and Iraq/Iran Border Areas, Updated and Consolidated Appeal for Urgent Humanitarian Action, 15 May 1991.
35   Jeff Drumtra, an Africa policy analyst, listed the following: being guilty, being unsure of one's own culpability, being afraid of unjustified prosecution, propaganda, security incidents in Rwanda, Burundi or Zaire, intimidation by the Interahamwe, loyalty to one's own group, homes occupied or destroyed, exhaustion. Drumtra, Jeff, *Site Visit Notes, Site Visit to Rwanda, Zaire, and Burundi*, 20 October to 17 November 1994, U.S. Committee for Refugees, 19 pages, 10-12.
36   *Burundi-Rwanda Voluntary Repatriation of Refugees*, Note on Voluntary Repatriation of Refugees, UNHCR, January 1995, 10.
37   *Global Report on UNCHR's Activities in Iraq*, 3.
38   Ibid., 7.
39   John Fawcett, International Rescue Committee, Interview 27 February 1997.
40   See Updated Plan of Action for the Inter-agency Humanitarian Programme, 1 September-31 December 1991 and UNHCR Information Bulletin No. 6, 3 October 1991, in Weller, ed., *Iraq and Kuwait*, 640-646.
41   *Global Report on UNCHR's Activities in Iraq*, UNHCR, 19.
42   *Asylum Under Attack, a Report on the Protection of Iraqi Refugees and Displaced Persons One Year after the Humanitarian Emergency in Iraq*, Lawyers Committee for Human Rights, New York, April 1992, 22-23. For details of UNHCR difficulties, see UNHCR, *Update on Operations within the Regional Humanitarian Plan of Action*, 5 December 1991, in Weller, ed., *Iraq and Kuwait*, 649.
43   *Asylum Under Attack*, Lawyers Committee for Human Rights, 22-23.
44   For details on the position of the government of Rwanda regarding IDPs see *The Policy of the Government of Rwanda Regarding Internally Displaced Persons*, a document of the Ministry of Rehabilitation and Social Integration, Republic of Rwanda, Kigali, undated document, the substance and tone of the text suggest that it was produced early autumn 1994. A copy can be found in the Documentation Centre of the Refugee Studies Programme, Oxford, 2.
45   Drumtra, *Site Visit to Rwanda, Zaire and Burundi*, USCR, 14.

46   Kent, Randolph, "The Integrated Operation Centre in Rwanda: Coping with Complexity" in Whitman, Jim and Pocock, David, eds., *After Rwanda, The Coordination of UN Humanitarian Assistance* (London: Macmillan Press Ltd, 1996), 63-85, 73.

47   *Oxfam Programme Update 21, Great Lakes Region - Rwanda Crisis*, 24 February 1995, 2.

48   *Oxfam Programme Update 22, Great Lakes Region - Rwanda Crisis*, 3 March 1995, 2.

49   Torrenté, *L'action de MSF dans la crise rwandaise*, MSF, 50.

50   Kent, "The Integrated Operation Centre in Rwanda," in Whitman and Pocock, eds., *After Rwanda*, 74-75.

51   Ibid., 75.

52   A good indicator of this overwhelming desire was that the large majority of Bosnian IDPs chose to register to vote in their 1991 municipality, *ICG Analysis of the 1997 Municipal Elections*, ICG Press Release, 14 October 1997, 3.

53   See for instance the Letter from the Society for Threatened Peoples denouncing forced repatriations of Bosnians, in *Bosnia Report*, Newsletter of the Alliance to defend Bosnia and Herzegovina, Issue 17, November 1996-January 1997, 10. See also *Who is Living in my House?* Amnesty International, 17.

54   Ibid., 15 and 23.

55   Ibid., 15 and 23.

56   *Going Fast Nowhere*, ICG Bosnia Report No. 23, 18-33.

57   Ibid., 25.

58   "Mediators Relieved by Peaceful Bosnian Voting," *Reuters* (Sarajevo), 16 September 1996. See also "Free and Fair are the Missing Bosnia Elements," *Los Angeles Times*, 13 September 1996.

59   UNHCR information note August/September 1996, quoted in the Amnesty International report, *Who's Living in my House?* 1, see also *Going Fast Nowhere*, ICG Bosnia Report No. 23, 16-17.

60   Hallegård, Carl, "Bosnia and Herzegovina: Problems and Progress in the Return Process," Vol. 1 (January-April 1998), *Forced Migration Review*, 21-24, 23.

61   UNHCR officer Tony Land, quoted in Rieff, David, *Slaughterhouse, Bosnia and the Failure of the West* (Reading: Vintage, 1995), 208.

62   Jessen Petersen, Soren, "La re-création de conditions de vie normales" in Domestici-Met, ed., *Aide Humanitaire Internationale*, 124-126, 124.

63   Statement of UNHCR at Donor Information Meeting, Geneva, 15 May 1991, in Weller, ed., *Iraq and Kuwait*, 617.

64   Ofteringer, Ronald and Backer, Ralph, "A Republic of Statelessness, Three Years of Humanitarian Intervention in Iraqi Kurdistan," Vol. 24, No. 2-3 (1994), *Middle East Report*, 40-45, 44.

65   See "The Crushing of Kurdish Civil Society" special feature of *Warreport*, Bulletin of the Institute for War and Peace Reporting, No. 47, November/December 1996, especially articles by WOOLLACOTT, Martin, "Why the West Must Help the Kurds," 24-25 and Keen, David, "Deprive and Rule," 52-53.

66   *Background Paper on Refugees and Asylum Seekers from Iraq*, Centre for Documentation and Research, UNHCR Geneva, September 1996 (On-line: http://www.unhcr.ch/refworld/country/cdr/cdrirq2.htm, no pagination).

67   Gunter, "A Kurdish State in Northern Iraq?" 76.

68   Keen, *The Kurds in Iraq*, SCF, 40.

69   According to Amnesty International and UNHCR, the reprisals could have caused around 30 000 victims, The Economist Intelligence Unit Country Report, Rwanda, 25. Moreover, many returnees were accused of killings by new settlers "squatting" the returnees' piece of land, *Human Rights World Report 1995*, Human Rights Watch, 43.

70   Drumtra, *Site Visit Notes, Site Visit to Rwanda, Zaire, and Burundi*, USCR, 12.

71   *Human Rights World Report 1995*, Human Rights Watch, 41-42.

72   Torrenté, *L'action de MSF dans la crise rwandaise*, MSF, 75.

73   *Africa Confidential*, Volume 35, No. 22, 4 November 1994, 4.

74   Fein, Helen, *The Prevention of Genocide, Rwanda and Yugoslavia Reconsidered*, working paper of the Institute of the Study of Genocide, copy in documentation centre of Refugee Research Programme, Oxford, 1994, 24.

75   Boulanger, Claire, "Les conditions judiciaires de la reprise de la vie normale," in Domestici-Met, ed., *Aide Humanitaire Internationale*, 126.

76   *Rwanda and Burundi: Horror of Genocide Hangs over the Region One Year Later*, Press Release, Amnesty International USA, New York, 6 April 1995.

77   *Justice et Droits de l'Homme au Rwanda; Justice and Human Rights in Rwanda*, talk by Dr. Joseph Mucumbitse, presented in a one-day conference: *Rwanda: Perspectives d'Avenir*, 12 May 1995, London: Westminster University, Association des Droits de l'Homme, Bruxelles.

78   ICRC report quoted in *Human Rights World Report 1995*, Human Rights Watch, 43.

79   *Rwanda: ICRC Sounds Alarm on Appalling Prison Conditions*, ICRC, Press Release 95/8, 31 March 1995 and *Rwandan Genocide to be in the Dock*, Human Rights Watch, Press Release, 9 November 1994.

80   Ibid. This point was also emphasised by José Kagabo (Centre D'études Africaines, Paris) in the course of the conference *Rwanda: Perspectives d'Avenir*, 12 May 1995, London.

81   *Rwanda and Burundi: Horror of Genocide Hangs over the Region One Year Later*, Amnesty International, 6 April 1995. Kent sees the absence of Western support for the Rwandan government as a major cause of its radicalisation regarding displacement issues. Kent, "The Integrated Operation Centre in Rwanda," in Whitman and Pocock, eds., *After Rwanda*, 79-80. Regarding the little help that Western states such as Belgium but above all France provided, see BA, Mehdi, *Rwanda 1994, Un Génocide Français*, L'Esprit Frappeur No. 4 (Paris, Vertige Graphic: 1997), 73-81.

82   *The International Response to Conflict and Genocide: Lessons from the Rwanda Experience*, Steering Committee of the Joint Evaluation of Emergency Assistance to Rwanda, March 1996, Study 4 "Re-building Postwar Rwanda" (Krishna Kumar, David Tardif-Douglin, Kim Maynard, Peter Manikas, Annette Sheckler and Carolin Knapp).

83   *Great Lakes Region: Still in Need of Protection: Repatriation, Refoulement and the Safety of Refugees and the Internally Displaced*, AFR/02/07/97, Amnesty International, 24 January 1997, 5-7.

84   *ICG in the Balkans, Past Achievements and Future Priorities, March 1996-March 1998*, ICG Bosnia Report No. 22, April 1997, 10.

85   Zilic, Ahmed and Risaluddin, Saba, *The Case of the Zvornick Seven* (London: The Bosnian Institute, 1997).

86   See Frelick, "Aliens in their Own Land," and the various ICG reports already mentioned.

87   Cigar, *Genocide in Bosnia*, 140.

88   Rieff, *Slaughterhouse*, 200.

89   *Information Notes on Former Yugoslavia*, UNHCR office of the Special Envoy for Former Yugoslavia, External Relation Unit, No. 11, November 1993, i.

90   *Confidential Note for Special Envoy (FYEO)*, Louis Gentile UNHCR, Banja Luka, 10 November 1993.

91   Ramsbotham, Oliver and Woodhouse, Tom, *Humanitarian Intervention in Contemporary Conflict, a Reconceptualisation* (Cambridge: Polity Press, 1996), 219-221.

92   Ogata (31 August 1993), quoted in ibid., 191.

93   Frelick, "Preventive Protection," 440.

94   UNHCR Information Bulletin, 11 June 1991, in Weller, ed., *Iraq and Kuwait*, 622.

95   John Fawcett (IRC), Interview, 27 February 1997.

96   Office of the Executive Delegate of the Secretary-General for a United Nations Inter-agency Humanitarian Programme for Iraq Kuwait and the Iraq/Turkey and Iraq/Iran border areas, 15 May 1991, Updated Appeal, 12 June 1991, in Weller, ed., *Iraq and Kuwait*, 636.

97   *The Economist*, 22 June 1991, 74.

98   Ofteringer and Backer, "A Republic of Statelessness," 44.

99   Mr. Perkins US, declaration to the UN Security Council, S/PV.3105, 11 August 1992, in Weller, ed., *Iraq and Kuwait* , 706-707.

100   Gunter, "A Kurdish State in Northern Iraq?" 57.

101   Kent, "The Integrated Operations Centre in Rwanda," in Whitman and Pocock, eds., *After Rwanda*, 67.

102   Both and Honig, *Srebrenica*, 116-117. See also Ramsbotham and Woodhouse, *Humanitarian Intervention in Contemporary Conflict*, 185.

103   In UNSC S/RES/836 (1993), 4 June 1993, the mandate of UNPROFOR was extended under chapter VII of the United Nations Charter to include the right to use "all necessary means, including the use of force" to protect the safe areas. Safe areas were proclaimed in UNSC S/RES/819 (1993), 16 April 1993 and UNSC S/RES/824 (1993), 6 May 1993.

104   Ramsbotham and Woodhouse, *Humanitarian Intervention*,179 and 184.

105   Quoted by Gaer, Felice, "UN Operations in Former Yugoslavia," issue 28 (September 1994), *Warreport*, 14-15, 14. In the same volume see comments by David Rieff on UN disregard for civilians. Rieff, David, "Accomplice to Genocide," 35-40.

106   Gentile, himself a protection officer in Banja Luka who put his career at risk by publicly protesting against ongoing Serb violence, "The quiet town where terror lurks," Louis Gentile, *New York Times*, 14 January 1994 and interview with Louis Gentile, 11 September 1998.

107   Hollingworth, *Merry Christmas Mr. Larry*, 240-254. UNHCR, *Banja Luka: Ethnic Cleansing has Another Name*, internal communication (BLK/HRV/HCR/0401/CMB/PBT/OSE), Louis Gentile, UNHCR representative in Banja Luka, 30 August 1993. For appraisal of UNHCR staff see Rieff, *Slaughterhouse*, 196.

108   Human Rights Watch, public release concerning ethnic cleansing in Bosnia

(untitled), 7 November 1994.

109 See for instance, *New wave of Ethnic Cleansing Before the "Referendum."* 26 August 1994 and *UN Must Act to Halt Renewed Wave of Ethnic Cleansing*, 3 September 1994, London briefings, Bosnia-Herzegovina Information Centre, London.

110 Accounts of the end of the war can be found for instance in Simms, Brendan, "An Enclave too far," Issue 18 (February-May 1997), *Bosnia Report* published by the Alliance to defend Bosnia i Herzegovina, 10 and *Strategic Survey 1995/1996* (London: International Institute for Strategic Studies, 1996), 126-138.

111 *Going Fast Nowhere*, ICG Bosnia Report No. 23, 1 May 1997, 26.

112 *Stabilisation Force, (SFOR) fact sheet*, NATO, 20 December 1996.

113 Evictions were regularly carried out in Croat-controlled territory. "70 persons evicted from West Mostar," *Agence France Presse*, 10 January 1997. In Banja Luka , harassment continued "Endangered Muslims Evacuated from Bosnian Town" *Reuters*, 9 March 1996. Haris Silajdzic - a wartime Bosnian prime minister - also complained about continued cleansing in "Dayton is not being implemented - a short analysis," *Bosnia Report*, Newsletter of the Alliance to defend Bosnia- Herzegovina, Issue 18, February-May 1997, 1-2, 2.

114 IPTF briefing for OSCE international election supervisors, Mostar, 10 September 1997.

115 *Kosovo: The Road to Peace*, ICG report, 12 March 1999, 6 (Lessons from Mistakes in Bosnia).

116 "Nato Force in Bosnia to shrink by half," *Reuters* News On-line, 11 November 1996.

117 Minear, Larry and Weiss, Thomas, *Mercy Under Fire, War and the Global Humanitarian Community*, (Oxford: Westview Press, 1995), 30.

118 HCR/CRHC/FC/2/Annexe I, 1. Despite the official line, there were some local arrangements. UNHCR officers in Banja Luka, for instance, organised, in the course of several months in 1993-1994, the departure to Croatia of several hundreds of Muslim residents desperate to leave a city in which their life was worth little [Interview with Louis Gentile, London 11 September 1998]. Some governments, such as that of the UK made explicit their reluctance to accept evacuation, except in certain dramatic medical cases which incidentally, were publicised. Statement by Baroness Chalker of Wallasey, Minister for Overseas Development, United Kingdom, International Meeting on Humanitarian Aid for Victims of the Conflict on the Former Yugoslavia, Geneva, 29 July 1992.

119 Interview with Allan Little, *Dani* (Sarajevo), reproduced in *Bosnia Report*, published by The Bosnian Institute, New Series No. 2, January-February 1998, 3-6, 4-5.

120 Ibid., 4-5.

121 *Update on the Yugoslav Region*, UNHCR internal documentation, 22 September 1993.

122 UNHCR, *The State of the World's Refugees* (New York: Penguin Books, 1993), 82.

123 "L'ONU tente de faire passer un nouveau convoi pour Srebrenica," *Le Monde*, 23 March 1993, 44; "Report de l'évacuation des Serbes de Tuzla," *Le Monde*, 24 March 1993, 4; "Faire Vivre Tuzla," Freimut Duve (social democrat MP in the Bundestag), *Le Monde*, 27 March 1993, 9.

124 Quoted in Both and Honig, *Srebrenica*, 115 (author's italics).

125   Rieff, *Slaughterhouse*, 209.

126   "Kurds flee as Iraqi army besieges town," *The Financial Times*, 8 October 1991, 4. "Equal in misery- Belatedly, the West is doing something for Kurds and Palestinians. But not enough," *The Financial Times*, 11 December 1991, 19.

127   "Clashes reported between Kurds and Iraqi troops," *The Financial Times*, 20 July 1991, 2.

128   *Asylum Under Attack*, Lawyers Committee for Human Rights, 21.

129   Ibid., 21.

130   Ibid., 20.

131   Ibid., 20.

132   "Turquie: soutenu par Washington, critiqué par Bonn, le gouvernement a lancé un nouveau raid aérien contre les bases séparatistes kurdes," *Le Monde*, 27 March 1992, 4. See also Ofteringer and Backer, "A Republic of Statelessness," 44.

133   Ofteringer and Backer, "A Republic of Statelessness," 44.

134   Landgren, "Safety Zones and International Protection," 443.

135   Keen, *The Kurds in Iraq*, SCF, 24-28.

136   Jean, François, ed., *Populations in Danger 1995, an MSF report* (London: 1995), 72-73.

137   Tiso, "Safe Haven Refugee Programs," 584-585 and 587. See also *The Economist*, 23 April 1994, 41-42.

138   Jean, ed., *Populations in Danger 1995*, MSF, 77.

139   "old caseload" refers to Rwandan Tutsi refugees from before the 1994 genocide.

140   For discrepancies in casualty numbers in Rwanda see UNDHA *Emergency Profile (Pilot Project) Rwanda*, 3 May 1995. See also "Rwanda refugees slaughtered," *The Independent*, 24 April 1995.

141   Both and Honig, *Srebrenica*, 110, 161-163. After the May 1995 hostage crisis, UNPROFOR soldiers were acting under a directive 2/95 -29 May 1995- stating that "the execution of their mandate [was] secondary to the security of the UN personnel," ibid., 8.

142   Ibid., 17 and 29.

143   Ibid., 28-30.

144   Ibid., 38-39.

145   Interview with Louis Gentile, London, 11 September 1998.

146   Both and Honig, *Srebrenica*, 48-88. Personal notes, conversation with survivors, Tuzla August 1995. "En Bosnie: la colonne de l'enfer" *Le Monde*, 17 October 1995, 14.

147   Both and Honig, *Srebrenica* , 177-178.

148   *Report of the Independent International Commission of Inquiry on the Events at Kibeho*, April 1995, 14 pages, submitted to the Rwandan government on 18 May 1995, 4-7.

149   *Report of the Independent International Commission of Inquiry on the Events at Kibeho*, 8.

150   "Rwandan army traps Hutus," *The Independent*, 20 April 1995. The ICRC, for instance, warned about the catastrophe. ICRC, 20 April 1995, Press Release 95/11, *Rwanda : ICRC Warns about Possible Human Disaster in Southern Camps* and Press Release 95/13, 22 April 1995, *Hundreds of Dead Among the Displaced Persons in Southern Rwanda.*

151   *Internally Displaced Persons, IOM Policy and Programmes*, IOM, 14-15. See also "Rwanda defends plan to close camps," *The Independent*, 22 April 1995.

152   Kent, "The Integrated Operation Centre in Rwanda," in Whitman and Pocock, eds., *After Rwanda*, 77.

153   70,000 is a conservative estimate provided by MSF. It is often claimed that about 120,000 persons resided in and around Kibeho.

154   ICRC News 17, 26 April 1995, *Rwanda: Wounded from Kibeho Camp Evacuated to Butare*. This bulletin also indicates that the other camps in the south-west of Rwanda were deserted and therefore that about 280,000 persons altogether were on the move and in need of help in south Rwanda.

155   IOC reports, 24 and 27 April 1995, quoted in DHA, *Emergency Profile (Pilot Project) Rwanda*, 3 May 1995. See also "Hutus trek home from camps at gunpoint," *The Independent*, 26 April 1995. "Refugees beaten to death on return," *The Independent*, 1 May 1995.

156   *Human Rights Watch/Africa and FIDH Commend Peaceful End to Kibeho Crisis but Warn Rwandan Judicial System Needs Immediate Action*, Human Rights Watch Africa, Federation International des Droits de l'Homme, Press Release, 11 May 1995, 1-2.

157   *Report of the Independent International Commission of Inquiry on the Events at Kibeho*, 12.

158   Ibid., 10.

159   IOC reports, 24 and 27 April 1995, quoted in DHA, *Emergency Profile (Pilot Project) Rwanda*, 3 May 1995.

160   Stockton, Nicholas, "Rwandan Refugees: Political Expediency or Humanitarianism?" (March/April 1997), *Crossline Global Report*, 14-16, 15.

161   Goddings, *Refugees or Hostages? Population Movements in the Great Lakes Region since 1990*, a paper presented at the conference "Towards Understanding the Crisis in the Great Lakes Region," St. Anthony's college, Oxford, 1 February 1997.

162   *Report of the Independent International Commission of Inquiry on the Events at Kibeho*, 8.

163   Human Rights Watch, Press Release, 29 November 1994.

164   "Des milliers de kurdes ont manifesté contre le retrait américain de Dohouk," *Le Monde*, 18 June 1991, 8.

165   Gunter, "A Kurdish State in Northern Iraq?" 48.

166   Ibid., 68-69.

167   Author's experience during stays in Tuzla (1996), Mostar (1997) and Vlasenica (1997).

168   *Who's Living in my House?* Amnesty International, 14.

169   *Registration of Bosnian Refugees for the September Elections*, Helsinki Committee for Human Rights in Serbia, 31 July 1996. For a detailed assessment of the abuse during elections preparations see *Why the Bosnian Elections Must Be Postponed*, ICG Bosnia Report No. 14, 14 August 1996.

170   Ogata, November 1992, quoted in Minear and Weiss, *Mercy under Fire*, 94-95.

171   For a discussion on the choice available to Kurds displaced and refugees in the Spring 1991 see Keen, *The Kurds in Iraq*, SCF, 8-9.

172   *Oxfam Update 21, Great Lakes Region - Rwanda Crisis*, 24 February 1995, 3-4.

173   Frelick, "Preventive Protection," 449 and "Aliens in their Own Land."

174   See for instance, Shacknove, "From Asylum to Containment," 522; Kirisci, "Provide Comfort and Turkey," Dowty and Loescher, "Refugee Flows as Grounds for International Action," Adelman, "The Ethics of Humanitarian Intervention,"

74-75. Also, the fear of chaos and of uncontrolled mass population movements appear clearly in the document: *Terms of Reference for Evaluation of Emergency Assistance to Rwanda*, ODA Evaluation Department, 7 December 1994, 1-2.

175   Rieff, *Slaughterhouse*, 198. See also Braumann, "Contre l'Humanitarisme," No. 177 (1991), *Revue Esprit*, 77-85 and "Les Limites de l'Humanitaire," Vol. 51 (1996), *Les Temps Modernes*, 303-319.

176   Torrenté, *L'action de MSF dans la crise rwandaise*, MSF, 51.

177   *Oxfam Programme Update 20, Great Lakes Region - Rwanda Crisis*, 17 February 1995, 3.

178   Frelick, "Preventive Protection," 447.

179   Ibid., 445.

180   Rieff, "Accomplice to Genocide," issue 28 (September 1994), *Warreport*, 35-40, 36.

181   Stallworthy, Guy, *An Evaluation of Care's Response to the 1994 Crisis in Rwanda*, a report for Care International, 18 February 1995, 6.

182   *Rwanda Update*, Report from the Jesuit Refugee Service, Fr. Mark Raper, Rome, 28 July 1994.

183   Keen, *The Kurds in Iraq*, SCF, 36.

184   *Burundi-Rwanda Voluntary Repatriation of Refugees*, UNHCR, Note on Voluntary Repatriation of Refugees, January 1995, 10.

185   Jessen Petersen, in Domestici-Met, ed., *Aide Humanitaire Internationale*, 124, author's translation.

186   Minear and Weiss, *Mercy under Fire*, 219-222. See also Weiss, "Triage, Humanitarian Intervention in an New Era," 59-68.

187   Minear and Weiss, *Mercy under Fire*, 38.

188   Ramsbotham and Woodhouse, *Humanitarian Intervention*, 191 and 221-222.

4   Restore Hope versus Restore Order

The 1992-1993 intervention in Somalia was chosen to test the book's claims. It is a test case in so far as, at first sight, the hypothesis (here the idea that protection is a function of containment) does not seem to hold. Several reasons explain this choice. First and foremost, none of the numerous studies of Somalia referred to forced displacement as a cause for international action.[1] Ramsbotham and Woodhouse summed up the conventional wisdom when writing "the threat to international peace and security [in the preamble of UNSC resolution 794] does not come from cross border disturbance but only from the fact of the humanitarian crisis within Somalia itself."[2] De Jonge showed that UN interventions could be classified using two simple criteria: conflict containment and the interest of one permanent member of the UNSC. However like others, she singled out Restore Hope as a case in which intervention was explained "by the magnitude of the humanitarian crisis there and the intense media coverage of this humanitarian disaster."[3] Indeed, involvement in Somalia was often heralded as an example of news media influence, a perspective which is indirectly challenged by the study. Furthermore, the case also displayed American leadership, an unusual feature given the three previous cases reviewed. Thus it requires attention. Besides, the Somali epic had such resonance that a research on humanitarian politics in the 1990s can scarcely afford to by-pass it.

Relief granted in Sudan, Mozambique or Chechnya were potential alternative test cases. However, engagement in Sudan and Mozambique dated back to the late 1980s, whereas the study was firmly set in the context of post-Cold War politics.[4] As for Chechnya, the case was disregarded on several accounts. The situation amongst CIS countries does not allow for easy distinctions between refugees and IDPs. Humanitarian institutions interfered on behalf of Chechen displaced persons in response to demands of the Russian authorities.[5] The latter insisted that Chechens who took refuge in Dagestan, Ingushetia and North Ossetia were to be called IDPs,[6] whereas many displaced persons saw themselves as refugees. Apart from this contention over labels, the conflict took place within Russia, a permanent member of the UNSC. This singularly affected the manoeuvring space of the UN.[7] Humanitarian action itself was limited to the borders of the breakaway republic. Finally, as with Sudan or Mozambique, information regarding Chechnya remains scant in comparison to the documentation available on Somalia. Given the limited amount of time and resources which could be spared for a test case, choosing Somalia made sense.

This chapter draws together the threads of the argument laid out in the previous two chapters and compares the conclusions to the Somali case. It comprises three sections. The first two are identically structured: each briefly summarises the conclusions of one of the above chapters, then gauges them against the study of involvement with Somali IDPs. The last part closes the chapter with an appraisal of the issues raised by the study of Somalia.

From Neglect to Unwanted Fame: the March of the Somalis

Chapter II holds that international protection was granted to IDPs so as to contain them within the borders of their states of origin. Thus it should be regarded as a tool of migration policies. The argument is based on a study of the decision-making processes, from the initial population movements until some areas were declared safe.

The emergence of action regarding Iraqi, Bosnian and Rwandan displaced persons followed one pattern. Early population displacements were met with indifference and the reiteration that a state's internal affairs were not for the international community to consider. As refugees reached neighbouring countries, however, the latter had no choice but to become involved. Two approaches were adopted. Some receiving states kept their borders open. A traditional refugee policy ensued with humanitarian aid distributions and refugee camps alongside borders, yet outside the refugees' country of origin. This took place in Iran, in April 1991, Croatia from May to July 1992, and in Tanzania in 1994. By contrast, when Turkey during the spring of 1991 and Croatia, from July 1992 onwards, started to deny entry to potential refugees, they propelled the world into action on behalf of IDPs. In Rwanda though, the international community interfered whereas Zaire did not explicitly close its borders. Interestingly enough, however, the UN institutions which raised the displacement issue readily stated their interest in preventing a new Tanzania-type exodus. Thus, stopping refugee outflows was a catalyst for action on behalf of IDPs. Finally, interventions themselves unfolded incrementally. Initial relief efforts that failed to

138

defuse border crises were complemented with more extensive measures: military protection of relief, establishment of no-fly zones when relevant and, last, safe area declarations.

Interventions were justified partly on humanitarian grounds partly on strategic, refugee-related, grounds. However, sudden Western desires to alleviate the plight of people stranded within their home countries was a weak argument on three counts. First, indifference greeted initial reports concerning threatened and displaced persons until people started to pour over borders. Second, protection measures were discussed in terms of their expected efficiency in stemming refugee outflows rather than in terms of their humanitarian impact. Third, the chronology of Western involvement itself suggests that protection was stepped-up as early measures failed to lessen refugee pressure on borders. These features of international engagement support the claim that protection for IDPs was produced in an attempt to defuse refugee and border crises. Indirectly this reading also challenges assumptions à propos of media influence on initial humanitarian engagement. Thus the claim needs to be put to the test.

As already mentioned, displacement is hardly ever associated with the 1992-93 intervention in Somalia. In fact, none of the UNSC resolutions in 1992 mentions refugee flow.[8] Whereas academics fiercely debate the exact role played by the media, no one doubts that action itself aimed at relieving suffering and fighting the famine. Focus on skeletal bodies, on graveyard towns such as Baidoa or Bardhera, eclipsed potential differences between displaced persons and residents. All were trapped by war, all were desperate for the meagre rations occasionally provided by overwhelmed ICRC officers. Indeed, Somalia may well be a case where the mass displacements of population caused by the war and the drought were irrelevant to international action. By late 1992, IDPs, the most vulnerable populations in Somalia, were cared for because they were starving, not to forestall any cross-border exodus. Nevertheless, the irrelevance of forced migration issues to understand the help granted to uprooted Somalis remains an assumption as long as it is not carefully investigated. In the light of the research findings, it is worth exploring.

Too Late for Many

Somalia disintegrated into chaos after the fall of its long-time dictator, Siad Barre, in January 1991. The different factions, until then united to oust the despot, fell on each other and completed the destruction of the country's infrastructure, resources, trade and social networks. Many peasants and nomadic groups moved to villages and towns after they were chased from their land by violence, or after they had sold the last cattle of their diminished herd. Having lost all means of autonomous survival, those displaced persons were, by far, the weakest and most needy of the Somali peoples. The conflict, however, was largely ignored by the international community despite mounting casualties, civilian distress and significant shifts of population since the overthrow of Siad Barre.[9] According to USAID, "By the end of 1991 there were already an estimated 20,000 casualties of the civil war, more than 600,000 refugees and several hundred thousand internally displaced persons."[10] In spite of numerous famine warnings and appeals by the ICRC as well as by leading politicians, the international community postponed its humanitarian and political involvement throughout the first half of 1992. UN action in particular was marked by inefficiency and procrastination.[11] This indifference had dramatic human costs as displaced Somalis, gathered around towns, became too weak even to be rescued. MSF was reported to claim that, according to an enquiry on 100,000 Somali displaced and resident in April 1992, 24% of the children and 10% of the adults had died in the previous year.[12] Today, it is estimated that around 350,000 persons died of hunger or related diseases in the course of 1991-92.

In the course of July and August 1992, the starvation of Somali populations became an object of the world's attention. According to Hirsh and Oakley, the UN Secretary General report of 22 July "estimated that a million Somali children were at immediate risk of malnutrition with four and a half million people in urgent need of food assistance. The pastoral economy was in ruin ... Farmers were unable to work their fields because of clan warfare in the most productive rain-fed and irrigated agricultural areas."[13] The emphasis on starvation suggests implicitly that Somali people were too weak to move, let alone to cross the country and reach the Kenyan or Ethiopian borders. This picture however is erroneous. In spring 1992, General Aideed's military operations in the south of the country had led to a new flow of refugees into Kenya and Ethiopia. According to the UNHCR, north-east Kenya, itself a region under drought, accommodated 120,000 Somali refugees in June 1992.[14] A month later however, the UN reported that 330,000 Somalis had reached Kenya.[15] Hirsh and Oakley state that, by July 1992, "there were 350,000 refugees already registered in Kenya, and thousands in Ethiopia as well, with an estimated 300,000 internally displaced. With 1,000 refugee a day crossing the border, the UN projected 500,000 refugees by the beginning of 1993."[16] In September 1992, UNHCR reported that over one million persons had fled the country.[17] Prunier writes:

> By the summer of 1992, the situation had reached a peak of chaos. Over one and a half million Somalis were displaced, either internally (in "Somaliland", in Mogadishu and in the far South) or externally (in Ethiopia, in Yemen, in Kenya and even, in the case of the wealthiest ones, in Europe and North America). The food situation had become catastrophic, especially in the Bay and Lower Shebelle provinces, with a 90 per cent child malnutrition rate and a 16.5 per cent death rate among the displaced in June 1992.[18]

The UNDP appointed a well-known refugee specialist, John Roggee, to assess the situation of Somali IDPs. His report in September 1992, reads as follows: "The total number of 'visible' displaced persons in South and Central Somalia is between 556,000 and 636,000 of which 50% are in the two parts of Mogadishu and about 8% in each Kismayo and Baidoa. ... Most are totally destitute and severely malnourished."[19] He also noted that, since May 1992, food scarcity was the cause of most flights: "Current out-migrations are almost all due to famine."[20] Noteworthy for the present book, the study also emphasised that people were mobile, in search of free food. Rumours that relief was available induced people to leave their village, or sometimes to return to them.[21]

Neighbouring countries were reluctant to accept Somali refugees despite international pressure to do so, and despite having little means of closing their borders. The Kenyan government in particular had been very reluctant to accept Somali refugees for months. By 1992 it was overwhelmed by the scope of the crisis.[22] Conditions in the border camps were disastrous and the Kenyan authorities did not always cooperate with international agencies.[23] Both Yemen and Saudi Arabia tried to refuse boat people the right to land on their coasts.[24] Finally, third country resettlement was most difficult as no Western nation would open its doors to destitute Somalis.[25] To sum up, the "discovery" of starvation in Somalia in the summer of 1992 coincided with a refugee crisis. Whether such a coincidence had any bearing on action remains to be worked out.

An Incremental Approach to Starvation

George Bush was said to be greatly distressed by a telex received from the US ambassador to Kenya, describing a day spent in the northern Kenyan refugee camps. The document was entitled "a day in hell." The visit also coincided with a mounting public campaign in the US congress. As the international relief machine entered into action, it became clear that issues of geography were central to the design of relief. Mohamed Sahnoun, the UNSG special representative in Somalia, explained in an interview with *Le Monde* how the insecurity and conflict prevented aid from being delivered where it was needed.

> The geography of Somalia is an obstacle to the delivery of this aid. The country spreads itself over miles. It is difficult to act everywhere. Hence, certain regions have been privileged, especially around Mogadishu. At the same time, the influx of aid in the capital city created intractable problems. The towns' population almost doubled in a few months ... For some time now, we have managed to provide food for some towns in the interior, such as Baidoa ... but the south of the country hardly gets any help, albeit this is the most populated area. It is necessary to re-balance the aid geographically.[26]

Starting in late August 1992, the food airlift targeted isolated regions in the south of the country as well as refugee camps in Kenya. However, the airlift relied on a "market-driven strategy"[27] by which Somalia was to be flooded with food so as to reduce its price on local markets. This approach itself hardly was an answer to the suffering of the weakest members of society. IDPs in particular faced a problem of income generation in addition to that of food scarcity. By September 1992 in Mogadishu, where 50% of the displaced had gathered, Roggee noted that although town markets were full, displaced persons had no means to purchase food. "While food is readily available in the market, there are virtually no opportunities for income-generating activities for the displaced."[28] Displaced persons were thus the least able to afford anything. Besides, flooding Somalia with food generated new displacement problems. Baidoa had become a "city of displacees" in which the availability of relief sustained the inflow of desperate villagers.[29] In Bardhera, displaced started to arrive as they heard rumours of incoming food convoys.[30] Finally, food control and food denial being part of warfare, looting increased. By the autumn, the UN claimed that only 20% of relief aid was delivered to the intended recipients.[31] Emphasis on looting surfaced in the wake of renewed fighting in the south of the country. Armed confrontations in September resulted in the withdrawal of humanitarian agencies from the town of Baidoa. The conflict also provoked a further exodus towards Kenya, despite continuing insecurity in border camps.[32] International reactions to these events are worth describing. Apart from the denunciations of looting to which the author shall return, the UN Secretary General asked UNHCR to involve itself in Somalia. In its own words, the institution "launched a cross-border operation in September 1992 with the initial aim of stabilising population movements inside Somalia itself and stemming the momentum of refugee flows into neighbouring countries."[33] The anxiety of UNHCR was echoed in the humanitarian plan presented by Mohamed Sahnoun to a donors' conference in October 1992. The "Hundred Days Plan for Accelerated Humanitarian Assistance" was, according to Hirsh and Oakley, "based on two broad objectives ... First, it intended to prevent further refugee outflows and encourage repatriation by providing for the immediate need of the populace. Second, in the longer view, it sought to revive and strengthen Somali civil society at the national, regional and local levels."[34] Clearly, UN agencies were concerned about the mass cross-border outflow towards Kenya.

International engagement in Somalia was dramatically enhanced in December 1992 with the creation of Operation Restore Hope whereby 40,000 troops, mainly American, were sent to ensure that aid distribution could take place unhampered by fighting and looting. However, Restore Hope represented no change in the options available to IDPs. The American intervention was the promise of an accelerated, and possibly more efficient, delivery of the Hundred Days Plan drawn up by the UN in the autumn. The essence of UN action itself remained unchanged, centred around the idea of providing food in order to stabilise populations. One might argue that quick access to relief could still make a difference between life and death to starving people. Although this is true, it should be remembered that, by the autumn, death rates were decreasing. The worse of the famine was over and the most vulnerable Somalis, the majority of whom were displaced persons, had already died.

Media influence? What Media Influence?

The above paragraphs make the point that the UN, who were very involved in designing relief for Somalis, had an instrumental perspective on aid. By the autumn, UN officials had identified that the solution to famine induced displacement was adequate food distribution. This reading, however, does not imply that media-induced humanitarianism did not have an impact. Instead, it suggests that media influence hardly affected the strategies that were designed for the uprooted. This study neither possesses the resources nor has the purpose to determine the exact role played by media reporting the US decision on Restore Hope. However, the some points that support the idea that journalists' influence on decisions affecting IDPs was limited should be highlighted.

Initially, it took much campaigning from determined politicians (Natsios and Kassebaum in the US and, to a lesser extent, Kouchner in France), particular NGOs (such as Save the Children UK), the ICRC, and later UN officials such as Mohamed Sahnoun and Boutros-Ghali to raise the profile of the crisis.[35] Somalia became a broadcast disaster as humanitarian programmes unfolded during the summer 1992. As a result, for that period at least, media coverage reflected political approaches rather than challenged them. Various studies exploring the complex mechanisms by which news media were drawn into reporting Somalia conclusively argued that critical reporting was not a trigger for initial humanitarian involvement in that country.[36] Once more, comparing chronologies of action and media coverage disputes readings of humanitarian action that grant much influence to journalism. In the months preceding the US landing on Somali beaches, reporting was focused on starvation. However, it was backed by consistent campaigning for further action. The latter was organised by the leading politicians and agencies already mentioned - plus other NGOs such as Care International - but also by UN officials.[37] The latter circulated reports alleging that up to 80% of the aid reaching Somalia was looted. This figure became crucial in the debate leading to the US intervention. According to African Rights, the figure not only was largely exaggerated but also ignored the particulars of delivering aid in African complex emergencies.[38] Apart from images correlating starvation to looting, other factors carried weight for intervention. Forceful action in Somalia was, for instance, perceived as a relatively easy military job which would deflect pressures to act in Bosnia.[39] Lewis and Mayall also insist that both procrastination and the December decision to interfere should be understood in the context of a convoluted election year in American politics. For them, there is no doubt that, in the end, Bush had a great impact on the decision.[40]

In summary, campaigning for further action in Somalia took various roads: US and UN administrations, diplomatic channels and media institutions. Thus to adjudicate on potential causes for Restore Hope, one needs to conduct an in-depth investigation of the decision making process itself. Drawing conclusions from correlations is not enough. Second, regarding media pressure, the fact that humanitarian agencies, including the UN, fed little abreast journalists with their reports may have been determinant in creating whatever CNN effect there was. In the conclusion of this work, more will be said on the responsibilities entailed in the campaigning power granted to humanitarian agencies by their knowledge of the field.

A Far-Ranging Narrative

Contrary to what is assumed implicitly in most writings on humanitarian action, the fear of mass out-migration was not a mere "additional factor"[41] for action with IDPs. Most often, it was the very motor of initial involvement, especially for neighbouring countries and UN agencies. In Somalia, as in the three other cases, options available to IDPs were designed by UN institutions and government officials before media coverage became part of the decision-making process. Initially, the suffering of displaced persons was ignored by the international community, this time for well over a year. Then an emerging refugee crisis, in Ethiopia but above all in Kenya, coincided with international attention being drawn to the horn of Africa. In addition to US members of Congress such as Kassebaum, UN leaders, namely Boutros-Ghali and Sahnoun, seemed to have shamed the UNSC members into action.[42] Sahnoun's energetic diplomacy, including criticism of UN apathy, contrasted with the absence of UN response to the crisis until the summer of 1992. It also took pictures of exhausted bodies in UNHCR camps in Liboy, Kenya, to raise interest in people's needs including those of IDPs. Overall though, UN institutions were explicitly concerned about mass migrations and they acted upon those anxieties. Furthermore, action itself unfolded incrementally. As the initial airlift, Provide Relief, failed to dampen the crises (both humanitarian and refugee), further steps were taken: first, a UNHCR cross-border operation, followed by a large humanitarian plan and, in December, by a full-scale military intervention. Indeed, all inferences of the hypothesis - indifference, coincidence of action and refugee flows and incremental approach to involvement - can be found in the international response to the Somali emergency. Media-induced pressure may well have led to Restore Hope but, as far as the uprooted persons were concerned, the intervention was incorporated in a UN-led approach to mass displacement.

The purpose of this section was to demonstrate the existence of displacement issues and their relevance to the emergence of international interest for starving Somalis. The extent to which this reading helps to understand action on behalf of IDPs remains to be examined though. Because of the simultaneity of the humanitarian and refugee crises and the scope of Restore Hope, it is not possible to challenge the claim that fighting starvation was the foremost aim of the international community on the mere basis of the findings so far. However, it is equally impossible to dismiss *a priori* the impact of UN desires to prevent people from spreading chaos in the whole region. Despite the fact that refugees brought light to the distress of Somalis, the 1992 mobilisation unfolded without explicit reference to displacement as an issue. Starvation was the only headline, the one subject matter. This is reflected not only in UN discourses but also in the work of academics on Somalia. All the studies that the author came across ignore the potential implications of fears of mass migration. In fact, an honest adjudication on perspectives requires a deeper understanding of the objectives governing action. The latter itself calls for a close study of unfolding aid programmes. The second part of this chapter discusses the implementation of humanitarian action for IDPs. Thus, it may provide a deeper grasp of the protection policies intended for IDPs and their aims.

Care and Control: Discord over Objectives

Chapter III examined patterns of relief distribution and long term commitments to safety pledges. The argument relied on overviews of aid and protection programmes but also on the detailed study of some dilemmas involving IDPs. Particular features of policies towards the displaced persons were highlighted: the insufficiency of armed protection, the absence of evacuations, the emphasis on early return and the superficiality of reconstruction. Drawing these characteristics together, the chapter claimed that both physical safety and relief were allocated to places, designated by the international community, for displaced persons to stay in or to return to. By contrast, provision for IDPs dwindled when they did not comply with decisions regarding their relocation, return and reintegration. The text also emphasised that, apart from Bosnia, the case of which requires further examination, aid and rehabilitation programmes were shallow and hardly improved the lot of displaced persons. These points provide grounds for the claim that the main purpose of protection policies for IDPs is to gain control over people on the move. In other words, the chapter argues that the policies implemented by the international community corroborated the initial priority given to containment over safety. It thus confirms the instrumentalisation of protection policies for IDPs.

Chapter III's claims raised numerous issues regarding the emergence of early warning systems and other new humanitarian practices and concepts, from Quick Impact Projects to the Right to Stay. This makes it all the more important to gauge the findings in a test case. In addition, it was pointed out that the patterns of relief distribution witnessed in Bosnia followed closely the rhythms of media coverage. This, once more, highlights that in complex emergencies, there is more than one potential cause for international involvement. Consequently, one cannot deduce causation from mere correlation. One needs to review closely the decisions taken. Chapter III did not pretend to provide a close examination of years of humanitarian action in three different parts of the world. Instead, it set out to highlight that a range of policies existed including some that had little to do with media-induced pressure. It could thus conclude by pointing out the importance of containment as a motor for action with regard to IDPs. It is therefore necessary to work out whether the primacy given to containment over safety in northern Iraq, Bosnia and Rwanda can be found in Somalia.

Building from case studies and reports, the following section seeks to capture humanitarian action as it applied to uprooted Somalis. The UN determined the overall orientation of the operation in a spirit very similar to other 1990s interventions. Focus was placed upon the factors that caused displacement: first food then violence. However, the UN failed to convince UNITAF commanders to attempt full-scale disarmament. Disagreements between the US and the UN came to the fore as the former focused exclusively on allowing food distributions. In the context of UNOSOM, return to villages was encouraged, sometimes forced upon displaced persons. Finally, reconstruction programmes waned into uncertainty as no national political solution could be worked out.

The Food/Safety Interplay in Somalia

The 1992-93 intervention was marked by a UN/US consensus regarding the food strategy and dissent concerning the provision of security. Neither assistance nor protection, however, significantly improved IDPs' situation.

"Food flooding" had been a two-edged sword from the start. In August 1992 it was agreed upon in order to fight starvation, through decreasing prices, and to stabilise populations on the move. UN officials made clear that food availability and displacement were twin problems to be solved jointly. Given that free food promoted displacement,[43] Roggee, in September 1992 insisted that "every effort be made to distribute it [food] beyond the district and regional towns."[44] For him, "Once food is known to be reaching the villages other displacees from further afield will likely begin to return."[45]

147

In the name of the emergency, the long term effects of "drowning" Somalia under American grain such as destroying local coping mechanisms, including traditional migrations,[46] or compromising redevelopment schemes, by denying local farmers a living, were overlooked. By the time the Marines were ready to land on Mogadishu's beaches, food flooding alone could bring only limited returns. The worse of the famine was over and the weakest members of the society dead. Although the airlift strategy had brought grain prices down, it had come too late. Furthermore, grain was still too expensive for many IDPs. Still, despite the fact that further mass staple dumping was likely to depreciate prices further, thus penalising farmers and preventing a return to the normal commercialisation of food,[47] this remained the chosen strategy of the UN and US. UNITAF's mission consisted primarily in taking control of the road network so as to ensure a rapid expansion of deliveries.

Although regional centres were taken over quite rapidly, UNITAF never achieved a complete coverage of the country. Thus, the operation little encouraged return to villages. It may even have exacerbated on-going displacement. However, it canalised internal migrations towards distribution centres - Mogadishu, Kismayo, Baidoa and Bardhera. Claims that Restore Hope saved hundreds of thousands of lives are seriously challenged by independent observers.[48] As far as IDPs who had survived the famine were concerned, the operation may have improved their immediate plight. But it certainly preserved and possibly enhanced their dependency. By May 1993, in Mogadishu, the town where most of the relief was concentrated, a survey showed that over 90% of the displaced persons relied mainly "on free food aid for their daily food supply."[49] The malnutrition rate amongst displaced children was also still significantly higher than that amongst the residential population.[50]

As mentioned, there were two initial drives behind the focus on food distributions in Somalia: starvation and cross-border displacement. By December however, the former was waning, although Western audiences might have just become aware of it. The UN though maintained a strategy of large scale distribution which consolidated displacement within Somalia and which proved detrimental to later development projects. By late 1993, the UN had come to acknowledge the problems it created:

> In many areas, the massive infusion of food aid in response to widespread starvation in Somalia has depressed prices for agricultural commodities. The on-going need for further emergency food aid in certain areas must be

148

balanced against longer-term efforts to reinvigorate the productive sector.[51]

Food however was only part of the story. Disagreements between the US, the UN and NGOs over what assistance entailed and, crucially, whether disarmament was part of UNITAF's mission surfaced from the early days of Restore Hope. American forces were given a UN mandate under chapter VII of the United Nations Charter which stipulated that they could use "all necessary means" to establish a secure environment for relief programmes. Later, another resolution confirmed that Western forces were entitled to disarm militias.[52] Although the UN expected UNITAF to engage in disarmament, the latter consistently refused. The protection of populations against looters, gangs and warlords was not UNITAF's aim. Consequently it was never sought nor achieved. Both Stedman and Stevenson claim that violence was never entirely contained by UNITAF.[53] The organisation African Rights contends that the arrival of US troops in the Somali capital led to a flight of looters from Mogadishu, resulting in increased insecurity in other parts of the country which were only later, sometimes never, controlled by Western troops.[54] In the same vein, Stevenson wrote in 1993: "Outside the areas of immediate military control, there is no more law and order than there was before the troops arrived - possibly even less."[55] Indeed, various analysts agree that Operation Restore Hope was ineffective in protecting Somali populations.[56]

A marked change in tone and approach emerged when UNOSOM took over from UNITAF in March 1993. UNOSOM owned wider ambitions regarding the pacification and reconstruction of Somalia.[57] However, it suffered from the same shortcomings as its predecessor. According to Ramsbotham and Woodhouse, UN forces covered only 40% of the Somali territory, thus leading to increased insecurity in the rest of the country.[58] In August 1993, for instance, the UNDHA reported increased banditry in Bardhera and along the Kenyan border. The region saw a surge in the hijacking of vehicles which slowed down cross-border operations.[59] Under UNOSOM, insecurity affected even the capital city:

The deteriorating security in Mogadishu since 5 June 1993 has greatly affected the operational capacity of humanitarian partner-organisations. ... At the same time, increasing military and militia activity has led to additional displacements of population within, and outside Mogadishu and a greater need for emergency medical care.[60]

As international troops engaged in a war against General Aideed and by extension against the population of Mogadishu suspected to support him, they hampered humanitarian work. Without warning, UN troops attacked civilian areas in the town as well as hospitals, making it impossible to organise medical evacuations.[61] Even in the early days of Restore Hope, and contrary to what is often assumed, international military intervention did not always boost the work of humanitarian NGOs. Looting was a permanent problem and aid workers became increasingly insecure. "Relief workers, valued by gunmen before Operation Restore Hope as a source of semi-legitimate 'protection' income, are now prime targets."[62] Finally, after the war waged against General Aideed had failed, both US and UN leaders turned back and started to re-negotiate with him.[63] Thus, after the warlord had been denounced as a great danger to his own people, he became a suitable partner to build peace in Somalia. This seeming inconsistency of international negotiators shows that civilian protection was less important than the safety of military troops and stabilisation. Not only civilian protection but UN pride was also subordinated to the search of a political solution for the country.

Behind the US/UN disagreement over disarmament lay a fundamental difference in purpose. Whereas the US focused on starvation and refused to deal with anything else than ensuring access for food deliveries, the UN wanted to restore order in the Somali society. For UN authorities, food availability was important because it was the motor of displacement thus disorder. As soon as it ceased to be so, they turned their attention towards other factors impeding stabilisation and return, particularly violence and the lack of infrastructure. However, mass food deliveries had already contributed to a further weakening of the country's ability to see for itself. Furthermore, UNOSOM was particularly ill-equipped to engage in a military struggle with the Somali strong man. Stedman pointed out the inconsistency inherent to the overall intervention: UNITAF, a peace enforcement operation decided without consultation of the local warriors was to be followed up by UNOSOM, a UN peace-keeping operation which, in theory, requires consent to be operational.[64] As for people on the move, all assistance and protection strategies combined in a particularly calamitous way as free food came too late, then increased immediate dependency on NGOs whose work was later compromised by the UN war.

Repatriation was at the core of the UN approach to the Somali crisis as early as summer 1992. One purpose of Roggee's study was to "examine or define strategies which may lead to repatriation and re-habilitation of the displaced."[65] As already mentioned, his recommendations made clear that relief was planned with return as an objective.

> For the populations more recently displaced by famine, only a sustained program of food delivery to their villages will induce them to return, and then only if they have the strength to undertake such journey or are assisted with transportation.[66]

NGOs and UN agencies became increasingly aware that, in addition to relief distribution, physical safety affected return programmes. Meuus wrote in June 1993: "A secure environment is a prerequisite before mass resettlement of the now displaced populations can take place."[67] A few months later the UN acknowledged that:

> Increased insecurity is the most significant constraint to resettlement. ... Problems of insecurity along access roads and on routes used by returnees are likely to be exacerbated as refugees and the displaced return with large resettlement packages.[68]

Before this, the UN reported a few repatriation "success stories" which are telling in themselves. In an Information Report published in August 1993, the UNDHA noted with satisfaction that about two-thirds of the displaced people registered by the ICRC before the organisation ended its operations had left Kismayo and Bardhera.[69] However, a more detailed picture of the situation in Kismayo reads as follows:

> The majority [of the returnees] are farmers who have spontaneously left Kismayo in view of the upcoming harvest in Juba Valley and as a result of the closing of ICRC Kitchens at the beginning of the month. The current displaced population in Kismayo was recently estimated by MSF Holland and WFP to be between 25,000 and 45,000.[70]

Whereas returns were prompted, at least partially, by the end of relief operations,[71] UN reports tended to present them as spontaneous.

Many of those who wish to return to their homes have already begun to do so spontaneously. In Kismayo, over 50 per cent of the displaced have been successfully resettled following political agreement in the area. In Baidoa, over 80 per cent of the displaced have returned home. In Bardera, most of the 20, 000 displaced have departed, although they are now being replaced by returning refugees.[72]

In Somalia, as in most other cases, the UN supervised only a minority of the population movements. Most flights but also most returns took place unrecorded and without Western material support. However, calling returns spontaneous suggests an absence of "compellence" not reflected in reality. In Kismayo, the end of ICRC relief distribution had some heavy costs for the herdsmen who had lost their only means of survival, and thus would not leave the camps. Whilst congratulating themselves on the spontaneous return of peasants, the UN admitted that phasing-out relief induced hardship:

> The situation is worsening for displaced herdsmen in Kismayo and Bardhere who are unable to plan for resettlement ... Since WFP and ICRC ended food distribution operations in the displaced camps in Bardhere and Kismayo, alarming reports have been received about the food situation of the remaining families. [73]

Curtailing aid without considering the absence of alternative means of survival for numerous displaced persons created resentment, and hence problems for the mission as a whole.

> The termination of ICRC's relief activities in Kismayo caused considerable tensions among the population during the month of July. A WFP ship attempting to dock at the port of Kismayo with 2,000 Mts. of food was prevented from entering the port when it was learned that the food was destined for a region further up the valley.[74]

To their credit, and maybe because of the problems highlighted above, UN agencies started to deal with the plight of the most destitute in Kismayo through re-launching both emergency and development-orientated relief.[75]

This example is interesting for two reasons. It shows that the UN emphasis on "spontaneous" returns may hide the fact that phasing out relief was introduced prior to departure from camps and in order to encourage it.

It also reveals that humanitarian agencies planning for withdrawal, either did not consider the circumstances of IDPs or used "withdrawing food aid" as a checking mechanism to see who would remain nevertheless, who would endure hardship, thereby determining who had no alternative but to rely on relief. Whatever the thoughts behind the exercise, "providing food" became an instrument of other policies. This in itself belies humanitarian principles.

This study cannot purport to evaluate Western-led reconstruction efforts in Somalia. But it seeks to highlight that some internationally sponsored efforts were created so as to encourage return rather than as an end in themselves. In fact, according to Cohen and Deng, the international community largely ignored local efforts to develop in the midst of conflict.

> In the early 1990s, under the most dangerous conditions, local citizens created their own organisations to provide educational and health services, employment and development opportunities and to mediate disputes. Clan elders, civic leaders, health professional and women's groups, among other sought to salvage what remained of civil society and provide a modicum of protection and assistance to displaced and other populations. When international assistance was provided however, it did not adequately take into account and build upon these local efforts.[76]

Development projects set up by humanitarian agencies were devoted to encourage the return of refugees from along the Kenyan border.[77] The total UN proposed budget for cross-border operations reached about $65 million. By comparison, the UN suggested to spend $23.7 million on health and nutrition, $12.74 million on water, $12.35 million on agriculture, $7.78 million on livestock, $20 million on employment, $10 million on education and $0.5 million on women.[78] Often, the re-habilitation of community structures were limited to designated return areas and integrated into repatriation plans.

> UNHCR's cross-border-cross-mandate operation is focusing assistance on communities in Somalia within a 150 kilometres of the Kenyan border. Assistance is delivered through quick impact projects designed to stabilise population movements, encourage refugees to return home and also to benefit the communities to which refugees will return.[79] ... Over the next ten months, action will be taken to create jobs, provide training and re-establish primary education. The provision of seeds and tools and activities to enhance livestock health is essential, as are programmes to

assist refugees and displaced persons to return to their areas of origin and become productive.[80]

Numerous agencies participated in the rehabilitation of wells, schools, health centres and in agricultural projects under UNHCR supervision. Return orientated development however produced particular patterns of development. The emphasis on contingency and on the ability to react speedily to any renewed or unexpected movement was a priority.

> Because movements home are often sudden and spontaneous, response plans also need to be formulated without delay. Contingency planning should include the ability to rapidly establish "transit" centres, mobile kitchens and health stations along routes which the displaced will pass on their way home.[81]

The wish to control fluid situations appears also in the fact that Quick Impact Projects included monitoring activities, the exact purpose of which was never made explicit.

> In order to plan for the resettlement of refugees in Lower Juba ... UNHCR will implement Quick Impact Projects in various sectors including water, health, agriculture and livestock ... The establishment of humanitarian agencies in this region, in addition to catering to the local population, will allow the humanitarian community to monitor the flow of families returning to home villages from displaced and refugee camps.[82]

However empowering certain provisions may seem, development remained inscribed in contingency planning, and thus limited. The weakness of development projects, added to the problems caused by previous emergency relief policies, made the transition from emergency to rehabilitation particularly arduous.[83] For example, according to the Somalia Task Force, food-for-work programmes were difficult to implement "because of the prior dumping of food commodities without reciprocal requirements."[84]

Despite the dedication of many aid workers, the overall reconstruction remained superficial. The situation of IDPs in Mogadishu illustrates this problem. According to various sources, numerous displaced, especially in Mogadishu expressed the desire to return home. Roggee noted this first.[85] Almost a year later a survey of displaced confirmed the following: "56.9% of the displaced wish to return home irrespective of the fact they have a source of income in Mogadishu."[86] Still the international intervention provided neither the security incentives nor the adequate development programmes that would encourage people to leave Mogadishu. Neither was there any provision made for those who did not want to return. In September 1992, Roggee had also warned that "irrespective of any programs aimed at inducing displaced persons to return to the land, many are likely to remain in the urban displacee camps in the longer term."[87] Hence the need to rehabilitate and resettle people within urban areas. UN institutions seemed to appreciate the situation.

> Many of the displaced persons in Somalia's urban centres have little desire to return to their homes. They have either broken ties with their traditional communities or have been unable to maintain them. Many of these persons, among them professionals and business people, have, in effect become new urban poor. In Mogadishu, for example, it is estimated that 40 per cent of recent arrivals are unwilling to return to their former areas. In the northern and central urban centres of Hargiesa, Galkayo and Bossasso the great majority of the displaced do not wish to return home.[88]

Despite presenting strategies that seem to take IDPs' wishes into account,[89] and being aware that security of the region was necessary before IDPs would return of their own accord,[90] the UN did little to address these issues. Plans to accommodate displaced people's choices were simply not implemented. By 1996, Kessler estimated that about one million persons were displaced in the Horn of Africa, most of them in Somalia.[91] Action on their behalf had been scaled down considerably since 1992. As in Sudan, UN programmes no longer attracted adequate funding.[92] With a few years of hindsight, the lack of interest for Somali displacees provides more evidence that the international community did not really care about Somali displaced persons. The only concern displayed consistently over years is the wish that they settle within their country. There is evidence that humanitarian practices and short-term development schemes such as food deliveries and quick impact projects were used for that purpose.

Food for Care, Food for Thought

Although only briefly portrayed, the Somali experience provides valuable insights concerning policies applied to IDPs. It suggests that food provision was used for stabilisation purposes by the UN more than by the US. The US also showed limited interest in dealing with hard-core Somali politics in the context of UNITAF. Their overwhelming concern with food distribution and death rates, despite the fact that starvation was no longer the main problem, supports the idea that the December landing was driven by issues unrelated to mass displacement. Occasionally however, UNITAF provided food as a substitute for safety. In January 1993 for example, UNHCR asked for international troops to be deployed at the Kenyan border so as to be able to accelerate the repatriation process from Kenya. Although no formal deployment took place, UNITAF provided some assistance in the Lucia area to support UNHCR's work.[93] This kind of occurrence suggests that "food as a substitute for protection" may be a valid understanding of the ways in which international protagonists acted when they only sought to satisfy public opinion. Even then the "food as substitute" perspective fails to make sense of UNHCR's demands for security. Given that UN institutions designed overall policies for IDPs, an emphasis on containment helps to better grasp the interplay between assistance and protection.

IDP's Options: Set by Others

Like chapter II, chapter III supports the hypothesis, i.e. the idea that protection is a device of containment policies. Not only was protection promised to people on the move in order to stem refugee exoduses, but it also was granted in ways that gave international actors a better control of the movements of the IDPs. Safety became a tool by which governments, warring factions, international mediators and humanitarian agencies tried to achieve political aims ranging from ethnic cleansing to stabilisation, repatriation and development. That warlords abused and targeted civilians in their personal pursuit of power and money is well known. That the international community, including its most revered humanitarian bodies, engaged in action that led to the subordination of civilian safety to other strategic purposes was more surprising and needed to be tested. The intervention in Somalia seemed to be the ideal hard case because of the emphasis on feeding and saving people and the absence of reference to displacement issues. The review of humanitarian action for Somali IDPs provided insight into two important debates: the impact of the media and, linked to it, the interplay between humanitarian assistance and protection.

This chapter readily concedes that the American intervention may have had more to do with American politics and, later, with images of starvation than forced displacement. Focus was limited to relief distribution, however inadequate that approach was from 1993 onwards. The US military's insistence that they should leave Somalia as soon as possible left no doubt about their unwillingness to engage with Somali politics although, in the end, the US remained heavily involved in UNOSOM. But UNITAF's work affecting IDPs took place within the context of a UN strategy which aimed explicitly at restoring order. In this context, assistance was to help to relieve famine, thus limiting displacement. Clearly, Restore Hope represented a muscular approach to relief distribution, one step beyond the consensus needed for peace keeping troops to operate. This shift in approach, if not in objectives, supports the idea that media presence may cause a change in policy methods - for instance bringing in food instead of tightening borders. In other words, news media coverage may affect tactics more than strategies regarding IDPs.

The belief that media coverage automatically increases the safety of vulnerable populations is popular. However, it is an assumption which relies on the idea that political figures first, grossly abuse civilians and second, do not want the world to know about it. Consequently, under scrutiny, even the worst warlords would feel compelled to limit the violence they usually unleash on civilians. Similarly, neighbouring states would swap harsh containment methods for more humane ones whenever journalists focus cameras on their handling of refugee outflows. As mentioned in the conclusion of chapter II, the findings highlight two problems with the view that containment objectives are wrapped in protection packages to satisfy the good conscience of Western TV viewers.[94] To start with, containment was an outspoken objective of governments and agencies engaged in humanitarian action. Somalia was no exception. UN officials were open about the need to stop displacement and start repatriation. Second, it seemed that all actors considered that protection was an efficient means of pre-empting exodus, and not only a cover-up for closed frontiers. In Bosnia, the candour with which UNHCR planned for stabilisation and return as early as September 1992 demonstrates its belief in the effectiveness of "preventive protection." In Somalia, the UN showed that they knew that IDPs' voluntary return depended on safety improvements. Hence safety provision was initially conceived not as a fig-leaf but as a tool, a point to which the author shall return.

To finish with insights concerning media influence, Somalia, like the other case studies, shows that a focus on media coverage brings only limited insights into policies affecting IDPs. In particular, it hardly makes sense of the nature and variations in resolves taken for people on the move. This chapter discussed both decision-making processes and patterns of implementation of strategies in the hope of providing a deeper grasp of protection policies for IDPs. It highlighted the fact that, as far as displacees were concerned, UNITAF brought no change in strategy. It also pointed out the disastrous consequences of mass food dumping. Therefore insights from working on the Somali crisis confirm the proposal that one needs to complement any study of media reporting with a focus on the specific humanitarian measures applied in the field.

Studying the delivery of aid in Somalia also yields interesting thoughts regarding the interplay between humanitarian assistance and protection. As briefly highlighted, although the failings of humanitarian missions are largely recognised within the humanitarian community, explanations and general understandings of the limits of humanitarian aid differ. Most UN and NGO analysts claim that major changes in the nature of conflicts are the source of difficulties for humanitarian agencies. In recent internal conflicts, civilians became the targets of attacks. As a result, offering protection to vulnerable populations entailed taking a stand against aggressors. This transforms a humanitarian agency into a political participant with the associated risk of becoming a target.[95] Being forced into the political arena is a daunting prospect for most humanitarian institutions and many try to back away from it through dissociating assistance from protection. Hence the tendency to separate assistance (food, medical support, shelter) from protection task (advocacy, visit of prisoners, evacuations, safe zones) judged eminently more political. UN mandates also reflected this desperate attempt at staying neutral when confining troops to the protection of convoys and UN personnel. However, in the context of Somalia, this reading made sense only for UNITAF. All other protagonists had more complex approaches to safety and relief policies. UN agencies in particular made choices that were eminently political. Western intervention contained, although did not necessarily stop, forced migrations in Somalia and allowed the repatriation of refugees, two explicit UN aims from the start. However, by the same token, Somali IDPs suffered from a succession of catastrophic decisions. Ignored when they needed food, many died. The airlift did not help uprooted persons as most were unable to generate the cash still needed to buy food. Later on, survivors were indeed fed, during Operation Restore Hope. Yet few were granted the means to rebuild a living. They also bore the brunt of badly handled force and dialogue to solve the political conflict.

The author claims that assistance and protection became political not only because new conflicts entailed targeting civilians but also because relief was used by the international community as an instrument to restore order via limiting forced displacement. Both conflict participants and the international community wanted to ensure that populations' whereabouts were controlled. Food provision was political in that it was used to achieve political purposes. Although the nature of new conflicts is important to understand humanitarian action, the objectives underlying international responses matter as much. The study also points out who really determined policies for people on the move. In all four cases, it suggests that news media little influenced agenda setting for people on the move. The latter was the task, thus the responsibility, of political actors, especially the UN. The coming conclusion confronts the findings to the literature survey and explores the themes of responsibility and accountability.

Notes

[1] Stevenson, Jonathan, "Hope Restored in Somalia?" No. 91 (1993), *Foreign Policy*, 138-154; Clark, Jeffrey, "Debacle in Somalia: Failure of the Collective Response," in Fisler Damrosh, ed., *Enforcing Restraint*, 204-239; Natsios, Andrew, "Food through Force: Humanitarian Intervention and US Policy," Vol. 17, No. 1 (1993), *The Washington Quarterly*, 129-144; Prunier, Gérard, *Civil War, Intervention and Withdrawal, 1990-1995* (July 1995), a writenet report available on-line: http://www.unhcr.ch/refworld/country/writenet/wrisom02.htm, no pagination; Hirsh, John and Oakley, Robert, *Somalia and Operation Restore Hope, Reflection on Peacemaking and Peace-Keeping* (Washington D.C.: United States Institute of Peace Press, 1995); Livingston, Steven and Eachus, T., "Humanitarian Crises and US Foreign Policy: Somalia and the CNN Effect Reconsidered," Vol. 12, No. 4 (1995), *Political Communication*, 413-429; Lewis, Ioan and Mayall, James, "Somalia," in Mayall, James, ed., *The New Interventionism 1991-1994, United Nations Experience in Cambodia, Former Yugoslavia and Somalia*, (Cambridge: Cambridge University Press, 1996), 94-124; Ramsbotham and Woodhouse, "Humanitarian Intervention in Somalia," in *Humanitarian Intervention*, 193-216; Mermin, Jonathan, "Television News and American Intervention in Somalia: The Myth of a Media Driven Foreign Policy," Vol. 112, No. 3 (1997), *Political Science Quarterly*, 385-403.

[2] Ramsbotham and Woodhouse, *Humanitarian Intervention*, 207.

[3] Jonge Oudraat, Chantal de, "The United Nations and Internal Conflict," in Brown, Michael, ed., *The International Dimensions of Internal Conflict* (Cambridge, Massachusetts: The MIT Press, 1996), 489-535, 522.

[4] Detailed discussions of displacement issues in Mozambique and Sudan can be found in Torrenté, Nicolas de, *The International Protection of Internally Displaced Persons*, Master of Arts in Law and Diplomacy Thesis, The Fletcher School of Law and Diplomacy, Medford, April 1992, 11-33 (Sudan) and 62-88

(Mozambique).

5   *Emergency Profile Chechnya Area*, HCWEB Pilot Project, Russian Federation 1995, UNDHA, 11 May 1995.

6   Robert, Bruce Ware and Kisriev, Enver, "After Chechnya: At Risk in Dagestan," Vol. 18, No. 1 (1998), *Politics*, 39-47, 42.

7   Jonge Oudraat, "The United Nations and Internal Conflict," in Brown, ed., *The International Dimensions of Internal Conflict*, 520.

8   UNSC Resolutions 733 (23 January 1992), 746 (17 March 1992), 751 (24 April 1992), 767 (24 July 1992), 775 (28 August 1992), 794 (3 December 1992).

9   Library of Congress Country Study, *Somalia*, on-line: http://lcweb2.loc.gov/frd/cs/sotoc.html#so0004, no pagination.

10   Situation Reports 5 (10 December 1991) and 6 (21 January, 1992), Office of Foreign Disaster Assistance, USAID, quoted in Hirsh and Oakley, *Somalia and Operation Restore Hope*, 18.

11   Sahnoun, Mohamed, *Somalia, the Missed Opportunities* (Washington: US Institute of Peace Press, 1994), 18-21. See also Clark, "Debacle in Somalia," in Fisler Damrosh, ed., *Enforcing Restraint*, Prunier, *Civil War, Intervention and Withdrawal, 1990-1995*.

12   "En Somalie, une détresse infinie," *Le Monde*, 3 June 1992, 7.

13   Hirsh and Oakley, *Somalia and Operation Restore Hope*, 23.

14   "En Somalie, une détresse infinie," *Le Monde*, 3 June 1992, 7.

15   "Sècheresse, famine et guerres civiles, l'ONU lance un nouvel appel à l'aide en faveur de la corne de l'Afrique," *Le Monde*, 17 July 1992, 5.

16   Hirsh and Oakley, *Somalia and Operation Restore Hope*, 23.

17   *Kenya, Ethiopia, Djibouti, Yemen and Saudi Arabia: The Situation of Somali Refugees*, Question and Answer Series, Documentary Information and Research Branch, Immigration and Refugee Board, Ottawa, Canada: September 1992, 1.

18   Prunier, *Civil War, Intervention and Withdrawal, 1990-1995*.

19   Roggee, John (Disaster Research Unit, University of Manitoba), *The Displaced Population in South and Central Somalia and Preliminary Proposals for their Re-integration and Re-habilitation*, a report to the UNDP, 4 September 1992, 1. 'Invisible' displaced, i.e. people supported by kinfolk, were not counted in the study, 11.

20   Ibid., 1 and 37-38.

21   Ibid., 15.

22   *Kenya, Ethiopia, Djibouti, Yemen and Saudi Arabia*, Immigration and Refugee Board, Ottawa, Canada, 2.

23   Ibid., 3-4.

24   Ibid., 5.

25   Ibid., 8.

26   "Somalie, un entretien avec l'envoyé spécial des Nations Unies M. Mohamed Sahnoun," *Le Monde*, 10 August 1992, 5 (author's translation).

27   Natsios, "Food through Force," 135.

28   Roggee, *The Displaced Population in South and Central Somalia*, 14.

29   Ibid., 16-17.

30   Ibid., 19-20.

31   Natsios, "Food through Force," 135.

32   "Somalie, le HCR cherche à enrayer l'afflux de réfugiés au Kenya," *Le Monde*, 25 September 1992, 6 and "Somalie: pour protéger les secours, l'ONU rappelle la

nécessité d'envoyer des casques bleus supplémentaires," *Le Monde*, 14 October 1992, 7.

33   UNHCR, *The State of the World's Refugees*, (New York: Penguin Book, 1993), 95.

34   Hirsh and Oakley, *Somalia and Operation Restore Hope*, 28.

35   Ibid., 36.

36   Livingston and Eachus, "Humanitarian Crises and US Foreign Policy," and Mermin, "Television News and American Intervention in Somalia." See also Livingston, *Clarifying the CNN Effect*, 7-8.

37   Ramsbotham and Woodhouse, *Humanitarian Intervention in Contemporary Conflict*, 206. See also Hirsh and Oakley, *Somalia and Operation Restore Hope*, 40.

38   African Rights, *Somalia Operation Restore Hope: A Preliminary Assessment*, London: May 1993, 59 pages, 2-4.

39   Ramsbotham and Woodhouse, *Humanitarian Intervention in Contemporary Conflict*, 206.

40   Lewis and Mayall, "Somalia," in Mayall, ed., *The New Interventionism*, 109-110.

41   Cohen and Deng, *Masses in Flight*, 304.

42   A dispute arose in the UNSC when the Secretary General accused Western leaders of caring only about a "war of rich people" in reference to Bosnia. "Le conseil de sécurité de l'ONU charge une mission technique de préparer une opération humanitaire d'envergure," *Le Monde*, 24 July 1992, 3; "La querelle entre M. Boutros-Ghali et le conseil de sécurité s'envenime," *Le Monde*, 29 July 1992, 5; "La Somalie à l'agonie," *Le Monde*, 30 July 1992, 1.

43   According to Steve Redding and Art Hansen: "Since the civil war, virtually everyone has either had to leave the country or has been permanently displaced following fighting. A large part of the population is nomadic, and so has not fixed place of residence. The war has taught Somalis how to be resourceful and, therefore, they can easily displace themselves if they is an opportunity to gain something by it through relief channels." Redding, Steve and Hansen, Art, "Somalia", in Hampton, ed., *Internally Displaced Persons*, 81-84, 82.

44   Roggee, *The Displaced Population in South and Central Somalia*, 2.

45   Ibid., 2.

46   Hampton, ed., *Internally Displaced Persons*, 77.

47   Ramsbotham and Woodhouse, *Humanitarian Intervention in Contemporary Conflict*, 210.

48   See in particular the studies by Stevenson, Ramsbotham and Woodhouse and African Rights already quoted.

49   Meuus, Wilma, *Household Survey of Displaced Camps in Mogadishu, May 1993*, draft report for Save the Children Fund, UK (SCF), Mogadishu, October 1993, 6.

50   Ibid., 7.

51   UNOSOM Division of Humanitarian Affairs, *Fourth Humanitarian Conference on Somalia*, Addis Ababa, Ethiopia, 29 November - 1 December 1993, Paper 2, *The Continuing Emergency*, 6 pages, 4.

52   Boucher-Saulnier, "Points de vue sur la protection de l'aide," in Domestici-Met, *Aide Humanitaire Internationale*, 201.

53   Stedman, "Conflict and Conciliation in Sub-Saharan Africa," in Brown, ed., *The International Dimensions of Internal Conflict*, 256.

54   African Rights, *Operation Restore Hope, A Preliminary Assessment*, 6.

55   Stevenson, "Hope Restored in Somalia?" 140.
56   Ramsbotham and Woodhouse, *Humanitarian Intervention in Contemporary Conflict*, 208-209. Stevenson, "Hope Restored in Somalia?" 138-154.
57   UNSC S/RES/814 (1993), 26 March 1993 outlines ambitious objectives in terms of disarmament, reconstruction and repatriation. On this issue see also Ramsbotham and Woodhouse, *Humanitarian Intervention in Contemporary Conflict*, 211.
58   Ibid., 210.
59   DHA/93/87 GE.93-02099, Information Report, Somalia, August 1993, 11 pages, 4.
60   UNOSOM, *Fourth Humanitarian Conference on Somalia*, Paper 2, 3.
61   Boucher-Saulnier, "Points de vue sur la protection de l'aide," in Domestici-Met, *Aide Humanitaire Internationale*, 208.
62   Stevenson, "Hope Restored in Somalia?" 139. See also African Rights, *Operation Restore Hope, A Preliminary Assessment*, 6-7.
63   Ramsbotham and Woodhouse, *Humanitarian Intervention in Contemporary Conflict*, 213.
64   Stedman, "Conflict and Conciliation in Sub-Saharan Africa," in Brown, ed., *The International Dimensions of Internal Conflict*, 255.
65   Roggee, *The Displaced Population in South and Central Somalia*, 6.
66   Ibid., 1.
67   Meuus, *Household Survey of Displaced Camps in Mogadishu*, SCF, 10.
68   UNOSOM Division of Humanitarian Affairs, *Fourth Humanitarian Conference on Somalia*, Addis Ababa, Paper 3, *Resettlement*, 2.
69   DHA/93/87 GE.93-02099, 1.
70   Ibid., 5.
71   Ibid., 1.
72   UNOSOM, *Fourth Humanitarian Conference on Somalia*, Paper 3, 2.
73   DHA/93/87 GE.93-02099, 5.
74   Ibid., 7.
75   Ibid., 5.
76   Cohen and Deng, *Masses in Flight*, 258-259.
77   Poor living conditions in the Kenyan border camps were themselves strong incentives to repatriate. "Given the Kenyan Government's attitude to the refugees, as well as the poor conditions in the border camps, conceivably many will return the moment they believe it safe and that food will be available." Roggee, *The Displaced Population in South and Central Somalia*, 34.
78   *UN Relief and Rehabilitation Programme for Somalia, Covering the Period 1 March-31 December 1993*, UNDHA, 11 March 1993, Tables I and II. These were UN proposed figures. The author ignores the extent to which these budgets were funded in the end.
79   Ibid., 37.
80   Ibid., 3.
81   Ibid., 34.
82   DHA/93/87 GE.93-02099, 6.
83   Somalia Task Force (network of academic specialists and NGO representatives whose purposes are policy discussion, information sharing and advocacy). *Post-UNOSOM Aid Strategies in Somalia: Recommendations to the Somali Aid Coordination Body*, November 1994, 4 pages, 3.

84   Ibid., 3.
85   Roggee, *The Displaced Population in South and Central Somalia*, 14-15.
86   Meuus, *Household Survey of Displaced Camps in Mogadishu*, 7 and 10.
87   Roggee, *The Displaced Population in South and Central Somalia*, 5.
88   UNOSOM Division of Humanitarian Affairs, *Fourth Humanitarian Conference on Somalia*, Paper 3, 3.
89   Ibid., 3.
90   *UN Relief and Rehabilitation Programme for Somalia*, UNDHA, 33.
91   Kessler, Peter, "Out of Sight, Out of Mind", Issue 103, I (1996), *Refugees*, (on-line: http://www.unhcr.ch/pubs/rm103/rm10308.htm, no pagination). Numbers vary according to estimates and definitions but clearly these figures exclude Sudanese displaced persons.
92   Redding and Hansen, "Somalia," in Hampton, ed., *Internally Displaced People*, 81-84, 84.
93   Hirsh and Oakley, *Somalia and Operation Restore Hope*, 86.
94   The Bosnian war also challenges the assumption that warlords never want their acts of violence publicised. Indeed, Bosnian Serb Nationalists used all media channels available to let the overall Bosnian population know about ethnic cleansing practices in the hope that, terrorised, they would choose to leave rather than resist. One could possibly argue that the Bosnian Serb nationalists' aim of ethnic separation was promoted through the wide publicity given to discourses about violence and to gruesome images. Unwittingly, the international media may have reinforced the political position of the advocates of violence in this respect.
95   UNHCR and ICRC regularly denounce the lack of security under which humanitarian workers operate and appeal for a reinforcement of security measures and international humanitarian law. See *UNHCR and International Committee of the Red Cross say Security of Humanitarian Operations under Threat*, UNHCR Press Release, 22 June 1998.

5 Fearing the Uprooted

The story told so far suggests that protection is a device of migration policies. This differs from perspectives presenting humanitarian action as a substitute for want of political will or a fig-leaf to cover unpopular diplomacy. Indirectly, it also questions the idea that much action for people on the move is a response to media-induced pressure. These views (humanitarianism as a substitute or as a cover) underlie most work on humanitarian intervention, including current reforms of action for people on the move. By contrast, the study reckons that, as far as IDPs were concerned, protection was more a containment tool than a disguise. Thus an emphasis on the instrumentality of safety policies helps to understand the crises reviewed. In particular, it makes sense of the variations in the assistance provided, and of the limited impact of media coverage. Such a standpoint also raises the issue of accountability both in policy making and academic research. More precisely, it highlights the necessity to reflect on the objectives of both endeavours. Questions such as "Who chooses policies regarding IDPs?" and "Which responsibilities are entailed in such choices?" are rarely faced in current policy circles. As for research, the findings suggest that the evaluation of international action for displaced persons requires a thorough assessment of the aims of policy makers. Otherwise, one might rely on dominant assumptions which are far from always being warranted. These are the themes developed in the three sections of this concluding chapter. The first section highlights the findings of the study and compares them to current understandings of action regarding IDPs. The second section explores the implications of the book's claims for policy and research design. The third, more tentative, outlines further research topics which can bring forth new perspectives on forced displacement policies.

Protection: Tool rather than Fig-Leaf

In short, a new explanation for the inadequacy of protection policies designed for IDPs in the early 1990s has been proposed: protection became inadequate because it was a means by which international organisations sought to control mass population movements.

The study supports the commonly held view that protection for displaced persons was inadequate during international interventions in northern Iraq, Bosnia, Somalia and Rwanda. International action was often limited to providing humanitarian assistance while the needs for safety against discrimination, harassment, physical abuse from armed forces and paramilitary troops were not adequately addressed. Cohen and Deng have provided further examples, also drawn from the 1990s, where responses to IDPs' needs materialised as forms of assistance falling short of fully-fledged protection.[1] So has the Global IDP Survey, pointing out that protection needs were often overlooked when population movements did not yield significant risks of cross-border migration. In the course of the 1990s, for instance, the UNDP worked and supported a Kenyan government which unleashed terror on displaced communities supporting opposition parties.[2] Overall, when intervention regarding IDPs took place, the emphasis often remained on short term relief rather than on providing safety against politically orchestrated violence. Even in Kurdistan, where protection was more extensive than either in Bosnia or Rwanda, UN guards were dispatched to ensure the safety of UN personnel and material, not that of civilians.[3] During the Bosnian war, given that the real means of protection were never deployed, humanitarian agencies often tried to avoid having military escorts for their convoys, as this made it harder to reach besieged populations.[4] Boucher-Saulnier denounced UN practices which, she claimed, were detrimental to real safety:

> The intervention of UN agencies was developed in the context of new concepts such as safety zone, corridors and humanitarian cease-fires. These 'peace bubbles' artificially created in the midst of conflicts do not stop the war and allow the victims' protection to be forgotten.[5]

However, whereas the research supports overall evidence that protection was inadequate, it suggests an understanding of the discrepancies between assistance and political protection different from mainstream thinking. Most observers of humanitarian work hold that assistance was used as a substitute for protection. Jon Bennett summarised it: "A common criticism of the UN system ... is that relief provision often becomes a substitute for adequate protection of civilians."[6] In other words, because the international community had no will to protect civilians, it organised relief provision, sometimes even the protection of relief as opposed to that of civilians, an attitude much criticised by NGO personnel and independent observers. Inherent in this criticism lies the idea that aid workers, while doing their job, unwittingly provided a fig-leaf for an absence of international commitment on behalf of war victims.[7] The idea that there was no policy but indifference also befits assumptions regarding the influence of media coverage, for in the absence of interest in people on the move, only media pressure could, occasionally, be a source of action.

Rather than holding humanitarian and strategic objectives as separate motors for action, the author suggested another approach whereby they could be linked and the former could be the device of the latter. This was the hypothesis to be explored. Chapters II, III and IV overall supported the suggestion. It was thus concluded from the study of four cases that assistance was the first stage in a continuum of measures which constituted international protection in the field. Overall protection for IDPs was a strategic resource deployed only in response to migration movements perceived to threaten valued orders and borders. This perspective implies that policies of containment were articulated from the beginning of international involvement, thus challenging the view that a policy vacuum was filled with responses to outraged Western audiences. It was also argued that protection could be enhanced or diminished depending on international goals concerning displaced populations.

Rethinking Forced Migration Policies

Viewing the deployment of protective measures as a device to limit exodus makes sense of the range of policies that were experimented by the international community. In particular, it enlightens the selectivity and timings of interventions, the general reluctance to evacuate people, the little emphasis on freedom of movement in contrast to the priority given to early returns. Even the 1992 UN working definition of IDPs, which is given in chapter I, reflects fears of uncontrolled population movements. In the following paragraphs, the author discusses dominant approaches to internal displacement, most of which shape recent reforms of humanitarian action, as well as the publication of the UN guiding principles on internal displacement. It is argued that, apart from the definition of IDPs itself, current reforms of the international humanitarian action system preserve the trends established in the early 1990s.

In 1994, UNHCR wrote that its activities concerning IDPs in armed conflict situations had involved the following:

Assisting the safe passage of civilians through front lines; facilitating, in acute life-threatening situations, in cooperation with the ICRC the organised evacuation of civilians; intervening with local authorities to prevent the involuntary return of the internally displaced to areas of danger; facilitating genuine freedom of movement, including the possibility for persons in danger to seek asylum; and promoting the right of the internally displaced persons to return - or not to return - voluntarily to their homes.[8]

This contrasts sharply with some points developed in this book. Evacuation in particular was rare, kept under tight international control and, whenever possible, directed away from borders. This happened whether the plight of IDPs was in the eye of the media (Northern Iraq, Bosnia, or Kosovo during the spring and summer 1998) or whether their fate was largely ignored (Burundi, Columbia, Sri Lanka). According to Tiso, in April 1994 "the United Nations and other world organisations considered aiding the mass exodus from the city [Gorazde] by evacuating civilians to other safe havens in Bosnia."[9] Occasionally, the ICRC and the IOM helped distressed populations to seek a safer place within the country. Deng and Cohen record that some NGOs have provided protection for IDPs through direct action, in particular "hiding or helping to evacuate IDPs."[10] However, the concept of evacuation does not even feature in their list of "strategies for improving protection."[11] Although, at the time of writing, humanitarian action is the object of many discussions and reforms, the trend consisting in trying to avoid international evacuations is not questioned.

Beyond evacuation lies the issue of freedom of movement embodied, in war zones, by humanitarian corridors. In theory, corridors represent an opportunity for vulnerable persons to keep moving in search of safer regions or to seek asylum abroad. Experience showed however that corridors were created and used for particular purposes that had little to do with freedom of movement. The UNHCR condemned the Bosnian Serb Nationalists for opening "one-way humanitarian corridors," that is occasionally allowing people to flee besieged areas.[12] Still, UNHCR itself created one-purpose corridors which not only had little to do with opening escape routes, but precluded this possibility. Jessen Petersen, from the UNHCR, pictures corridors uniquely as a better way to provide for besieged populations.[13] Although freedom of movement is now encapsulated into principle 14 and 15 of the UN guiding principles on internal displacement,[14] the international community scarcely supports movements, especially when flight entails seeking asylum. In June 1998,

NATO considered deploying troops to cordon off the borders between Kosovo, Albania and Macedonia. The option however was not pursued, officially to avoid trapping refugees in the making.[15] Nevertheless, until NATO's intervention in March 1999, issues of evacuations and freedom of movement in Kosovo were not discussed. Whereas humanitarian action and the OSCE monitoring were justified in the name of protection, fleeing to safe places abroad in search of safety was not an option that the international community wanted Kosovar displaced persons to consider. During the two months' war between NATO and Yugoslavia, hundreds of thousands of persons poured into Albania and Macedonia, some deported, most by their own means, on foot, with battered cars and tractors. Refugees who reached Albania were welcome there, according to the 1951 Geneva Convention. In contrast, Macedonian authorities multiplied humiliating treatments, many of which were contrary to international law. For instance, they left thousands stranded in a no-man's land at the border and they insisted that refugees go through customs. They also forcibly removed refugees to Albania.[16] Furthermore, in the course of the war, the whereabouts of hundreds of thousands displaced Kosovars were unknown. Although fears for their safety were great, neither the organisation of evacuation nor the creation of safe escape roads were considered. Not only were evacuation and freedom of movement low priorities on the humanitarian agenda, but also they were, and they remain, largely framed out of debates on action regarding IDPs. The right to escape a conflict is one that Western governments and institutions do not want to discuss.

In contrast to evacuation, early return became gradually established as a principle of humanitarian action in the 1990s.[17] The UNHCR executive Committee Conclusion No. 40 (XXXVI) states: "From the outset of a refugee situation, the High Commissioner should at all times keep the possibility of voluntary repatriation for all or part of a group under active review."[18] The case studies highlighted that, in the rush to return people home, insecurity in return areas was overlooked. This echoes other experiences. Displaced Georgians, 300,000 persons who had fled Akhazia in 1993, faced a similar situation. The UNSC insisted that their repatriation go ahead despite the fact that the UNHCR itself denounced the lack of security which they would face upon return.[19] Cases of manipulation of the idea of voluntary return are numerous. In Peru, assistance for IDPs depended on whether they accepted to return to rural areas of origin, a plan favoured by a government struggling to reverse urban migration, or if they wanted to resettle.[20] The government of Azerbaijan tried to discourage IDPs from resettling "in an effort to promote their return to

Nagorno-Karabakh."[21]   Cutting off aid to avoid dependency and encourage return also took place in Burundi in 1995 and greatly exacerbated tensions there.[22] In the context of the war in Kosovo, it is striking to see how Western leaders had decided, from the first days of the mass exodus, that "all Kosovar wanted to return home" which was then presented at the top international community objective. As a result, the dispatching of refugees to Western countries took place under special "temporary protection" measures that did not allow the Kosovar who might want it to apply for asylum. Last, the case studies highlighted that, despite this emphasis on return, the lack of reconstruction particularly affected the uprooted. The UNHCR's commitment to development is questioned in that its pet concept "Quick Impact Projects" often appear to be no more than "fast exit strategies."[23] Despite their appeal (small, cost-effective, local and gender-orientated projects), the projects often failed to spark off development because of lack of financial commitment in the long term. In fact, the lack of long-term assistance characterised prominent UN reconstruction schemes such as projects in Cambodia or El Salvador.[24] Even in Bosnia, despite heavy international presence, the extent to which reconstruction benefits IDPs remains unclear.

Until very recently, there were no specific provisions regarding the conditions under which IDPs could voluntarily return home. Thus the idea of "voluntary return" was an *ad hoc* extension of the principle of voluntary repatriation for refugees. The problem however is that the 1951 Refugee Convention, although very clear on the point of non-refoulement, exhibits a legal gap in what is called the "cessation clause." The latter entails the idea that international protection can stop once the cause for the initial exodus has ceased to be. Whereas the idea that protection can cease is inscribed in the convention, the detailed circumstances under which this clause applies were never specified. They were left to governments and UN bodies to decide upon. The implications of such a lull are currently experienced by numerous refugees. For years the Indonesian government detained about 4,000 Vietnamese boat people in a military-run camp on the Galang Island. Once the democratisation process started in Vietnam, the international community then decided that UNHCR should phase out its assistance to these persons. In UNHCR staff's own words, these people:

> ... live without many options: all have been individually screened by trained adjudicators, and all have been found to have no real claim to refugee status. Because they face no persecution in Viet Nam, and since no resettlement countries will accept them, the Indonesian authorities

have decided that they should go home. They can go voluntarily, under the auspices of UNHCR, or they can face deportation. [25]

Numerous problems are raised by increasingly restrictive refugee practices, including that of refusing or delaying access to asylum for people fleeing wars until it is judged safe for them to return. This is achieved either by detaining them in camps such as in Galang or by keeping them in a legal vacuum as in the case of Bosnian refugees who were granted "temporary protection" in Western Europe.[26] In other words, the concept of "voluntary repatriation" has been replaced by that of "safe return," a process by which governments and international agencies decide when people should go home, and then enforce it.[27] Interestingly enough, in this respect, IDPs should be in a stronger legal position than refugees, for it is widely accepted that citizens have a free choice of residence in their own country. Nevertheless, the case studies suggest that IDPs had very little say regarding the return and rehabilitation plans drawn for them. Humanitarian support was put to the service of restoring the order upon which governments and international agencies had settled. Domestici-Met wrote that the international community readily "denies emancipation while organising nutrition."[28] The author would rather contend that it organised nutrition in ways that restored order, sometimes to the detriment of emancipation. But whereas the international community vehemently denounces certain abuses of voluntary return, it does not explore its own participation in the practice. After the massacres at Kibeho, the RPA was - mildly - criticised for using violence in closing the camp. Still, the difference between military violence and the previous IOC decision to cut off relief to a population that could not sustain itself is only a matter of degree on a constraint scale. Since Kibeho, the UN guiding principles on repatriation emphasise that IDPs should be free to return or resettle in their country.[29] A whole section is devoted to improving the conditions of return. The text however does not specify who is qualified to decide on return and resettlement issues and, in particular, who decides when protection can stop. Deng and Cohen argue that "It is essential to consider the views of the internally displaced in designing and implementing programs for them because they know better than anyone else how to meet their protection and assistance needs."[30] However, in his initial work as the UN special representative for IDPs, Deng emphasised the need to work with states and the modalities by which to persuade governments to cooperate with UN bodies. Little was said regarding how to work with people on the move, how to listen to them.

171

The above has presented a rather stern picture whereby humanitarian practices for uprooted people were subordinated to and instrumental in the containment of exoduses and the restoration of stability in collapsed countries. Over recent years, a debate about the activities that should be entailed in protection missions developed in legal and humanitarian circles. The UNHCR attempted to define its protection activities for IDPs. These were to include the following:

> ... monitoring the treatment of threatened minority groups, intervening with the authorities to request protective action, investigating and prosecuting specific cases, providing assistance and protection in temporary relief centres, and helping governments provide personal documentation ... helping civilians secure safe passage through front lines, relocating and evacuating civilians from conflict areas, assisting besieged populations unable or unwilling to move from their home, intervening with local authorities to prevent the involuntary return of the internally displaced to areas of danger, alerting governments and the public to human rights abuses and promoting the right of the internally displaced to return voluntary to their homes.[31]

Discussions were further enhanced with the publication, in January 1998, of the "UN Guiding Principles on Internal Displacement" designed to fill gaps in international protection for displaced persons.[32] In the process, the 1992 working definition of IDPs was revised. The definition used by the UN is now the following: IDPs are persons, or groups of persons "who have been forced or obliged to flee or to leave their homes or habitual places of residence, in particular, as a result of, or in order to avoid the effects of, armed conflicts, situation of generalized violence, violation of human rights or natural or human made disasters and who have not crossed an internationally recognised state border." As Frelick made clear, there were several problems with the working definition that prevailed during the 1990s, not least the following:

> The IDP definition, unlike the refugee definition, did not mention a government's willingness or ability to protect displaced persons. By making *location* the essence of the IDP definition, and not the right to be protected, it did not offer the restoration of one's rights in another location as a durable solution.[33]

This, according to Frelick, made return to own's home the only acceptable outcome in the eyes of the international community. It was a mistake which he claimed "needlessly complicated the search for acceptable - not ideal - solutions."[34] However, the author would contend that the 1992 definition simply reflected the prevailing approaches to forced displacement: throughout the 1990s, issues of space, location and relocation were of utmost importance. Interestingly enough, the new definition enlarges the concept of "home." What is now needed, according to Frelick, is "to place the focus away from location on the need for protection."[35] Nevertheless, even Frelick does not address the question of choice "Who decides what is best, ideal or acceptable?"

Although not binding, the principles are an attempt to provide a "yardstick for monitoring the treatment of IDPs."[36] Whether they will make any impact on field practices, however, remains to be seen. So far the international community has refused either to create an agency responsible for IDPs or to attribute this function to an existing agency. UNHCR was prompted but remained reluctant to engage in more than it already does. As a result, responsibility for IDPs was left to inter-agency cooperation (through the Inter-agency Standing Committee on which Francis Deng sits) chaired by the Emergency Relief Coordinator. Kosovo was a baptism of fire for the Guiding Principles. In 1998 and early 1999, however, the protection mechanism failed to apply. IDPs' suffering was played down throughout 1998 and early 1999, so long as the international community wanted to negotiate with Slobodan Milosevic. In contrast, as war was waged, IDP's persecution was highlighted during NATO briefings. However, because of the withdrawal of the OSCE verifiers and of all humanitarian agencies, they were, in effect, abandoned to their fate. In the light of these events, the author would strongly support the defence of an individual's "right to flee." Although, as mentioned above, escaping is not an option that governments favour, it is important to bear in mind that it can be a matter of survival.

The News Media: Limited Influence

As already mentioned, this study indirectly challenges assumptions regarding media influence, many of which shape writings concerning international action regarding IDPs. The purpose of this section is to clarify which understandings of the role of the media are supported by the above findings. Thus, the author will review the range of positions regarding media influence before discussing them in relation to the argument developed in the study.

The strongest proponents of the CNN factor hold that media presence provides the key to understanding international humanitarian action.[37] This reading underlies numerous studies of interventions in the 1990s. Authors usually point out that humanitarian policies emerged as pressures to act increased in response to disasters or following a better reporting of humanitarian catastrophes. This contrasts with international leaders' indifference towards threatened people, displayed in the early days of each crisis. George Bush held for weeks during the repression of the Kurdish revolt that the US would not interfere in the "internal matters" of Iraq. According to Stromseth: "*As* television reports brought their [Kurds'] suffering into homes around the world, Western governments could no longer characterise the situation in Iraq as a strictly 'internal' matter."[38] The most comprehensive case for media-induced intervention in Iraq was put forward by Martin Shaw. In a study of media reporting, he pointed out an outstanding emphasis on Kurdish suffering, expectations and the responsibility of Western decision makers.[39] Similar readings can be found regarding Western policy in Bosnia. It is often emphasised that the airlift of Sarajevo was established a few days only after a mortar bomb exploded in the city square provoking the "bread-line massacre." Likewise, UMPROFOR was expanded to secure humanitarian deliveries in the wake of the Roy Gutman/ITN reports on Serb-run detention camps.[40] A comprehensive policy to fight ethnic cleansing was set up three months after the Bosnian war started. Christopher Bennett, himself a journalist by training, suggested that killings would have carried on longer without the work done by journalists.[41] As for Rwanda, Western reluctance to be involved was displayed first with the withdrawal of UNAMIR, second with multiple attempts to prevent the word genocide from being used in reference to the massacres. Prunier depicted the situation in those terms:

> The press was at first stunned into incomprehension, but then after a fortnight articles began to pour out, documenting the magnitude of the disaster. But TV coverage of the genocide was not available given the near impossibility of catching killers in the act. This was later to prove an important factor, *since* in contemporary Western society events not seen on a TV screen do not exist. And since the refugee exodus to Zaire and a cholera epidemic later in July and August were covered by TV, the relative perception of the two events shifted in the international consciousness.[42]

Except for Shaw, the above quoted authors presumed a direct causal link between media reporting and Western action. Stromseth and Prunier in particular used terms such as "since" and "as" which indicate a temporal correlation but also suggest a causal link. The idea that media reporting created humanitarian action is supported by the fact that some of the horrors uncovered (detention camps; genocide) were plausibly known by policy makers and kept quiet. As mentioned at the end of chapter II, this belief in the impact of media reporting does not easily hold in the cases reviewed. Recent literature cast more doubts as to whether journalists uncovered truths upon which politicians would rather not have had the public focus. Close examinations of international action in Somalia revealed that the media echoed policies that were already well under way rather than engendered them. Mermin showed that "stories on Somalia appeared just after the articulation of demands for intervention in Washington in the summer and fall of 1992. Journalists ultimately made the decision to cover Somalia, but the stage for this decision had been set in Washington."[43] Livingston and Eachus supported this finding and argued that because news agendas typically reflected the agendas of officials, the media served as instrument of those officials who were "most adept at using news to further their policy goals."[44] Interestingly enough, Shaw agreed with both studies on Somalia.[45] Such a position leaves room for debate.

Media influence however was rarely presented as the only key to understanding initial humanitarian action. More often, it was considered a necessary yet insufficient condition for intervention. Following the distinction between strategic and humanitarian concerns for international intervention, Adelman, Kirisci, Loescher, Dowty, Roberts claimed that two conditions were necessary for Western states to react: refugee pressure and a strong media presence.[46] They claimed that Western states reacted only when people crossed borders *en masse* **and** CNN filmed their misery.[47] Adelman, in his detailed study of Operation Provide Comfort, concluded: "Mass exodus and demonstrated suffering in that exodus would seem to be jointly sufficient conditions independent of any objective verification of human rights violation."[48] Shaw himself emphasised the need of strategic reasons for interventions in the case of Rwanda:

> ... despite its limitation, the media coverage [in Rwanda] constituted, as in Kurdistan, the chief pressure for intervention. The fact that intervention did not follow reflects the fact that, in Rwanda, as well as in other cases we have examined, there were no strongly perceived Western strategic

interests and no connection of responsibility which the Kurds were able, it now appears uniquely, to exploit.[49]

Adelman however articulated the link between media and refugee flows further by suggesting that strategic motives were more important than media-led humanitarianism. He wrote "the ground for intervention is mass exodus producing a threat to peace and security."[50] Doing so, he joined a small group of writers (generally from a refugee studies background) who see refugee containment as the main aim of international action. As a result, for Adelman, human rights protection was a side effect or, in other words, a collateral benefit, of an intervention the primary purpose of which was to stop an exodus. "A by-product of that intervention may be the defence of the civil rights of the minority population."[51] In this context, the role attributed to news media remains unclear. Tiso and Frelick, for instance, in their respective studies of safe areas and preventive protection hardly mentioned media coverage. On the other hand, none of these authors explicitly denied that news media influenced humanitarian action. Plausibly, such authors may agree with Nick Gowing's view that their impact was superficial in that it was often short-term and affected tactics rather than strategies. This leads to a slightly different, yet powerful, argument that seems to underlie much of the writing on containment, although is explicit in none. Containment alone matters. It is forced on people ruthlessly *until* CNN arrives. When CNN is present, though, states use patently humanitarian approaches, ranging from aid to safe zones, to convince people to stay at home. In other words, the presence of journalists alters the means used by international actors to contain people within the bounds of their collapsed home states.

To sum up, the first reading presented the media as a necessary and sufficient condition for international action. A second position suggested that both strategic and humanitarian pressures are necessary to stir the international community into action.[52] Finally, the last perspective saw refugee outflow as a necessary and sufficient condition for action. Implicitly, it presented the media as an instrument which restrained interveners' behaviour and obliged states to protect civilians rather than contain them by force.

From this short review, it is clear that the initial triggering role of news media is open to debate. Whether coverage triggers humanitarian intervention or reflects such policies is still a matter of contention. Often, however, the causal link between news media reporting and international involvement is postulated rather than explored.[53] This is particularly true of humanitarian agencies reports.[54] A confusion between correlation and causation underlies numerous studies and reports of international action. Overall, people who study the role of news media in depth (Gowing, Mermin, Livingston and Eachus, even Shaw) are more cautious, yet still divided, regarding its initial impact.

The depth of media influence on policy is also disputed. Authors who consider that news reporting creates policy against the will of decision-makers fear that humanitarian action might replace the search for political settlements.[55] Authors who consider that both media coverage and refugee flows are necessary conditions for action tend to emphasise and discuss "new humanitarian practices" emerging from the combined desires to ensure protection and prevent refuge outflow.[56] Those who look at humanitarian action as a media-managed cover for on-going hard core strategic diplomacy suspect a more superficial impact. Nick Gowing makes the point that, except in times of "policy panic" (those particular moments when there is no clear policy line), the media only affect the tactics of international policies not the strategic aims.[57] Indeed, whereas all of these writers agree that media-induced humanitarian policies act as fig leaves, the question remains whether they cover a policy vacuum[58] or would-be unpopular diplomacy, such as the tacit partition of Bosnia. In the first case, media-induced humanitarian action becomes the only game in town; thus wavering media interest can affect policy dramatically. Shaw, for instance, argues that in Iraq, "media coverage affects the form of intervention as well as whether intervention takes place" and thus concludes that media coverage is and integral part of policy making.[59] In the second case, media influence is merely tactical, to use Gowing's terminology.

The research findings suggested that the role of the media was indeed limited, that news media neither initiated nor significantly shaped action for IDPs. The study showed that important decisions concerning people on the move were taken almost independently from media pressure. Even in the test case of Somalia, the UN seemed to have forged policy options before TV crews and newspaper journalists interfered. Thus although the media played a role, their impact occurred within a policy framework set not only by governments but also by major humanitarian bodies. Hence the author agrees with the view that containment is the top priority of international actors and that protection is instrumental. However, whereas she agrees that protection is a tool, she disagrees significantly regarding the nature of that instrumentality. Protection for IDPs was less a media device than a containment policy device. To sum up, the present research supports sceptical views on the impact of the media. The findings suggest in particular that the media act within policy frames. Humanitarian strategies for IDPs were designed largely before media involvement and were not significantly changed by coverage. Although control of media channels, and more importantly of the framing of reports became objects of constant struggles among humanitarian agencies, politicians and journalists themselves, all Western interveners assumed a common approach for people on the move: containment through protection.

The idea of relief developed in order to contain populations is important in itself, for it challenges the idea that humanitarianism is a cover for either political indifference or unpopular diplomatic concessions to aggressors.[60] The study holds that the protection plans initially designed were deemed efficient ways of forestalling exodus. This was particularly explicit in Bosnia. Discussions about preventive protection in the summer of 1992 made it clear that "international protection" was believed to be an answer to the refugee exodus. However surprising this may sound today, one must bear in mind that in 1992 safe areas had good press. The idea of preventive protection had been first experimented within Sri Lanka by UNHCR to stem an exodus to India. Two years down the road, that project was considered a success. Thus it should come as no surprise that policy makers genuinely believed that they could kill two birds with one stone: that humanitarian aid would reduce the pain and thus stop the flow.

Whereas the principles of preventive protection were not a matter of contention, debates raged about how to contain people, which degree of protection was needed and thus which military means required. In this context, media coverage echoed voices that shouted loudest. Most often, mainstream positions were simply reflected. Occasionally, alternative policies were articulated possibly with effects on decision-makers, as Shaw contends regarding Iraq in 1991. Still, even seemingly strategic U-turns such as George Bush's decision to send troops to northern Iraq, to Somalia, or the proclamation of Srebrenica a safe area, represented no policy change for the displaced persons trapped in these areas. These were merely promises of better tactics to achieve unchanged aims. Indeed, as far as IDPs were concerned, media influence was limited to debates over tactics. This is not to say that media pressure had no impact on policies for the uprooted whatsoever but to help assess the depth of its influence : news media may have had some influence on "how to achieve things," but not on "what should be done."

The fact that containment-based approaches were never really questioned raises issues regarding the framing of humanitarian need in the media. Here the role of UN agencies, even of NGOs must be emphasised. Because of their unique position in the field and their knowledge of the situation, humanitarian organisations have the possibility to take control of the editorial line.[61] The case studies provide multiple evidence of NGOs and UN agencies feeding the media with their stories so as to win governments policies via public pressure. Somalia itself provides a telling story about how NGOs occasionally manage to recruit journalists to their cause.

> Most observers credit the *New York Times*' July 19 front page story and photo with playing a key role in sparking greater media attention, particularly as other editors soon followed the *Times*' lead. ICRC's Loane recalls having taken an initially hesitant Jane Perlez, the *Times'* correspondent, on his visit to Baidoa. Before being exposed to the horror, she had asked: 'Why don't Somalis take more responsibility for themselves?'[62]

Relations between humanitarian agencies and the media are more complex than usually allowed for. As hinted at already, the presence of cameras may induce all political protagonists to use distress for their own purposes, not only fighting parties but also mediators and humanitarian agencies.[63] Although the latter acknowledge that media reporting is, in essence, detrimental to long-term humanitarian work, they also choose to participate in the creation of "televised emergencies."[64] Over recent years, NGO analysts have been reflecting on how to develop cooperation between aid workers and journalists for a more powerful advocacy work. Given the findings of the study, such efforts may be of little benefit to people on the move. In fact, Gowing warned that unprofessional handling of sensitive information about displaced persons can lead to catastrophic policies that contribute to their vulnerability.[65] By contrast, internal advocacy within the UN for the adoption of policy principles or policy lines could be explored further. Take, for instance, the assumption that the very presence of foreigners, be they aid workers, international observers, journalists, or even expatriates, can reduce abuses because of the latter's presumed links to the outside world. Experiences in Bosnia, Rwanda and Zaire lead most analysts to agree that, "the much-used equation 'presence equals protection' no longer bears closed scrutiny."[66] Still very few persons reflect on why this approach was implemented in the first place. As early as summer 1992 in Bosnia, Tadeusz Mazowiecki, entrusted by the UN to investigate the detention camps, did not manage access to all of them.[67] The protective power of the UN and the protective power of information were already clearly limited. The failure to protect adequately has led many humanitarian agencies to reflect on the aims of warring parties but also on their own strategies. More needs to be done however. For with the possibility of influencing world views on displacement disasters come responsibility and accountability.

There is no "Lack of Will"

Clarity and Accountability in Action

Interveners, including leading humanitarian agencies, both designed and implemented containment approaches for uprooted persons using the provision of safety as a policy tool. In some circumstances, this approach could put both IDPs and aid workers in very difficult situations, the former being trapped and the latter having no leverage to help. In the cases surveyed, most implementing partners (NGOs) worked within the guidelines set among UN agencies (UNHCR, UNDHA, DPKO). As far as uprooted persons were concerned, even the work of UNITAF in Somalia can be examined as part of an overall UN designed approach. UNITAF however had its own rationale and was powerful enough to ignore UN views when they did not suit its objectives. Very few implementing partners have such a standing of their own, allowing them to criticise the UN. MSF for instance, tried to distance itself from enforced returns in Rwanda. More than once, it highlighted the failure of the UN humanitarian machinery in providing for the needs of IDPs.[68] Other NGOs courageously raised their voices against UN-led relief programmes.[69] However for many small organisations, it remains difficult to refuse to play by UN rules. Apart from the exclusion and thus the financial implications that might result, small agencies would lose the opportunity to work on massive, well-known projects. Such a rebellious institution may also be labelled un-cooperative, an ominous reputation to acquire given that much time and energy is currently spent on how to improve coordination in complex emergencies.[70]

The tensions that result from different perspectives on how to deal with IDPs reflect divergent basic priorities. As Boucher-Saulnier made clear, the real battle of the UN is the defence of peace and international security.[71] In 1992, Boutros-Ghali, then UN Secretary General, wrote about peace-making:

"If, for instance, assistance to displaced persons within a society is essential to a solution, then the United Nations should be able to draw upon the resources of all agencies and programmes concerned."[72]

That "If" highlights the condition under which IDPs are of interest to the UN community: when their fate is encompassed in a UN-designed solution to solve an unstable situation. One cannot, however, presume that the search for and design of solutions to international security problems will consistently coincide with rescuing, or listening to vulnerable populations. Certain solutions may imply silencing them. One MSF worker brought this perspective on the issue:

> The international community at large, and Western governments in particular have to accept that it is not the role of humanitarian organisations to provide the solutions to a problem. Our role is to help the people in danger ... we should not accept our action being used as a political fig-leaf.[73]

The search for a "global solution" indeed differs markedly from a deliberate priority given to relieving suffering. Great is the difference in purpose between the UN and some NGOs. But the real problem for MSF is not that care became a fig-leaf for political inaction. The problem is that care became a part of the UN-conceived "solution," namely containment. In that sense, care was more than a cover-up. Thus the metaphor of the fig-leaf is incomplete, if not inaccurate, in picturing abuses of humanitarian work. Both the UN and NGOs perceived care and an emphasis on protection as an essential part of their work. However, it was for different reasons, and this mattered. Occasionally, care for IDPs was an end in itself. This may have be the case for some NGOs. For the UN, providing care was a means of preserving borders and thus order. Still, although they might be reluctant to acknowledge it, containment was the overall framework for action in which NGOs took part. This might not automatically lead to policy problems, but it can. Hence the necessity for all those who care for IDPs to question and sometimes face the ambiguities of their work, as well as the global strategies to which they participate.

Objectives matter. Furthermore the maintained confusion between humanitarian and migration goals works to the detriment of the former. In Bosnia especially, preventative protection turned out to be a process by which false safety promises accompanied a closed-doors policy for the uprooted.

Even in Sri Lanka, where preventive protection was presented as a complete effort to address the roots of the problem, the Open Relief Centres did not necessarily prevent initial uprooting. As places of first refuge, they limited the flights and contained civilians. Indeed, preventive protection measures did not always reduce uprooting, they reduced pressure at borders, a significant nuance. At first sight, the emphasis on human rights issues, on addressing the root causes of conflicts, that is, dealing with refugees in camps, was welcome both by human rights activists and development workers. However, concerns for IDPs rights were rooted in a fear of exodus and thus limited by it. By 1992, life for the uprooted in Sri Lanka was plagued by violence and destitution.[74] In three cases out of the four reviewed, reconstruction efforts were superficial or waned after the major repatriation movements had taken place.

Clarifying objectives is the first stepping stone to improve humanitarian praxis. However, the author does not claim that the issues of migration and humanitarianism can be easily separated. This would be not only naive but possibly counter-productive. Take, for instance, the concept of early reconstruction, a process by which return is accelerated through engaging development projects in a war context. In 1992, Roggee already noted a new approach in post-war development in which early return in war zones and reconstruction were intertwined, "a new paradigm in which early reconstruction initiatives are seen as ways in which to promote and accelerate the re-establishment of security."[75] As such, reconstruction and security can be linked into positive dynamics. However, this does not render the question of purpose irrelevant The issue is less to separate forcefully development from migration projects, but to make plain the logical links between objectives and to clarify whether the core purpose of intervention has to do with people's emancipation or the control of their whereabouts.

Laying down objectives is not only essential for a better grasp of humanitarian deeds, or a prerequisite for improving future practices. It is also necessary for accountability, an issue difficult to articulate yet essential to approach sensibly.[76] Without a clear grasp of the objectives for action in the first place, both the processes of evaluation and accountability are flawed. Alternatively, different understandings of initial objectives might lead to construct divergent judgements on events. For instance, the fall of Srebrenica in 1995 can be approached differently, depending on understandings of the role of the UN in the besieged pocket. If emphasis is placed on the humanitarian mission, on UN desperate efforts to rescue civilians from a fratricidal war, then the focus rests on achievements, on

182

lives saved. In this light, although the fall of Srebrenica was a failure, the UN were still perceived as having mitigated the abuses of human rights and the massacres ensuing. In contrast, one can emphasise the fact that, in 1993, the international community decided not to evacuate most displaced persons from the besieged town, although most were desperate to be taken out.[77] Instead it promised to provide for them and to protect them. After they had heard that their town was declared a safe area, civilians in Srebrenica were ecstatic. According to Louis Gentile of UNHCR, the initial sense of relief and trust in the UN was such that most weapons were brought to the UN troops and civilian pressure to be evacuated decreased. Gentile is adamant that, in the weeks following the declaration, not only the aid workers, but also the UN Canadian troops, felt morally invested with the protection of people.

> The atmosphere in Srebrenica has been calm and relaxed since the arrival of a CANBAT company on 18 April 1993 ... The demilitarisation of the town was completed on 21 April (12:00) and weapons are no longer seen in town. ... The local authorities in Srebrenica have no intention of evacuating civilians from the pocket (although they have allowed the evacuation of the sick, wounded and disabled, by helicopter and may allow further limited evacuation/freedom of movement of refugees if the situation stabilizes). CANBAT [the Canadian Battalion] has a mandate and moral obligation (according to Canadian C.O. Lt Colonel Gebert) to protect the population of Srebrenica now that the town has been demilitarised. The CANBAT mandate is supported by a UN Security Council Resolution declaring Srebrenica a UN "Safe Haven." However, it is unclear whether the CANBAT troops have the capacity to defend the town should Bosnian Serb forces decide to recommence their attack.[78]

Likewise, in May 1993, the population of Zepa was overwhelmingly grateful to the UN for its presence and support.[79] However, neither effective protection nor humanitarian aid were ever adequately provided. This contributed to further raids for food on the part of the besieged Bosniaks in Srebrenica, in the winter of 1994-95 which, in turn, deepened the violence and hatred between the two sides. From this standpoint, responsibility and accountability look different. The UN failure to protect the civilian population might require accountability. In a similar vein, one could argue that the international community is partly responsible for what happened in Kibeho, especially given the means of pressure and help that Western institutions had on the Rwandan Government.[80]

The purpose of the above is not to allocate blame but to suggest a potential way of approaching the issue of accountability in dealing with vulnerable uprooted persons. Extreme failures, like Kibeho or Srebrenica, may help to clarify the links between choice and responsibilities. Displaced persons were little involved in the decision-making processes concerning their own fate. The international community limited their options or, as in the case of Srebrenica, made the choice for them. Only occasionally did IDPs manage to vote with their feet. By July 1995, the IDPs who were trapped in Srebrenica could not be held responsible for being in the wrong place at the wrong time. Nor could they be held responsible for the choices they did not make. It is true that the authorities in Srebrenica did not want further evacuations in 1993. Likewise, the RPF in Rwanda wanted to close the camps. Still, these positions also suited international bodies and the UN joined in these policies. However, the UN did not take responsibility for what happened. Only Tadeusz Mazowiecki publicly resigned after the fall of Srebrenica. The author would thus suggest that if, in the context of international policies, civilians' choice is curtailed on account of safety promises, then responsibility rests with the self-proclaimed rescuers. By contrast, the more choice individual civilians have, the more their responsibility is enhanced and that of the international community diminished. Clearly, this is a tentative suggestion which, to be credibly defended, would require a discussion beyond the scope of this book. It should nonetheless be borne in mind, as it differs from current approaches to responsibility detailed below.

Over recent years, responsibility became a key theme for reflection developed by Francis Deng, the UNSG high representative for IDPs. However, the responsibility there emphasised is, by and large, that of states.[81] From a UN perspective, "stronger national institutions would reduce the risk of dependence on external assistance and ease coordination difficulties between government and agencies."[82] Cohen and Deng make clear that the overall strategy of the international community regarding IDPs is to reinforce and monitor states' activities and structures for IDPs wherever they exist.[83] Sri Lanka, for instance, is thought to have taken a positive responsibility vis-à-vis displaced persons because it acknowledged the problem and co-operated with the international community to solve it.[84] This contrasts with the attitude of the Sudanese regime. This position, though, relies on the assumption that states producing forced migrants are weak, institutionally and financially, or under special strain, say an environmental catastrophe, therefore require only international support and expertise to solve their displacement problem. In practice, however, government structures often actively participate in enforced displacement policies such as in the cases of Iraq, Bosnia and Rwanda. Occasionally, as in Somalia, there was no such state structure left. UN protagonists, including Francis Deng, although aware of the ambiguities of their emphasis on the state, make it plain that they prefer to deal with central authorities able to take responsibility for people on the move. This is a continuation of the policies that affected displaced persons since the end of the Cold War. In a study of Somalia, an independent group of academics and NGO representatives came to the conclusion that persistent Western attempts at maintaining a central government were indeed part of the problem.

> The failure of the U.N. mission in Somalia is to a large degree the extension of a bankrupt donor policy which for decades has supported and reinforced overly centralised governments in Mogadishu whose legitimacy came primarily from the barrel of a gun. The U.N. and donor governments have spent the last year [1993] obsessing over the re-creation of a centralised authority in Mogadishu. This has greatly exacerbated the conflict.[85]

For years after 1992, Somalia had no central government. Both safety and economic activities are organised only at local level. However, whereas an empty seat in the UN general assembly represented a problem for the institution, the absence of Somalia's central authority did not make its citizens, both displaced and residents, necessarily worse off.[86] Another problem with the current UN approach is that some governments, such as those in Colombia or Uganda, understood that acknowledging and emphasising that they have an internal displacement problem might attract more help and support from the UN. As NGOs workers pointed out, so far this has not changed the life of IDPs, given that conventions signed and promises made to international visitors rarely had practical implications.[87] Because of its interest in IDPs though, the UN share responsibility. Although state responsibilities both in creating and solving forced displacement issues are important, UN agencies and international actors bear heavily on policy design for people on the move. After all, if Karadzic had had his will, there would have been no IDPs in Bosnia. The Bosnian Muslim population would have gone entirely in exile. It was the intervention of the international community that contributed to the maintenance of hundreds of thousands of displaced persons in Bosnia, the survival of most, but also the death of some. Again, it is necessary for humanitarian agencies, both UN and NGOs, to face the ambiguities at the core of their work.

For UN personnel, it can be tempting to present protection projects which were designed to reduce refugee flows as responses to humanitarian needs. A good illustration can be found in Clarance's description of the Open Relief Centres'policy in Sri Lanka. Whereas he detailed plainly the context in which the project emerged and laid emphasis on UNHCR's desire to forestall the new exodus towards India, he wrote later in the article: "ORCs were developed after June 1990 as a pragmatic response to the humanitarian needs emerging from the ground situation in the Mannar district."[88] Forestalling refugee flows was relegated to being a positive side effect of the policy. As a result, Clarance never questioned the implications that trying to prevent an exodus may have had on an ORC project. The flexibility that Clarance emphasised[89] is far from negligible. The UNHCR also claimed that the ORCs did not serve as alternative to flights to India.[90] However, when fighting resumed in 1995, tens of thousands of people were displaced but remained in their country. Francis Deng, after visiting the place, drew attention to the fact that IDPs were particularly liable to be picked up during cordon searches and "sent to various areas in which the security situation was precarious."[91] In a similar vein, Natsios presented the prevention of spill over of the Somali people and conflict as a positive consequence of humanitarian intervention. "Intervention in complex emergencies makes eminently good policy sense as a preventive measure to keep chaos from spreading beyond national boundaries."[92] In fact, Natsios distinguished short-term humanitarian objectives "declining death rate from disease and starvation" from long term political objectives such as the restoration of civil order.[93] Interestingly enough though, he also wrote:

> Somalia became a case study in confusing objectives. Relief issues became operationally subordinate to diplomatic and military issues, although these latter were of only secondary importance to the protection of the relief effort itself.[94]

Conflicting priorities is the core problem highlighted by Natsios. However, in his study, he still assumed that the main purpose of international interventions was to relieve immediate suffering. He may have been right with regard to UNITAF, but he partly missed the point as far as the UN intervention was concerned.

Indeed a major obstacle to thorough investigations of objectives governing work with uprooted populations is the fact that humanitarian actors themselves often mis-represent their work and its purpose. A study of the project "Seeds of Hope" designed to avert famine in post-genocide Rwanda showed the extent to which international agencies favour standardised procedures that suit their needs and justify their existence and funding requirements.[95] As humanitarian agencies now spend much time and efforts reflecting on the themes of evaluation, responsibility and accountability,[96] it is essential that they face what they are about. Why do we intervene? What do we really seek to achieve for ourselves? For others? These questions are the stepping stones of honest, thus useful, evaluation and accountability procedures. So long as humanitarian actors, in particular UN institutions, remain ambiguous over their own purposes, the question of responsibility will be by-passed.

Research: Focus on Purpose

Deploring the absence of any study of Serb war aims, Noel Malcolm, a specialist of Balkan history, wrote at the end of the Bosnian war: "It is not clear what Western politicians can really mean when they claim that their policies have at least "contained" the conflict within the former Yugoslavia."[97] Indeed, to grasp what Western politicians might mean by "containing the conflict," it is crucial to study not only Serbian war aims but also Western war aims, what they intended to do in the first place, which fears dominated. There is indeed no "lack of will." Nevertheless, writers often seem to miss the contradictions inherent to the ambient humanitarian discourse and sometimes take for granted that protection from starvation or violence is the ultimate aim of the game. As was argued earlier in this book, research on IDPs remains incomplete, sometimes out of focus, simply because academics tend either to be little interested in IDPs *per se* or to rely on unwarranted assumptions regarding the role of the media and the aims of intervention. This section highlights the dangers that researchers face when they remain unclear about the aims of the policies investigated.

In an article entitled "Cruel Wars and Safe Havens: Humanitarian Aid in Liberia 1989-1996," Quentin Outram suggested that ECOMOG, the Nigerian peace-keepers troops, provided a *de facto* safe zone in Monrovia throughout the war, except briefly in 1992 and in the spring of 1996.[98] Creating such a haven was not the mandate of ECOMOG. However, its massive military presence, its maintenance of links with the outside world and its provision of a base for humanitarian agencies helped to improve the situation of Monrovia's residents, including that of numerous displaced persons. Indeed, civilians were better off in Monrovia than in the rest of the country where fighting restricted humanitarian access. Outram thus concluded that pessimist perspectives on safe havens, which prevail since the fall of Srebrenica, should be tempered in the light of the relatively positive experience in Liberia. However, as he himself outlined, the safety of populations was not the mandate of Ecomog. The primary aim of the ECOMOG troops seemed to have been to prevent Charles Taylor from taking over the country. Benefits provided by its military presence, although crucial for people, were secondary. This became clear in April 1996 when Monrovia was looted. Neither the safety of civilians nor that of humanitarian workers were of much interest to the Nigerian troops. The interest of the article is that it illustrates that some humanitarian ends can be achieved *en route* or as a by-product of other projects. Furthermore, Outram highlighted the problems posed by internal divisions within the safe haven, especially the violence of leaders against their own people.[99] The fact that neither in Liberia, nor Rwanda, Bosnia or northern Iraq, occupation forces tried to deal with law and order in the zones they controlled, confirms the idea that safety never was a priority. However, Outram was ill-advised to extend his conclusion to safe havens in general. For his paper illustrates indeed the limits of the kind of protection that is a by-product of other endeavours. It also highlights the necessity to clarify objectives before evaluating humanitarian action.

Similarly, Jeremy Ginifer investigated the potential benefits of limited disarmament for the protection of IDPs without considering the question of the purpose of international intervention.[100] Although it described the problems of disarming populations who often do not trust in the internationally sponsored peace processes,[101] the article made the point that limited forceful disarmament was feasible and enhanced the protection of displaced populations. Leaving aside the difficulties of enforcing arms control on a limited territorial area, which were not dealt with adequately, the term "protection disarmament" used throughout the article shows that Ginifer took for granted that the protection of vulnerable populations was the aim of humanitarian operations in general, and of disarmament operations in particular.[102] Whereas he described disarmament as a means rather than an end, he assumed that protection was the end.[103] Again, strategic issues were simply tucked away from the humanitarian problematic. When referring to the Rwandan crisis, Ginifer ignored the fact that resolution 918 was taken amid discussions on refugee movements.[104] He then wrote about Operation Turquoise that it was "authorised to protect civilians and prevent mass movements of refugees."[105] The impact of Operation Turquoise was then declared

188

"positive" without any clear reference to evaluation criteria, although Ginifer does mention that the operation limited refugee outflow. Overall, because of a lack of clarity regarding the purposes of international action in the Great Lake area, the assessment of the causes of disarmament failures remains unconvincing. Once more, the role of the media in promoting action is postulated. Once more, a lack of political will was declared to be the end reason for failure,[106] except possibly in Somalia where the "wrong methods" were employed.[107] Only the French in Rwanda were perceived to have a form of political agenda and interests other than humanitarianism. The author would contend that seeing protection not as an end but as a device to be promised or delivered to control population movements may help understand why disarmament, itself a function of protection, was so often only half heartily attempted. Going one step further, it seems that Ginifer implicitly adopted the assumption of the UN and of numerous governments, that mass displacement was itself dangerous. This position led him to declare that somehow mobility was the problem.

> Displaced persons are difficult to protect. They are mobile, awkward to track and they move across international boundaries. This makes them physically vulnerable unless they are congregated where they can be protected.[108]

This kind of statement implied that only solutions that increased control over population should be considered. Not surprisingly, Ginifer recommended "a more active policy of cordoning off camps and establishing checkpoints" to collect weapons, overall an increased control of "movement" in and out of the zones to be demilitarised.[109] Such an approach dismisses the fact that people flee for their lives, and it may seriously endanger this essential freedom of movement. Given the book's findings, that protection attempts remain superficial so long as people do not threaten borders *en masse*, any proposal to increase direct international control of population movements raises prospects of an international community evermore directly engaged in the incarceration of the victims. To sum up, Ginifer refers to means but does not relate them to ends and thus proposes solutions far from entailing the emancipation of the displaced persons themselves. To a great extent, IDPs remain the "objects" of policy-making and of academic enquiry.

Ginifer's article encapsulated the problems of not questioning the discourse of mainstream humanitarian operators. The risk, then, is to adopt the implicit values that shape the policy evaluated, as Ginifer readily accepted the idea that mobility was the problem.

Underneath Belief in News Media

An observer should also bear in mind the assumptions that underline faith in the impact of news media on humanitarian action. Most people writing on the influence of the media on humanitarian practices work on a common assumption. However insufficient, sometimes distorting, the effect of news media are perceived to be, it is assumed that media influence naturally leads to a greater involvement in relieving suffering. In other words, there is an ambient in-built conviction that media presence always improves, however little or insufficiently, the fate of people in danger. This often leads to the assumption that the outcomes of humanitarian crises handled under TV scrutiny are necessarily better for civilians than if the events had not been covered. By contrast, events ignored by the media are assumed to bear consequences for civilians worse than if they had reached newspapers and television headlines. To give an example, the presence of numerous journalists in Sarajevo is presumed to have indirectly limited the bombing of the city and its inhabitants. By contrast, the absence of Western journalists in Somalia until the summer of 1992 is deemed partly responsible for the violence of the clan war in 1991-92, as well as for Western indifference. Such allegations would require serious investigation. However, because of its widespread acceptance, the assumption that media presence improves the lot of vulnerable populations is hardly ever up for discussion. In the same vein, the possibility that media coverage itself may immediately worsen the life conditions of vulnerable persons is hardly considered. Yet, as mentioned in chapter II, mediatisation can also be a process of instrumentalisation. And the use of suffering for one's particular political purposes is a constant temptation. Once more, only a close look at the decisions taken and implemented can lead to knowing whether the presence of reporters actually improved the fate of the people appearing on the small screen. So far however, studies of the decisions taken and implemented on the ground have tended to be dissociated from the search for causes of humanitarian involvement and especially from the study of news media's impact. Not only should media influence be considered in conjunction with other potential causes for action, but to know whether media impact changes policy, one needs to pay attention to the very decisions taken, the alternative discussed, the modalities of implementation etc. The fact that "something is being done" coincidentally to intense media

190

coverage and public outcry does not tell whether policy is being changed. To sum up, because of its strength, the assumption that media coverage influences political action for the benefit of civilians is not only over-simplistic but also detrimental to sound analyses of political action.

At the other end of the spectrum, specialists in forced migrations such as Tiso and Frelick, not only ignore the potential influence of the media but do not compare their findings on containment to alternative perspectives on the same events. The reasons of this absence of dialogue among academics lies in a simple division of tasks and interests. Authors interested in humanitarian action do not spare time to work on media, and the media influence studies. By contrast, media specialists are not ultimately interested in the type of decision taken on the ground and the process by which they are reached. Few people really seek to explore this interface, that is, study the decisions taken on the ground and relate one's findings to the debate over media influence. Nevertheless, such a study would be necessary to acquire some solid ground to be able to adjudicate between motives for action. Gowing's study of the Eastern Zaire crisis in late 1996 and early 1997 highlights the tangles between protection and information handling.[110] In particular, he showed how insensitive information handling can put displaced persons at risk, as warring parties used humanitarian agencies's information concerning the location of displaced persons for their own purposes. It is a frightening text which sobers immediately any enthusiasm for the impact of news media. Yet it may pave the way for more sophisticated accounts of the issues.

To conclude on media issues, this book indirectly questioned the idea that news media automatically improves the lot of displaced persons, and that aid workers and journalists can easily team up to help devastated populations. This approach relies on numerous assumptions which are not always warranted. Some of these are listed below, as a reminder of the themes to be borne in mind in further research or action. They are the following:

1. Warring parties do not want their deeds known.
2. Warring parties cannot manipulate and use humanitarian information for their own purpose.
3. Western governments react to public outrage rather than make the news themselves.
4. "what is being done" is a change of policy.
5. Policies implemented are those wished by aid workers, let alone by displaced persons.

191

The Human Costs of Preserving Borders

There are numerous ways of exploring the extent to which protection is instrumentalised and the prevalence of order, of population control over civilian safety. Below are some suggestions for further work arising from the book's findings.

Mobility as Obstacle to the Search for Order

The link between border control and international intervention with people on the move should be investigated further. It is noteworthy that it took three weeks to send troops to stop forced migrations in northern Iraq, three months in Rwanda but more than three years in Bosnia. One difference among the cases was the following. Despite Turkey, Iran or Zaire attempts at re-creating border zones, Iraqi and Rwandan frontiers remained porous throughout the crises, and cross-border population movements largely uncontrolled. By contrast, Bosnia was a closed trap for its displaced persons. Unlike Rwandan Hutus and Iraqi Kurds, Bosnians could not escape. This distinction, combined with the claim that IDPs protection is an instrument of containment policies, renders the following suggestion plausible. Bosnian IDPs were not significantly protected precisely because they could not leave their country. The exact role of the international community in this progressive "incarceration of the victims," to borrow Chimni's expression, still needs exploring. As part of it, more attention could be devoted to the issue of evacuation, not only in terms of comparing practices to speeches but also in terms of investigating why and how international evacuations are framed out of the current debate over humanitarian reforms.

The Western search for orderly and controllable events could also be investigated further. It is fascinating indeed that the concepts of order and disorder are absent from the dominant humanitarian rhetoric yet are prominent in policy documents or mission statements, such as that of the IOM, an organisation particularly active with people on the move.[111] This work is not an argument against the recreation of political order *per se*. But it pointed out that, during endeavours regarding IDPs, the quest for order could run counter to basic issues of personal safety. Such evidence flies in the face of the accepted idea that war victims are always better off immobile, close to their homes, than on the move. There is indeed a human cost in insisting that people should remain within dangerous and volatile situations, and this should be part of the policy-making discussions.

Besides, by undertaking to prevent movements or to repatriate in ways that seek to recreate the initial state of affairs, Western protagonists also refuted the possibilities of social change. In fact, they prevented displaced persons from choosing and therefore assuming responsibility for their future. Apart from the fact that such an exercise is bound to fail because forced displacement on its own entails dramatic changes within societies, it reflects a very conservative agenda. It was the preservation of some entrenched feudal orders that undermined aid work with Rwandan refugees and displaced persons. Given that whole communities had fled together, aid workers found it easier to use the power structures and leaders in place despite their authoritarian nature.[112] However, working with the very leaders who had organised the genocide and the exodus had ominous implications for most displaced persons. This led to reflection regarding the desire to deal with leaders who control situations, no matter who they are. Still, further thought is required on the role of Western institutions in the creation of the circumstances in which displaced persons make choices. To that purpose, more attention should be devoted to Western information policies towards uprooted populations.

Among the issues just highlighted, the implications of preventing escapes are of particular relevance to both practitioners and academics. Thus the book will close with a few rough thoughts on this theme.

Civilian Bodies as Front Line

In June 1993, the BSA arrested non-Serbs in Doboj and forced them to stand as a living front line in combat areas nearby. This was a blatant violation of humanitarian law and was denounced as such. At the same time however, the international community agreed with the leaders of Srebrenica that mass evacuation be stopped after it was declared a safe area.[113] Despite agreements among aid workers that the town was too overpopulated to be sustainable,[114] large-scale evacuation was ended, thus transforming thousands of displaced persons into the front line of the war of resistance against ethnic cleansing campaigns. It became clear, as the war went on, that the very presence of civilians was the asset that allowed the Bosnian government to preserve territory. However, because the maintenance of civilians in war zones was done in the name of opposing ethnic cleansing, it was not questioned. In fact, in Europe, the concept of ethnic cleansing was constructed as such an evil that the nature of the policies proposed to oppose it could hardly be challenged without one exposing oneself to the condemnation of siding with the cleansers. This happened despite the fact that the Western emphasis on the "right to stay" and policies of "preventive protection" were openly dictated by migration concerns. Speaking for the European Community member states, Baroness Chalker plainly declared:

> We believe that the key to alleviating the problem of migrant flows is to try to stem the flow of displaced persons by providing sufficient assistance to enable them to be cared for within the former Yugoslav Republics.[115]

The problems of Linda Chalker were "migrant flows" to the European Community, Slovenia and Croatia were to act as buffer zones and humanitarian assistance was the key instrument to tackle unwanted population movements. Both concepts, "the right to stay" and "preventive protection," were created to implement Western refusal to accept Bosnian refugees. Without much investigation, they were accepted as the only ways to fight ethnic cleansing. This drove numerous aid workers to despair of their own tasks:

> What I found in the field was total despair among the delegates who could do nothing to help people. They felt that to leave them in their villages was to condemn them to death and trying to protect them there would be useless. The only thing that seemed of any use was to help them to make for a safe place until some political arrangement enabled them to return. It seemed to us hypocrisy for the political negotiators to say that nothing should be done that might possibly encourage "ethnic cleansing." We saw only one way out - to help people to get away and at the same time denounce "ethnic cleansing."[116]

When aid workers helped people to escape, they were accused of giving in to ethnic cleansing. In fact, it was the Western emphasis on ethnic cleansing itself that hindered analysis by disallowing the fact that people were fleeing for their lives. At the core of preventive protection policies lay the assumption that people wanted to claim this "right to stay." But were they really asked? This right to stay in particular presupposes that they still had a home they valued. To people who had already lost their homes, their land, their families and were desperate to leave for a safe country, the international community imposed not a right but a "duty to remain" to use Barutciski's terminology. In effect, the very presence of IDPs meant that it was too late for early warnings or for preventive protection policies. Thus, the emergence of such humanitarian rhetoric regarding persons already uprooted needs to be examined cautiously. This is all the more important, given that Bosnian displaced persons were not an unfortunate minority for whom an overall well-intended policy had unforeseen ill-effects. On the contrary, they were the very persons for whom the policy was designed in the first place. At the beginning of the war, they were the majority of the intended recipients of humanitarian action. By the end of the war, they still represented almost half the beneficiaries of international aid.[117] Hence the need to question the design of international responses to ethnic cleansing as a whole.

The emphasis on the evil of cleansing also obscured the fact that the interventions did not always oppose practices of ethnic cleansing. For example, the idea that "safe areas" challenged cleansing only emerged in spring 1993. In a UN debate held late 1992, both the UNHCR and the US had raised concerns that the creation of safe areas might encourage the logic of ethnic partition. Christopher Tiso recorded that inhabitants of the villages surrounding Gorazde left for the town when it was declared safe, hence making it easy for the BSA to close on the city. General Morillon castigated the authorities in Tuzla for not abiding by General Mladic's demand that Serbs be "evacuated" from the multi-ethnic town. Indeed, the "right to stay" applied to some people rather than others, to the Bosniak inhabitants of Srebrenica in 1993, many of whom did not want it, but not to the Serbs in Tuzla or to those of Sarajevo in 1996.

In all the cases reviewed, the choice of individuals was subordinated to that of their leaders and of international authorities. Few had to do with what the victims themselves wanted. Nevertheless, it was in the name of their suffering that policy, whether bringing more aid, creating safe havens or repatriating was justified. It is rarely acknowledged that this suffering resulted not only from enemy persecution but also from the fact that both leaders and the international community used these persons' bodies to resist certain population movements that did not suit their political endeavour. The language of protection hid the fact that the international community acted on the assumption that civilians could be used for state matters. In other words, it obscured the fact that people were presumed to belong to states, as a property.

Notes

1   Cohen and Deng, *Masses in Flight*, 162.

2   Binaifer, Nowrojee, "Regional Profile: Kenya," in Hampton, ed., *Internally Displaced Persons*, 65-68, 67. See also Abdullahi, Ahmednasir, "Ethnic Clashes Displaced Persons and the Potential for Refugee Creation in Kenya," Vol. 9, No. 2 (1997), *International Journal of Refugee Law*, 196-206. It is a revealing article not least because the author insists on the potential for a refugee crisis generated by the Kenyan government in the hope to attract attention upon internal displacement issues.

3   Torrenté, *The International Protection of Internally Displaced Persons*, 54.

4   Boucher-Saulnier, "Points de vue sur la protection de l'aide," in Domestici-Met, ed., *Aide Humanitaire Internationale*, 205, author's translation.

5   Ibid., 204, author's translation.

6   Bennett, Jon, "Forced Migration Within National Borders: the IDP Agenda," No. 1 (January-April 1998), *Forced Migration Review*, 4-6, 6.

7   MSF is an organisation particularly vocal about the "lack" of political will of the international community. It organised international days to raise awareness about populations in danger. MSF, *Population in Danger, Appeals by Doctors without Borders or Médecins sans Frontières*, E-mail posting regarding the publication of *Population in Danger 1995*, 16 November 1994.

8   EC/SCP/87 - 17 August 1994 - *Protection Aspects of UNHCR Activities on behalf of Internally Displaced Persons*.

9   Tiso, "Safe Haven Refugee Programs," 589.

10   Cohen and Deng, *Masses in Flight*, 201-202.

11   Ibid., 202-207.

12   For instance in the course of the BSA offensive in Eastern Bosnia in winter 1993, *UNHCR Update on Former Yugoslavia*, Geneva, 12 February 1993, 2 pages.

13   Jessen Petersen, "Corridors and Convoys," in Domestici-Met, ed., *Aide Humanitaire Internationale*, 194.

14   The UN guiding principles can be found in Davies, ed., *Internally Displaced People*, 209.

15   "Nato planners prepare for air-land operation," *The Guardian*, 9 June 1998, 11.

16   Personal communication, Daoud Sarhandi, International Medical Corp officer on the Macedonian border, April 1999.

17   Barbero, Julie, "Refugee Repatriation during Conflict: A New Conventional Wisdom," Vol 12, No. 8, *Refuge*, 7-11.

18   Quoted in Clarance, "Open Relief Centres," 324.

19   Domestici-Met, "L'aide humanitaire: terrain de consensus et espace de controverses," in Domestici-Met, ed., *Aide Humanitaire Internationale*, 25.

20   Cohen and Deng, *Masses in Flight*, 261.

21   Ibid., 261.

22   UN General Assembly, A/50/558, Annex: *Report on Internally Displaced Persons* prepared by the Representative of the Secretary-General Mr. Francis Deng, 20 October 1995.

23   Reilly, Rachel, Summary of paper discussions and debates during the conference *People of Concern*, Geneva, 21-23 November 1996, panel: *Returnees: the Meaning and Modes of Reintegration*, 18, UNHCR Centre for Documentation

and Research.

24   Stedman, "Negotiation and Mediation in Internal Conflict," in Brown, ed., *The International Dimensions of Internal Conflict*, 373.

25   Lander, Brian, UNHCR protection officer, Galang Indonesia, "Far from Paradise," issue 104, No. 2 (1996), *Refugees*, (on-line: http://www.unhcr.ch/pubs/rm/104/rm10403.htm, no pagination). The article reflects only the author's position. On this issue, see also Helton, Arthur, "Displacement and Human Rights: Current Dilemmas in Refugee Protection," Vol. 47, No. 2 (1994), *Journal of International Affairs*, 379-389, 393-395.

26   European Community, Ad Hoc Immigration Group, *Resolution on Certain Common Guideline as regards the Admission of Particularly Vulnerable Groups of Persons from the Former Yugoslavia*, Copenhagen, 1 June 1993. See also Frelick, Bill, "Barriers to Protection: Turkey's Asylum Regulations," Vol. 9, No. 1 (1997), *International Journal of Refugee Law*, 8-34.

27   Duffield, Mark, "Normalising the Crisis, from Complex Emergencies to Social Reconstruction" in Edkins, Jenny, ed., *The Politics of Emergency*, Manchester Papers in Politics, 2/97, Department of Government, University of Manchester, December 1997, 73 pages, 7-13, 12.

28   Domestici-Met, "L'aide humanitaire," in Domestici-Met, ed., *Aide Humanitaire Internationale*, 25.

29   UN Guiding Principles, in Davies, ed., *Internally Displaced People*, 205-213, principles 15, 209 and 28, 212-213.

30   Cohen and Deng, *Masses in Flight*, 260. This also includes a reference to a positive UNHCR experience with involving IDPs into decision making.

31   Ibid., 256.

32   Copies of the UN Guiding Principles on Internal Displacement can be found in Davies, ed., *Internally Displaced People*, 205-213 or Cohen and Deng, *Masses in Flight*, 305-316. For interesting comments on the debates surrounding their elaboration, see Klin, Walter, *Guiding Principles on Internal Displacement*, paper presented at the Conference on Internally Displaced Persons, Overseas Development Institute, London, 20 July 1998. See also Bagshaw, Simon, *Internally Displaced Persons at the Fifty-Fourth Session of the United Nations Commission on Human Rights, 16 March-24 April 1998*, unpublished paper.

33   Frelick, "Aliens in their Own Land."

34   Ibid.

35   Ibid.

36   Cohen, Roberta, "Recent Trends in Protection and Assistance for Internally Displaced People," in Davies, ed., *Internally Displaced People*, 3.

37   Minear, Scott, Weiss, *The News Media*, 1.

38   Stromseth, "Iraq's Repression of its Civilian Population," in Fisler Damrosh, ed., *Enforcing restraint*, 84 (italics added).

39   Shaw, Martin, *Civil Society and Media in Global Crises, Representing Distant Violence*, (London: Pinter, 1996), 88.

40   Minear, Scott, Weiss, *The News Media*, 57.

41   Bennet, *Yugoslavia's Bloody Collapse*, 3.

42   Prunier, *The Rwanda Crisis*, 273-274 (italics added). See also Minear, SCOTT, Weiss, *The News Media*, 62-67.

43   Mermin, "Television News and American Intervention in Somalia," 403.

44   Livingston and Eachus, "Humanitarian Crises and US Foreign Policy," 427.

45   Shaw, *Civil Society and Media in Global Crises*, 171. Shaw does not explain why.

46   Dowty and Loescher, "Refugee Flows," Adelman, "The Ethics of Humanitarian Intervention," Kirisci, Kemal, "Provide Comfort and Turkey, Decision Making for Humanitarian Intervention," (on-line: http://snipe.ukc.ac.uk/international/papers.dir/kirisci.html, no pagination) and Roberts, *Humanitarian Action in War*.

47   Roberts, *Humanitarian Action in War*, 10.

48   Adelman, "The Ethics of Humanitarian Intervention," 73.

49   Shaw, *Civil Society and Media in Global Crises*, 173. The fact that Shaw points out the lack of strategic motives to explain the absence of timely intervention in Rwanda renders his absence of focus on strategy in his main study on Iraq all the more inconsistent.

50   Adelman, "The Ethics of Humanitarian Intervention," 74.

51   Ibid., 75.

52   Strategic pressures include mass refugee flow. As for humanitarian pressures, they entail mass suffering regularly displayed on TV screens.

53   See for instance Weiss, "Triage: Humanitarian Intervention in a New Era," 63.

54   For example, see UNHCR, *Global Report on UNHCR's Activities in Northern Iraq since April 1991*, Geneva, 1 September 1992, 1, or Mercier, *Crimes without Punishment*, 147.

55   Minear, Scott, Weiss, *The News Media*, 74.

56   Roberts, *Humanitarian Action in War*, 8.

57   Gowing, Nick, "Real Time Coverage from War, Does it Make or Break Government Policy?" in Gow, James, Paterson, Richard and Preston, Alison, eds., *Bosnia by Television*, (London: British Film Institute Publishing, 1996), 81-91, 89-91.

58   For Roberts "The fact remains that alongside the growth of humanitarian action there has been a policy vacuum. Major powers and international organisations have lacked long-term policies addressing the substantive issues raised by the conflict of the 1990s." Roberts, *Humanitarian Action in War*, 9.

59   Shaw, *Civil Society and Media in Global Crises*, 180-181.

60   Stedman writes on Somalia: "The humanitarian intervention saved lives in the short term but did not solve the country's deeper problems. The intervention was more palliative than cure." Stedman, "Conflict and Conciliation in Sub-Saharan Africa," in Brown, ed., *The International Dimensions of Internal Conflict*, 257.

61   On the necessity for both aid workers and journalists to take stock of their complementarity see Westermann, Simone, "Media and Relief Workers: Changing Relations," Vol. 5, No. 2, Issue 28 (March April 1997), *Crosslines Global Report*, 21-23. See also Weiss, "Nongovernmental Organisations and Internal Conflict," in Brown, ed., *The International Dimensions of Internal Conflict*, 455.

62   *Humanitarian Aid in Somalia, September 1990-May 1993*, Refugee Policy Group, Draft Discussion Paper, Washington DC, March 1994, 54 pages, 17.

63   For a recent detailed study of the complexity of information handling, see Gowing, Nik, *New Challenges and Problems for Information Management in Complex Emergencies, Ominous Lessons from the Great Lakes and Eastern Zaire in late 1996 and early 1997*, Conference Paper, London, 27 and 28 May 1998, 79 pages.

64 Minear, Scott, Weiss, *The News Media*, 11-12.
65 Gowing, *New challenges and Problems for Information Management in Complex Emergencies*, 21-34 and 47-66.
66 Bennett, "Forced Migration within National Borders," 6.
67 E/CN.4/1992/S-1/9 UN Economic and Social Council, Commission of Human Rights, report submitted by Tadeusz Mazowiecki pursuant to paragraph 14 of the Commission resolution 1992/S-1/1 of 14 August 1992.
68 Cohen and Deng, *Masses in Flight*, 200.
69 Ibid., 200.
70 The need for better co-ordination was emphasised after each of the crises reviewed. See for instance Natsios, Andrew, "The International Humanitarian Response System," Vol. 25, No. 1 (1995), *Parameters*, 68-81.
71 Boucher-Saulnier, "Points de vue sur la protection de l'aide," in Domestici-Met, ed., *Aide Humanitaire Internationale*, 203.
72 Boutros-Ghali, Boutros, *An Agenda for Peace, Preventive Diplomacy, Peace-making and Peace-keeping*, report of the Secretary-General pursuant to the statement adopted by the summit meeting of the Security Council on 31 January 1992, UN Department of Public Information, New York, 1992 (author's italics).
73 World Council of Churches, "Statements on Uprooted People," 7, quoted in Cohen and Deng, *Masses in Flight*, 200.
74 Commission de l'immigration et du statut de refugié, Direction générale de la documentation, de l'information et des recherches, *Sri Lanka: les possibilités de fuites intérieures*, Series "Questions et Réponses," Ottawa, Canada: December 1992.
75 Roggee, *The Displaced Population in South and Central Somalia*, 43.
76 The issue of the accountability of humanitarian actors in forced migration contexts was a theme developed notably by Barbara Harrell-Bond and her colleagues in the Refugee Research Programme in Oxford, UK. See for instance Harrell-Bond, Barbara, Voutira, Eftihia and Leopold, Mark, "Counting the Refugees: Gifts, Givers, Patrons and Clients," Vol. 5, No. 3/4 (1992), *Journal of Refugee Studies*, 205-225.
77 Gentile, Louis (UNHCR) *Internal Report on the Situation in Srebrenica*, Belgrade, 14 April 1993, 3 pages, 1.
78 Gentile, Louis (UNHCR representative in Srebrenica), *Internal Report on the Situation in Srebrenica*, Belgrade, 21 April 1993, 2 pages, 1. Gentile's use of the term "Safe Haven" shows that, at the time, the subtle differences developed in later UN rhetoric between safe haven and safe area were not grasped by field workers.
79 Gentile, Louis (UNHCR representative in Zepa), *Zepa, The Second Safe Area*, internal report regarding the situation in Zepa, 7 June 1993, 6 pages, 1 and 4.
80 The issue of responsibility of the humanitarian community in the politics of the post-genocide Rwanda was emphasised by José Kagabo (Centre D'études Africaines, Paris) in the course of the conference "*Rwanda : Perspectives d'Avenir, Perspectives on the Future of Rwanda*," Friday 12 May 1995.
81 Deng, Francis, *Sovereignty and Accountability, a Framework of Protection, Assistance and Development for the Internally Displaced*, Summer 1995.
82 McLean, Jennifer, "National Response to Internal Displacement," No. 1 (January-April 1998), *Forced Migration Review*, 10-11, 11.
83 Cohen and Deng, *Masses in Flight*, 262.

84   Ibid., 261-262. See also McLean, "National Response to Internal Displacement," 11.
85   Somalia Task Force, *Post-UNOSOM Aid Strategies in Somalia*, 1. The damage on reconstruction created by an externally generated agenda has been described in Bartoli, Andrea, "Somalia and Rwanda vs. Mozambique: Notes for Comparison on Peace Processes," in Girardet, Edward, ed., *Somalia, Rwanda and Beyond*, (Geneva: Crosslines Global Report, 1995), 195-202.
86   Karen von Hippel (Department of War Studies, King's College London), talk on Somalia presented at the Conference on Regional Security in a Global Context, 7 April 1998.
87   Conference on IDPs ODI London 20 July 1998, discussions on case studies, Columbia and Sudan, reference also to Uganda.
88   Clarance, "Open Relief Centres," 325. Mannar was chosen because it was the area of last refuge for displaced on their ways to India. The Maddhu Shrine in the jungle was chosen because it was an important crossroad, 326.
89   Ibid., 327.
90   Sen, Sumit, *International Law of Internally Displaced Persons: the Role of the UNHCR*, Master of Philosophy Dissertation submitted to the Jawaharlal Nerhu University, New Delhi, 1995, 106.
91   A/50/558, Annex: *Report on Internally Displaced Persons* prepared by the Representative of the Secretary-General Mr. Francis Deng, 20 October 1995.
92   Natsios, "Food through Force," 143.
93   Ibid., 131.
94   Ibid., 133.
95   Pottier, "Agricultural Rehabilitation and Food Insecurity," 56-75.
96   The *Forced Migration Review*, Vol. 8 (August 2000) contains 20 pages devoted to the issue of accountability, 4-24.
97   Malcolm, "Bosnia and the West," 6.
98   Outram, Quentin, "Cruel Wars and Safe Havens: Humanitarian Aid in Liberia 1989-1996," Vol. 21, No. 3 (1997), *Disasters*, 189-205.
99   Ibid., 202. Nicolas de Torrenté, MSF worker in Liberia, gave illustrations of the abuses, including forced displacement and starvation, inflicted on people by local warlords. Oxfam Conference on Human Rights, London, SOAS, 14th March 1998.
100   Ginifer, Jeremy, "Protecting Displaced Persons Through Disarmament," Vol. 40, No. 2 (1998), *Survival*, 161-176.
101   Ibid., 164.
102   Ibid., 162.
103   Ibid., 162.
104   Ibid., 169.
105   Ibid., 169.
106   Ibid., 171.
107   Ibid., 165.
108   Ibid., 163.
109   Ibid., 167.
110   Gowing, *New Challenges and Problems for Information Management in Complex Emergencies*.
111   International Organisation for Migration - IOM - *Internally Displaced Persons*, 1.
112   Reynolds, *Development in a Refugee Situation*, 2.

113   Gentile, Louis (UNHCR), *Internal Report on the Situation in Srebrenica*, Belgrade, 21 April 1993, 2 pages, 1.

114   Ibid., 1-2.

115   Transcript of the statement by Baroness Chalker on behalf of the European Community and its member states, *International Meeting on Humanitarian Aid for Victims of the Conflict on the Former Yugoslavia*, Geneva, 29 July 1992.

116   Mercier, *Crimes without Punishment*, 6.

117   *Information Notes on Former Yugoslavia*, No. 6/95, UNHCR Office of the Special Envoy for Former Yugoslavia, Zagreb, Croatia, June 1995, 7.

Bibliography

This bibliography is confined to listing works and documents cited in the text or notes of this book (excluding news reports for which full references have been given in the notes). Html addresses are correct at the time of writing.

UN Documents

ECOSOC (Economic and Social Council)
E/CN.4/1992/S-1/9, Commission of Human Rights, report submitted by Tadeusz Mazowiecki pursuant to paragraph 14 of the Commission resolution 1992/S-1/1 of 14 August 1992.

E/CN.4/1995/50, *Internally Displaced Persons*, report of the representative of the Secretary-General Mr. Francis Deng submitted pursuant to Commission on Human Rights resolutions 1993/95 and 1994/68, 2 February 1995.

UNDHA (United Nations Department of Humanitarian Affairs)
DHA/93/87 GE.93-02099, *Information Report, Somalia*, August 1993.

UNOSOM Division of Humanitarian Affairs, *Fourth Humanitarian Conference on Somalia*, Addis Ababa, Ethiopia, 29 November-1 December 1993, Paper 2, *The Continuing Emergency*, 6 pages.

UNOSOM Division of Humanitarian Affairs, *Fourth Humanitarian Conference on Somalia*, Addis Ababa, Ethiopia, 29 November-1 December 1993, Paper 3, *Resettlement*, 5 pages.

UN Relief and Rehabilitation Programme for Somalia, Covering the Period 1 March-31 December 1993, 11 March 1993.

94/0279, *Rwanda Civil Disturbance*, DHA - Geneva Daily Information Report No. 32, 26 August 1994 (information provided by UNREO - United Nations Rwanda Emergency Office).

Emergency Profile Chechnya Area, HCWEB Pilot Project, Russian Federation 1995, 11 May 1995.

Emergency Profile (Pilot Project) Rwanda, 3 May 1995.

UNDP (United Nations Development Programme)
Roggee, John, (Disaster research Unit, University of Manitoba), *The Displaced Population in South and Central Somalia and Preliminary Proposals for their Re-integration and Re-habilitation*, a report to the UNDP, 4 September 1992.

UNDPI (United Nations Department of Public Information)
Boutros-Ghali, Boutros, *An Agenda for Peace, Preventive Diplomacy, Peace-making and Peace-keeping*, report of the Secretary-General pursuant to the statement adopted by the summit meeting of the Security Council on 31 January 1992, New York, 1992.
The United Nations and the Situation in Rwanda, reference paper, New York, April 1995.

UN General Assembly
A/50/558, Annex: *Report on Internally Displaced Persons*, prepared by the Representative of the Secretary-General Mr. Francis Deng in accordance with paragraph 16 of the Commission for Human Rights resolution 1995/57 of 3 March 1995 and Economic and Social Council decision 1995/273 of 25 July 1995, 20 October 1995.

UNHCR (United Nations High Commissioner for Refugees)
Statement of the High Commissioner for Refugees at the Donor Information Meeting, Geneva, 15 May 1991, UNHCR Information Service.
Global Report on UNHCR's Activities in Iraq since April 1991, Geneva, 1 September 1992.
UNHCR Information Bulletin No. 6, 3 October 1991.
UNHCR Update on Operations Within the Regional Humanitarian Plan of Action, 5 December 1991.
HCR/IMFY/1992/2, *A Comprehensive Response to the Humanitarian Crisis in the Former Yugoslavia*, 24 July 1992.
HCR/CRHC/FC/2, 31 August 1992, *Comprehensive Response to the Humanitarian Crisis in Former Yugoslavia*, working document for the second meeting of the CRHC follow-up Committee, Geneva, 4 September 1992.
HCR/CRHC/FC/2/ Annex I, *UNHCR/UNICEF Joint Statement on the Evacuation of Children from Former Yugoslavia*, 13 August 1992.
HCR/CRHC/FC/2/Annex 2, *Inter-Agency Assessment Mission to Former Yugoslavia*, 9-16 August 1992.
Update on Ex-Yugoslavia, 13 August 1992.
Humanitarian Issues Working Group of the International Conference on the Former Yugoslavia, working document, prepared for the meeting of 4 December 1992, 30 November 1992, 8 pages plus annex entitled *Note on the Deployment of UNPROFOR and its Incidence on UNHCR Operations in Bosnia and Herzegovina*.
Statement by the United Nations High Commissioner for Refugees at the Meeting of the Humanitarian Issues Working Group of the International Conference on Former Yugoslavia, Geneva, 4 December 1992.
Ogata, Sadako, United Nations High Commissioner for Refugees, *Refugees, a Multilateral Response to Humanitarian Crises*, Elberg Lecture on International Studies, University of California, Berkeley, 1 April 1992

204

(on-line: http://www.unhcr.ch/refworld/unhcr/hcspeech/1ap1992.htm, no pagination).

UNHCR Update on Former Yugoslavia, Geneva, 12 February 1993.

Internal Report on the Situation in Srebrenica, Louis Gentile, Belgrade, 14 April 1993.

Internal Report on the Situation in Srebrenica, Louis Gentile, Belgrade, 21 April 1993.

Zepa, The Second Safe Area, internal report regarding the situation in Zepa, Louis Gentile, UNHCR representative in Zepa, 7 June 1993.

Banja Luka: Ethnic Cleansing has Another Name, internal communication (BLK/HRV/HCR/0401/CMB/PBT/OSE), Louis Gentile, UNHCR representative in Banja Luka, 30 August 1993.

Update on the Yugoslav Region, internal documentation, 22 September 1993.

UNHCR Report on Former Yugoslavia, September 1993.

Confidential Note for Special Envoy (FYEO), Louis Gentile, UNHCR representative in Banja Luka, 10 November 1993.

Information Notes on Former Yugoslavia, UNHCR office of the Special Envoy for Former Yugoslavia, External Relation Unit, No. 11, November 1993.

UNHCR Rwanda Appeal, May 1994.

UNHCR Warns of Impeding Bukavu Crisis, UNHCR Update on Rwanda, Geneva, 12 August 1994, 2 pages.

EC/SCP/87, *Protection Aspects of UNHCR Activities on behalf of Internally Displaced Persons*, 17 August 1994.

Burundi-Rwanda Voluntary Repatriation of Refugees, Note on Voluntary Repatriation of Refugees, January 1995.

Information Notes on Former Yugoslavia, No. 6/95, UNHCR Office of the Special Envoy for Former Yugoslavia, Zagreb, Croatia, June 1995.

Background Paper on Refugees and Asylum Seekers from Iraq, Centre for Documentation and Research , Geneva, September 1996, (On-line: http://www.unhcr.ch/refworld/country/cdr/cdrirq2.htm, no pagination).

Reilly, Rachel, Summary of paper discussions and debates during the conference *People of Concern*, Geneva, 21-23 November 1996, UNHCR Centre for Documentation and Research - CDR.

UNHCR and International Committee of the Red Cross Say Security of Humanitarian Operations under Threat, Press Release, 22 June 1998.

United Nations Inter-Agency Humanitarian Programme for Iraq Kuwait and the Iraq/Turkey and Iraq/Iran border areas

United Nations Regional Humanitarian Plan of Action Relating to the Crisis between Iraq and Kuwait, Second Update, 9 April 1991.

Updated and Consolidated Appeal for Urgent Humanitarian Action (including foreword by the executive delegate of the Secretary-General), 15 May 1991.

Updated Plan of Action for the Inter-Agency Humanitarian Programme, 1 September-31 December 1991.

UNSC (United Nations Security Council)
S/RES/688 (1991), 5 April 1991 [Iraq]
S/RES/733 (1992), 23 January 1992 [Somalia]
S/RES/746 (1992), 17 March 1992 [Somalia]
S/RES/751 (1992), 24 April 1992 [Somalia]
S/RES/752 (1992), 15 May 1992 [BiH]
S/RES/757 (1992), 30 May 1992 [Former Yugoslavia]
S/RES/758 (1992), 8 June 1992 [BiH]
S/RES/761 (1992), 29 June 1992, [BiH]
S/RES/764 (1992), 13 July 1992 [BiH]
S/RES/767 (1992), 24 July 1992 [Somalia]
S/RES/771 (1992), 13 August 1992 [BiH]
S/RES/775 (1992), 28 August 1992 [Somalia]
S/RES/776 (1992), 14 September 1992 [BiH]
S/RES/781 (1992), 9 October 1992 [BiH]
S/RES/786 (1992), 10 November 1992 [BiH]
S/RES/787 (1992), 16 November 1992 [BiH]
S/RES/794 (1992), 3 December 1992 [Somalia]
S/RES/814 (1993), 26 March 1993 [Somalia]
S/RES/816 (1993), 31 March 1993 [BiH]
S/RES/819 (1993), 16 April 1993 [BiH]
S/RES/824 (1993), 6 May 1993 [BiH]
S/RES/836 (1993), 4 June 1993 [BiH]
S/RES/893 (1994), 6 January 1994 [Rwanda]
S/RES/909 (1994), 5 April 1994 [Rwanda]
S/RES/912 (1994), 22 April 1994 [Rwanda]
S/RES/918 (1994), 17 May 1994 [Rwanda]
S/RES/925 (1994), 8 June 1994 [Rwanda]
S/RES/929 (1994), 22 June 1994 [Rwanda]

UNSG (United Nation Secretary General)
S/1994/470, 20 April 1994, UN Secretary-General Report [regarding the situation in Rwanda].
S/1994/728, 20 June 1994, Letter dated 19 June 1994 from the Secretary-General addressed to the President of the Security Council [regarding provisions offered for UNAMIR II].
S/1994/798, 6 July 1994, Jean François Mérimée, French ambassador to the United Nations, Letter to the UN Secretary-General, dated 2 July 1994.
S/1994/924, 3 August 1994, Report of the Secretary-General on the Situation in Rwanda.

World Food Programme [WFP]
WFP in Former Yugoslavia, Assistance to Refugees, Displaced Persons and Other War-affected Populations,   Situation Report, January 1993;
    Situation Report No. 2, March 1993;

Situation Report No. 3, May 1993;
Situation Report No. 4, July 1993;
Situation Report No. 5, September 1993;
Situation Report No. 6, November 1993.
World Food Programme in Former Yugoslavia, *Winter Programme for Bosnia-Herzegovina, WFP Proposal for the Pre-positioning of Contingency Food Stocks*, June 1993.

Humanitarian Agencies' Documents (ICRC and NGOs)

African Rights
*Somalia Operation Restore Hope: A Preliminary Assessm*ent, London: May 1993.
Rwanda: Who is Killing, Who is Dying, What is to be Done? Discussion paper, May 1994, Refugee Studies Programme Documentation Centre, Oxford.

Amnesty International
EUR/48/05/93, *Bosnian Refugees: A Continuing Need for Protection in European Countries*, London, July 1993.
EUR/63/01/97, *Who is Living in my House? Obstacles to the Safe Return of Refugees and Internally Displaced People*, Amnesty International report on the repatriation programme in Bosnia-Herzegovina, London, 19 March 1997.
Rwanda and Burundi: Horror of Genocide Hangs Over the Region One Year Later, Press Release, Amnesty International USA, New York, 6 April 1995.
AFR/02/07/97 *Great Lake Region: Still in Need of Protection: Repatriation, Refoulement and the Safety of Refugees and the Internally Displaced*, 24 January 1997.

CARE (several departments)
Wallace, Steve, *Comments on the Rwanda Disaster and Care's Response to it* (draft), Care Rwanda in Kenya, 14 June 1994.
Rwanda-Emergency Update, Care Britain, 16 January 1995.
Stallworthy, Guy, *An Evaluation of Care's Response to the 1994 Crisis in Rwanda*, (draft for feedback), 18 February 1995.

Christian Outreach
Reynolds, R., *Development in a Refugee Situation: the Case of Rwandan Refugees in Northern Tanzania*, June 1994, consultancy report for Christian Outreach and Tear Fund (Copy in Refugee Studies Programme, Oxford).

Helsinki Committee for Human Rights in Serbia
Bisersko, Sonja, *Registration of Bosnian Refugees for the September Elections*, Belgrade, 31 July 1996.

Helsinki Watch (a division of Human Rights Watch)
War Crimes in Bosnia-Hercegovina, A Helsinki Watch Report, August 1992.

Human Rights Watch
Untitled press release regarding ethnic cleansing in Bosnia, New York, 7 November 1994.
Rwandan Genocide to be in the Dock, Press Release, 9 November 1994.
Untitled press release regarding the absence of funding for the field operation of Tadeusz Mazowiecki, the Special Rapporteur for the Former Yugoslavia of the United Nations Commission on Human Rights, New York and Brussels, 29 November 1994.
Human Rights Watch/Africa and FIDH Commend Peaceful End to Kibeho Crisis but Warn Rwandan Judicial System Needs Immediate Action, Human Rights Watch Africa, Federation international des Droits de l'Homme, Press Release, 11 May 1995.
Human Rights World Report 1995, London, 1995.

ICG (International Crisis Group)
Why the Bosnian Elections Must be Postponed, Bosnia Report No. 14, 14 August 1996.
Going Fast Nowhere, Refugees and Internally Displaced Persons in Bosnia and Herzegovina, Bosnia Report No. 23, 1 May 1997.
ICG in the Balkans, Past Achievements and Future Priorities March 1996-March 1998, Bosnia Report No. 22, April 1997.
Analysis of the 1997 Municipal Elections, Press Release, 14 October 1997.
Kosovo: The Road to Peace, Kosovo report No. 13, 12 March 1999.

ICRC (International Committee of the Red Cross)
ICRC Activities in the Region of Former Yugoslavia, Fact Sheet, Geneva, July 1994.
Public Statements Issued by the ICRC on its Activities in Rwanda, April-August 1994, 10 August 1994.
Rwanda: ICRC Sounds Alarm on Appalling Prison Conditions, Press Release 95/8, 31 March 1995.
ICRC Warns about Possible Human Disaster in Southern Camps, Press Release 95/11, 20 April 1995.
Hundreds of Dead among the Displaced Persons in Southern Rwanda, Press Release 95/13, 22 April 1995.
Rwanda: Wounded from Kibeho Camp Evacuated to Butare, ICRC News 17, 26 April 1995.
Annual Report 1994 on Rwanda, 30 May 1995.

IOM (International Organization for Migration)
Internally Displaced Persons, IOM Policy and Programmes, Geneva, April 1997.

Jesuit Refugee Service
Rwanda Update, Report from the Jesuit Refugee Service, Fr Mark Raper, Rome, 28 July 1994.

Lawyers Committee for Human Rights
Asylum Under Attack, a Report on the Protection of Iraqi Refugees and Displaced Persons One Year after the Humanitarian Emergency in Iraq, New York, April 1992.

MSF (Médecins sans Frontières)
Populations in Danger, appeals by Doctors without Borders or Médecins sans Frontières, E-mail posting regarding the publication of the report *Populations in Danger 1995*, 16 November 1994.
Jean, Francois, ed., *Populations in Danger, 1995*, a Médecins Sans Frontières report, (London, 1995).
Torrenté, Nicolas de, *L'action de MSF dans la crise rwandaise, un historique critique*, avril-décembre 1994, a report for MSF, Version définitive, juillet 1995.

Oxfam
Niedrum, Susanne (coordinator for the inter-agency information sharing effort), University of Leeds Department of Civil Engineering, *Rwanda Situation Update*, (faxed summary of information compiled from information from Oxfam, MSF, Human Rights Watch, Accord, CARE and Amnesty International over the 3rd and 4th May 1994), 5 May 1994.
The Rwandan Crisis, "Information from Oxfam" leaflet, Oxfam, Oxford 1994.
Vassal-Adams, Guy, *Rwanda: An Agenda for International Action*, (Oxford: Oxfam Publication, 1994).
Programme Update 20, Great Lakes Region - Rwanda Crisis, 17 February 1995.
Programme Update 21, Great Lakes Region - Rwanda Crisis, 24 February 1995.
Programme Update 22, Great Lakes Region - Rwanda Crisis, 3 March 1995.
Programme Update 25, Great Lakes Region - Rwanda Crisis, 24 March 1995.

RPG (Refugee Policy Group)
Humanitarian Aid in Somalia, September 1990-May 1993, draft discussion paper, Washington D.C., March 1994.

SCF (Save the Children Fund)
Keen, David, *The Kurds in Iraq: How Safe is their Haven Now?* a report for Save the Children Fund, London, June 1993.
Meuus, Wilma, *Household Survey of Displaced Camps in Mogadishu, May 1993*, draft report for Save the Children Fund (UK), Mogadishu: October 1993.

Somalia Task Force
Post-UNOSOM Aid Strategies in Somalia: Recommendations to the Somali Aid Coordination Body, November 1994.

USAID (United States Agencie for International Development)
Rwanda Report, August 5-8 1994.
Rwanda Report, August 16-18 1994.

USCR (United States Committee for Refugees)
Mass Exodus, Iraqi Refugees in Iran, Issue Brief, Washington, July 1991.
The Rwanda Crisis Advocacy Action Alert 2, 27 June 1994.
Drumtra, Jeff, *Site Visit Notes, Site Visit to Rwanda, Zaire, and Burundi*, October 20 to November 17 1994, a report for USCR.

Government and military bodies

Bosnia-Herzegovina Information Centre, London
New Wave of Ethnic Cleansing Before the "Referendum." London briefing, 26 August 1994.
UN Must Act to Halt Renewed Wave of Ethnic Cleansing, London briefing, 3 September 1994.

European Community
Transcript of the statement by Baroness Chalker on behalf of the European Community and its member states, *International Meeting on Humanitarian Aid for Victims of the Conflict on the Former Yugoslavia*, Geneva, 29 July 1992.
Resolution on Certain Common Guideline as regards the Admission of Particularly Vulnerable Groups of Persons from the Former Yugoslavia, Ad Hoc Immigration Group, Copenhaguen, 1 June 1993.

France
Transcript of the statement of Bernard Kouchner, Ministre de la Santé et de l'Action Humanitaire, *International Meeting on Humanitarian Aid for Victims of the Conflict on the Former Yugoslavia*, Geneva, 29 July 1992.Germany

Germany
Transcript of the statement of Rudolf Seiter, Federal Minister of the Interior, *International Meeting on Humanitarian Aid for Victims of the Conflict on the Former Yugoslavia*, Geneva, 29 July 1992.

Immigration and Refugee Board, Commission de l'immigration et du statut de refugié, Ottawa, Canada.
Kenya, Ethiopia, Djibouti, Yemen and Saudi Arabia: The Situation of Somali Refugees, Question and Answer Series, Documentary Information and Research Branch, Ottawa, Canada, September 1992
Sri Lanka: les possibilités de fuites intérieures, Series "Questions et Réponses", Direction générale de la documentation, de l'information et des recherches, Ottawa, Canada, December 1992.

Independent International Commission of Inquiry on the Events at Kibeho
Report of the Independent International Commission of Inquiry on the Events at Kibeho, April 1995.

NATO (North Atlantic Treaty Organisation)
Stabilisation Force (SFOR), Fact Sheet, 20 December 1996.

Pan African Movement
Rwanda Fact Finding Mission Report, 5-8 June 1994.

RPF (Rwandese Patriotic Front)
Letter of the First Vice Chairman RPF, Patrick Mazimhaka, Mulindi, 7 May 1994.
Rwanda Victims Humanitarian Appeal to International Community, Rwandese
Patriotic Front - RPF - Patrick Mazimhaka (First Vice Chairman - RPF),
Brussels, 8 May 1994.

Republic of Rwanda
Circular to all NGOs, UN and International Organisations, Republic of Rwanda,
Ministry of Rehabilitation and Social Integration, Kigali, 25 July 1994.
The Policy of the Government of Rwanda Regarding Internally Displaced Persons,
Republic of Rwanda, Ministry of Rehabilitation and Social Integration, Kigali,
undated document, the substance and tone of the text suggest that it was
produced in the autumn of 1994.
Communiqué of the Regional Summit on Rwanda, Presidents of Kenya, Burundi,
Rwanda, Tanzania, Uganda, Zambia, Nairobi, 7 January, 1995.

Slovenia
Transcript of the statement of Joze Pucnik, Vice-President of the Government of
the Republic of Slovenia, *International Meeting on Humanitarian Aid for
Victims of the Conflict on the Former Yugoslavia*, Geneva, 29 July 1992.

United Kingdom
Transcript of the statement of Baroness Chalker of Wallasey, Minister of Overseas
Development, *International Meeting on Humanitarian Aid for Victims of the
Conflict on the Former Yugoslavia*, Geneva, 29 July 1992.
Terms of Reference for Evaluation of Emergency Assistance to Rwanda, United
Kingdom, Overseas Development Administration London - ODA, Evaluation
Department, 07 December 1994.

Interviews and personal notes
Fawcett, John, head office of IRC (International Rescue Committee) in northern
Iraq in spring 1991. Interview, February 1997.
Gentile, Louis, UNHCR, interview. London, 11 September 1998.
IPTF briefing for OSCE international election supervisors, Mostar (Bosnia), 10
September 1997, (author's personal notes).

Pamphlets, conference and research papers
BA, Mehdi, *Rwanda 1994, Un Génocide Français*, L'Esprit Frappeur No. 4 (Paris,
Vertige Graphic: 1997).

Bagshaw, Simon, *Internally Displaced Persons at the Fifty-Fourth Session of the United Nations Commission on Human Rights, 16 March-24 April 1998*, unpublished paper.

Cohen, Roberta, *International Protection for Internally Displaced Persons, Next Steps*, Washington DC: RPG focus paper No. 2, January 1994.

Cohen Roberta, *Internally Displaced Persons: an extended role for UNHCR*, discussion paper, UNHCR conference on people of concern, November 1996.

Deng, Francis, *The International Protection of IDPs*, conference paper, Symposium on Refugees and Forced Population Displacements in Africa, organized by Organization of African Unity and United Nations High Commissioner for Refugees, Addis Ababa, 8-10 September 1994.

Deng, Francis, *Sovereignty Responsibility and Accountability, a Framework of Protection, Assistance and Development for the Internally Displaced*, concept paper for the Brookings Institution, Refugee Policy Group - RPG - Project on Internal Displacement, summer 1995.

Edkins, Jenny, ed., *The Politics of Emergency*, Manchester Papers in Politics, 2/97, Department of Government, University of Manchester, December 1997, 73 pages.

Fein, Helen, *The Prevention of Genocide, Rwanda and Yugoslavia Reconsidered*, Working paper of the Institute of the Study of Genocide, 1994.

Franche, Dominique, *Rwanda, Généalogie d'un Génocide*, (Paris, éditions des mille et une nuits, 1997).

Godding, *Refugees or Hostages? Population Movements in the Great Lakes Region since 1990*, a paper presented at the conference "Towards Understanding the Crisis in the Great Lakes Region," St. Anthony's college, Oxford, 1 February 1997.

Gowing, Nik, *New Challenges and Problems for Information Management in Complex Emergencies, Ominous Lessons from the Great Lakes and Eastern Zaire in late 1996 and early 1997*, Conference Paper, London 27 and 28 May 1998, 79 pages.

Hippel, Karen von, (Department of War Studies, King's College London), talk on Somalia presented at the Conference on Regional Security in a Global Context, April 7th 1998.

Independent Commission on International Humanitarian Issues, *Refugees: the Dynamics of Displacement: a Report for the Independent Commission on International Humanitarian Issues* / Foreword by the co-chairmen Sadruddin Aga Khan, Hassan Bin Talal, (London: Zed Books, 1986).

Kirisci, Kemal, "Provide Comfort and Turkey, Decision making for Humanitarian Intervention,"
(on-line: http://snipe.ukc.ac.uk/international/papers.dir/kirisci.html,   no pagination).

Klin, Walter, *Guiding Principles on Internal Displacement*, paper presented at the Conference on Internally Displaced Persons, Overseas Development Institute, London, 20 July 1998.

Library of Congress Country Study, *Somalia*, (reflects information available as of mid 1992), online: http://lcweb2.loc.gov/frd/cs/sotoc.html#so0004, no pagination.

Livingston, Steven, *Clarifying the CNN Effect: An Examination of Media Effects According to Type of Military Intervention*, Research Paper R-18, June 1997, The Joan Shorenstein Center on the Press, Politics and Public Policy, Harvard University, Cambridge MA.

Loescher, Gil, *Refugee Movement and International Security*, Adelphi Paper No. 268, Summer 1992, (London: Brassey's for the International Institute for Strategic Studies - IISS, 1992).

MacDowall, *The Kurds*, A minority Rights Group Report, published by Minority Rights Group, London: September 1991.

Mucumbise, Joseph (Association des Droits de l'Homme, Bruxelles), *Justice et Droits de l'Homme au Rwanda; Justice and Human Rights in Rwanda*, talk presented in the conference: Rwanda: Perspectives d'Avenir, 12 May 1995, London: Westminster University.

Prunier, Gérard, *Civil War, Intervention and Withdrawal, 1990-1995*, A writenet report, (online: http://www.unhcr.ch/refworld/country/writenet/wrisom02.htm, no pagination).

Roberts, Adam, *Humanitarian Action in War*, Adelphi paper, No. 305, (Oxford: Oxford University Press, 1997).

Rutinwa, Bonaventure, *Short Notes on the Plan of Action for Voluntary Repatriation of Refugees in the Great Lakes Region*, Paper presented at the International Workshop on the Refugee Crisis in the Great Lakes Region, Arusha Tanzania, August 16-19, 1995.

Sen, Sumit, *International Law of Internally Displaced Persons: the Role of the UNHCR*, Master of Philosophy Dissertation submitted to the Jawaharlal Nerhu University, New Delhi, 1995.

Steering Committee of the Joint Evaluation of Emergency Assistance too Rwanda, *The International Response to conflict and Genocide: Lessons from the Rwanda Experience*, March 1996, comprising: Synthesis report (John Erikson); Study 1: *Historical perspective: Some explanatory factors* (Tor Sellstrom and Lennart Wohlgemuth); Study 2: *Early Warning and Conflict management* (Howard Adelman, Astri Suhrke, Bruce Jones); Study 3 *Humanitarian Aid and Effects* (John Borton, Emery Brusset and Allastair Hallam); Study 4 *Re-building postwar Rwanda* (Krishna Kumar, David Tardif-Douglin, Kim Maynard, Peter Manikas, Annette Sheckler and Carolin Knapp).

International Institut for Srategic Studies, *Strategic Survey 1995/1996*, (London: International Institute of Strategic Studies, 1996).

Torrenté, Nicolas de, *The International Protection of Internally Displaced Persons*, Master of Art in Law and Diplomacy Thesis, The Fletcher School of Law and Diplomacy, Medford, April 1992.

213

Zilic, Ahmed and Risaluddin, Saba, *The Case of the Zvornick Seven*, (London: The Bosnian Institute, 1997).

Articles in journals

Abdullahi, Ahmednasir, "Ethnic Clashes Displaced Persons and the Potential for Refugee Creation in Kenya," Vol. 9, No. 2 (1997), *International Journal of Refugee Law*, 196-206.

Adelman, Howard, "The Ethics of Humanitarian Intervention: The Case of the Kurdish Refugees," Vol. 6, No. 1 (1992), *Public Affairs Quarterly*, 61-87.

Barbero, Julie, "Refugee Repatriation during Conflict: A New Conventional Wisdom," Vol 12, No. 8 (1992), *Refuge*, 7-11.

Barutciski, Michael, "EU States and the Refugee Crisis in the Former Yugoslavia," Vol. 14, No. 3 (1994), *Refuge*, 32-35.

-------------------------, "The Reinforcement of Non-Admission Policies and the Subversion of UNHCR: Displacement and Internal assistance in Bosnia-Herzegovina (1992-1994)," Vol. 8, No. 1/2 (1996*)*, *International Journal of Refugee Law*, 49-110.

Bennett, Jon, "Forced Migration within National Borders: The IDP agenda," No. 1 (January-April 1998), *Forced Migration Review*, 4-6.

Braumann, Rony, "Les limites de l'humanitaire," Vol. 51 (1996), *Les Temps Modernes*, 303-319.

-----------------------, "Contre l'humanitarisme," No. 177 (1991), *Revue Esprit*, 77-85.

Chomsky, Noam, "The Middle East in the New World Order, A Post War Teach in" (1991), *Z Magazine*, The Chomsky Archives on-line: http://wwwwdsp.ucd.ie/~daragh/articles/a_z_saygoes.html, no pagination.

Clarance, William, "Open Relief Centres: A Pragmatic Approach to Emergency Relief and Monitoring during Conflict in a Country of Origin," Vol. 3, No. 2 (1991), *International Journal of Refugee Law*, 320-328.

Dowty, Alan and Loescher, Gil, "Refugee Flows as Grounds for International Action," Vol. 21, No. 1 (1996), *International Security*, 43-71.

Frelick, Bill, "'Preventive Protection' and the Right to Seek Asylum: A Preliminary Look at Bosnia and Croatia," Vol. 4, No. 4 (1992), *International Journal of Refugee Law*, 439-454.

-----------------, "Barriers to Protection: Turkey's Asylum Regulations, Vol. 9, No. 1 (1997), *International Journal of Refugee Law*, 8-34.

Frelick, Bill, "Aliens in their Own Land: Protection and Durable Solutions for Internally Displaced Persons," in United States Committee for Refugees, *World Refugee Survey 1998*, (on-line: http://www.refugees.org/world/articles/internallydisplaced_wrs98.html, no pagination).

Gagnon, V.P. Jr., "Ethnic Nationalism and International Conflict: The Case of Serbia," Vol. 19, No. 3 (1994-95), *International Security*, 130-166.

Ginifer, Jeremy, "Protecting Displaced Persons Through Disarmament", Vol. 40, No. 2 (1998), *Survival*, 161-176.

Gunter, Michael, "A Kurdish State in Northern Iraq?," Vol. 20, No. 2 (1994), *Humboldt Journal of Social Relations*, 45-94.

Hallegård, Carl, "Bosnia and Herzegovina: Problems and Progress in the Return Process," Vol. 1 (January-April 1998), *Forced Migration Review*, 21-24.

Harrel-Bond, Barbara, Voutira, Eftihia and Leopold, Mark, "Counting the Refugees: Gifts, Givers, Patrons and Clients" Vol. 5, No. 3/4 (1992), *Journal of Refugee Studies*, 205-225.

Helton, Arthur, "Displacement and Human Rights: Current Dilemmas in Refugee Protection," Vol. 47, No. 2 (1994), *Journal of International Affairs*, 379-389.

Heusch, Luc de, "Anthropologie d'un génocide: le Rwanda," No. 579 (1994), *Les Temps Modernes*, 1-19.

Jacobsen, Peter, "National Interest, Humanitarianism or CNN: What Triggers UN Peace Enforcement After the Cold War?" Vol. 33, No. 2 (1996), *Journal of Peace Research*, 205-215.

Jaeger, Gilbert, "The Recent Concept and Policy of Preventive Protection," Vol. 14 (January 1994), *Refugee Program Network*, 20-21.

Kessler, Peter, "Out of Sight, Out of Mind," Issue 103, No. 1 (1996), *Refugees* (on-line: http://www.unhcr.ch/pubs/rm103/rm10308.htm, no pagination).

Kingsley-Nyinah, Michael, "What may be Borrowed, What is New?" No. 4 (April 1999), *Forced Migration Review*, 32-33.

Kirisci, Kemal, "Refugee Movements and Turkey," Vol. 29, No. 4 (1991), *International Migration Review*, 545-560.

Kisriev, Enver and Robert, Bruce Ware, "After Chechnya: At Risk in Dagestan," Vol. 18, No. 1 (1998), *Politics*, 39-47.

Lander, Brian, "Far from Paradise," issue 104, No. 2 (1996), *Refugees* (on-line: http://www.unhcr.ch/pubs/rm/104/rm10403.htm, no pagination).

Landgren, Karin, "Safety Zones and International Protection: A Dark Grey Area" Vol. 7, No. 3 (1995), *International Journal of Refugee Law*, 436-458.

Lebas, Jacques, "Paradoxes de L'humanitaire," Vol. 51 (1996), *Les Temps Modernes*, 314-321.

Livingston, Steven and Eachus, T., "Humanitarian Crises and US Foreign Policy: Somalia and the CNN Effect Reconsidered," Vol. 12, No. 4 (1995), *Political Communication*, 413-429.

Loescher, Gil, "The European Community and Refugees," Vol. 65, No 4 (1989), *International Affairs*, 617-636.

Malcolm, Noel, "Bosnia and the West, A Study in Failure," (Spring 1995), *The National Interest*, 3-14.

McLean, Jennifer, "National Response to Internal Displacement," No. 1 (January-April 1998), *Forced Migration Review*, 10-11.

Mendiluce, Jose-Maria, "Meeting the Challenge of Refugees: Growing Co-operation between UNHCR and NATO," Vol. 42, No. 2 (1994), *NATO*

Review, (on-line edition: http://www.nato.int/docu/review/articles/9402-5.htm, no pagination).

Mermin, Jonathan, "Television News and American Intervention in Somalia: The Myth of a Media Driven Foreign Policy," Vol. 112, No. 3 (1997), *Political Science Quarterly*, 385-403.

Natsios, Andrew, "Food through Force: Humanitarian Intervention and US Policy," Vol. 17, No. 1 (1993), *The Washington Quarterly*, 129-144.

----------------------, "The International Humanitarian Response System," Vol. 25, No. 1 (1995), *Parameters*, 68-81.

Ofteringer, Ronald and Backer, Ralph, "A Republic of Statelessness, Three Years of Humanitarian Intervention in Iraqi Kurdistan," Vol. 24, No. 2-3 (1994), *Middle East Report*, 40-45.

Onishi, Akira, "Global Early Warning System for Displaced Persons: Interlinkages of Environment, Development, Peace and Human Rights," Vol. 31, No. 3 (1987), *Technological Forecasting and Social Change*, 269-299.

Outram, Quentin, "Cruel Wars and Safe Havens: Humanitarian Aid in Liberia 1989-1996," Vol. 21, No. 3 (1997), *Disasters*, 189-205.

Pellicer, Olga, "Successes and Weaknesses of Recent UN Operations in the Field of International Security," Vol. 47, No. 2 (1995), *International Social Science Journal*, 305-314.

Posen, Barry, "Military Responses to Refugee Disasters," Vol. 21, No 1 (1996), *International Security*, 72-111.

Pottier, Johan, "Agricultural Rehabilitation and Food Insecurity in Post-war Rwanda, Assessing Needs, Designing Solutions," Vol. 27, No. 3 (1996), *IDS Bulletin*, 56-75.

Roberts, Adam, "Humanitarian War: Military Intervention and Human Rights," Vol. 69, No. 3 (1993), *International Affairs*, 429-450.

--------------------, "A New Age in International Relations?," Vol. 67, No. 4, (1991), *International Affairs*, 509-525.

Rutinwa, Bonaventure, "Beyond Durable Solutions: An Appraisal of the New Proposals for Prevention and Solution of the Refugee Crisis in the Great Lake Region," Vol. 9, No. 3 (1996), *Journal of Refugee Studies*, 312-325.

---------------------------,"How Tense is the Tension between the Refugee Concept and the IDP Debate?," No. 4 (April 1999), *Forced Migration Review*, 29-31.

Shacknove, Andrew, "From Asylum to Containment", Vol. 5, No. 4 (1993), *International Journal of Refugee Law*, 516-533.

Snyder, Jack, "Science and Sovietology: Bridging the Methods Gap in Soviet Foreign Policy Studies," Vol 40, No. 2 (1988), *World Politics*, 169-193.

Stevenson, Jonathan, "Hope Restored in Somalia?," No. 91 (summer 1993), *Foreign Policy*, 138-154.

Stockton, Nicholas, "Rwandan Refugees: Political Expediency or Humanitarianism," Vol. 5, No. 2 (1997), *Crossline Global Report*, 14-16.

Tiso, Christopher, "Safe Haven Refugee Programs: a Method of Combatting International Refugee Crises," Vol. 8, No. 4 (1994), *Georgetown Immigration Law Journal*, 575-601.

Weiner, Myron, "Bad Neighbors, Bad Neighborhoods, An Inquiry into the Causes of Refugee Flows," Vol. 21, No. 1 (1996), *International Security*, 5-42.

Weiss, Thomas, "Triage, Humanitarian Intervention in an New Era," Vol. 11, No. 1 (1994), *World Policy Journal*, 59-68.

Westermann, Simone, "Media and Relief Workers: Changing Relations," Vol. 5, No. 2, Issue 28 (1997), *Crosslines Global Report*, 21-23.

Zetter, Roger, "Labelling Refugees: Forming and Transforming a Bureaucratic Identity," Vol. 4, No. 1 (1991), *Journal of Refugee Studies*, 39-62.

Books

Al-Nauimi, Najeeb and Meese, Richard, eds., *International Legal Issues Arising under the United Nation Decade of International Law, proceedings of the Qatar International Law Conference' 94* (The Hague: Martinus Nijhoff Publishers, 1995).

Bennet, Christopher, *Yugoslavia's Bloody Collapse: Causes, Course and Consequences* (London: Hurst and Company, 1995).

Bisersko, Sonja, ed., *Yugoslavia's Collapse War Crimes* (Belgrade: Centre for Anti-war Action, 1993).

Both, Norbert and Honig, Jan Willen, *Srebrenica, Record of a War Crime* (London: Penguin Book, 1996).

Brown, Michael, ed., *The International Dimensions of Internal Conflict* (Cambridge, Massachusetts: The MIT Press, 1996).

Campbell, David, *Politics Without Principles, Sovereignty, Ethics, and The Narratives of the Gulf War* (London: Lynne Rienner Publishers, Inc., 1993).

Chaliand, Gérard, *The Kurdish Tragedy* (London: Zed Books Ltd., 1994).

Cigar, Norman, *Genocide in Bosnia: the Policy of "Ethnic Cleansing"* (College Station, Texas: A&M University Press, 1995).

Cohen, Roberta and Deng, Francis, *Masses in Flight, The Global Crisis of Internal Displacement* (Washington D.C.: Brookings Institution Press, 1998).

Cohen, Roberta and Deng, Francis, ed., *The Forsaken People, Case Studies of the Internally Displaced* (Washington D.C.: Brookings Institution Press, 1998).

Cushman, Thomas and Mestrovic, Stjepan, ed., *This Time We Knew, Western Response to Genocide in Bosnia* (New York: New York University Press, 1996).

Davies, Wendy, ed., *Rights Have No Borders, Worldwide Internal Displacement* (Norwegian Refugee Council, Global IDP Survey: Oslo/Geneva; 1998).

Domestici-Met, Marie-José, ed., *Aide humanitaire internationale: un concensus conflictuel* (Paris: Economica, 1996).

217

Dowty, Alan, *Closed Borders: the Contemporary Assault on Freedom of Movement* (London: Yale University Press, 1987).

Drüke, Luise, *Preventive Action for Refugee Producing Situations,* European University Studies Series XXXI, Political Science, Vol./Bd. 150 (Peter Lang, Frankfurt am Main, 1993).

Fisler Damrosh, Lori and Scheffer, David, ed., *Law and Force in the New International Order* (Boulder: Westview press, 1991).

Fisler Damrosh, Lori, ed., *Enforcing Restraint, Collective Interventions in Internal Conflicts* (New York: Council on Foreign Relations Press, 1993).

Garde, Paul, *Journal de voyage en Bosnie Herzegovine* (Paris: La Nuée Bleue, 1994).

Girardet, Edward, ed., *Somalia, Rwanda and Beyond* (Geneva: Crosslines Global Report, 1995).

Gutman, Roy, *A Witness to Genocide* (London: Element Books, 1993).

Hampton, Janie, ed., *Internally Displaced Persons: A Global Survey* (London: Earthscan Publications Ltd, 1998).

Harrell-Bond, Barbara, *Imposing Aid* (Oxford: Oxford University Press, 1986).

Hirsh, John and Oakley, Robert, *Somalia and Operation Restore Hope, Reflection on Peace-making and Peace-keeping* (Washington D.C.: United States Institute of Peace Press, 1995).

Hollingworth, Larry, *Merry Christmas Mr. Larry* (London: Heinemann, 1996).

Hyden, G. and Brattan, M., ed., *Governance and Politics in Africa* (London: Lynne Rienner Publisher, 1992).

King, Gary, Keohane, Robert and Verba, Sidney, *Designing Social Inquiry: Scientific Inference in Qualitative Research* (Princeton New Jersey: Princeton University Press, 1994).

Kroyenbroek, Philip and Sperl, Stepan, ed., *The Kurds, A Contemporary Overview* (London: Routledge, 1992).

Lemarchand, René, *Rwanda and Burundi* (London: Pall Mall Press, 1970).

Little, Alan and Silber, Laura, *The Death of Yugoslavia* (London: Penguin Book, 1995).

Loescher, Gil, *Beyond Charity, International Co-operation and the Global Refugee Crisis* (Oxford: Oxford University Press, 1993).

Loescher, Gil and Monahan, Lisa, eds., *Refugees and International Relations* (Oxford: Oxford University Press, 1989).

Loescher, Gil and Scanlan, John, *Calculated Kindness: Refugee Problems in America's Half Open Door, 1945 to the Present* (New York: Free Press, 1986).

Maass, Peter, *Love Thy Neighbour, A Story of War* (London: Papermac, 1996).

Malcolm, Noel, *Bosnia, a Short History*, 2nd edition (London: Papumac, 1996).

Mayall, James, ed., *The New Interventionism 1991-1994, United Nations Experience in Cambodia, Former Yugoslavia and Somalia* (Cambridge: Cambridge University Press, 1996).

Mercier, Michelle, *Crimes without Punishment* (London: Pluto Press, 1995).

218

Minear, Larry, SCOTT, Colin and Weiss, Thomas, *The News Media, Civil War and Humanitarian Action* (Boulder Colorado: L. Rienner, 1996).

Minear, Larry and Weiss, Thomas, *Mercy under Fire, War and the Global Humanitarian Community* (Boulder Colorado: Westview Press Inc., 1995).

Nye, Joseph and Smith, Roger, ed., *After the Storm, Lessons from the Gulf War* (Lanham, Maryland: The Aspen Institute, 1992).

Prunier, Gérard, *The Rwanda Crisis, History of a Genocide, 1959-1994* (London: Hurst and Company, 1995).

Ramsbotham, Oliver and Woodhouse, Tom, *Humanitarian Intervention in Contemporary Conflict, a Reconceptualisation* (Cambridge: Polity Press, 1996).

Rieff, David, *Slaughterhouse, Bosnia and the Failure of the West* (Reading: Vintage 1995).

Rohde, David, *End Game, the Betrayal and Fall of Srebrenica: Europe's Worst Massacre since World War II* (Boulder, Colorado: Westview Press, 1997).

Sahnoun, Mohamed, *Somalia, the Missed Opportunities* (Washington: US Institute of Peace Press, 1994).

Shaw, Martin, *Civil Society and Media in Global Crises, Representing Distant Violence* (London: Pinter, 1996).

UNHCR, *The State of the World's Refugees* (New York: Penguin Books, 1993).

UNHCR, *The State of the World's Refugees* (New York: Penguin Books, 1995).

Waal, Alex de, *Rwanda Death Despair Defiance*, 2nd edition (London: African Rights 1995).

Weller, M., ed., *Iraq and Kuwait, the Hostilities and their Aftermath*, Cambridge International Document Series, Volume 3 (Cambridge: Grotius Publication Limited, 1993).

Whitman, Jim and Pocock, David, eds., *After Rwanda, the Coordination of UN Humanitarian Assistance* (London: Macmillan Press Ltd., 1996).

Index

drift 32, 42n, 166-7
and disarmament 188-9
of expatriates 53
"in-country" 5, 16-7, 75
international 16, 34, 64, 79
and media 191
officers 110
temporary 67-8, 170-1
through presence 1-2
preventive 8, 16, 23, 67-8, 71, 78,
107, 157, 176, 178, 181-2,
194-5
variation in 122-4
see also United Nations Guiding
Principles on Internal
Displacement, UNHCR, safe
areas, safety
public order 192

Quick Impact Projects 146, 153-4, 170

reconstruction issues 94, 103, 103-6,
146, 149, 170, 182
Refugee
Convention see Geneva Convention
on refugees
crises 10, 20, 22, 34, 57-61, 64,
141, 145
flow 9, 19, 24, 34, 39n, 52, 61, 138-
41, 143, 176-7, 194
law 17
protection 21
quota policies 61, 67
regime 27
repatriation 5, 8, 21, 63, 70, 102-3,
116, 153-4, 169-71
testimomy 53
see also Bosnia, IDPs, Kosovo,
Kurds, Rwanda, Somalia, UNHCR
regional stability 60-1
repatriation, see refugee repatriation,
return
Republican Guards, see Iraq
resettlement 48
Responsibility
and humanitarian action 18
in policy making and research 37,
43n, 165, 180-7
of states 184

return, 29, 170
forced 101-2, 109, 116-9, 122-3,
147, 151-2, 168, 171-2
safe 171
rights
minority 8
right to stay 146, 194
see also human rights
RPA (Rwandese Patriotic Army) 73,
124, 117, 171
Rwanda 26, 28-9, 31, 35-6
Arusha Accords 50, 55
assistance to IDPs 22, 58, 72-4,
95-7
disarmament 188-9
ethnic and social issues 33
forced return 101, 109, 116-119
genocide 53, 55, 84n, 105, 175
human rights 105, 109
Hutu population 50, 52
Interahamwe (paramilitaries) 52, 73
Kibeho 2, 105, 116-8, 123, 171, 183
NGOs 125
Open Relief Centres 99
Operation Turquoise 69, 72-3, 78,
89n, 188
property disputes 105
protection issues 109
Radio Mille Collines 74
reconstruction 104-5
refugees 50, 60
safe area 69
Tutsi populations 33, 52, 50
See also France, RPF, RPA,
UNAMIR, WFP

safe areas 12-3, 19, 23, 45, 74, 107, 139,
166, 176, 178, 187-8
See also Bosnia, Iraq, Rwanda
safety 38, 99, 188
promises 45, 93, 181
and return issues 151
Sahnoun, Mohamed 142-5
sanctions
against Serbia 52, 106
against Iraq 48, 104
Santer, Jacques 66
Sarajevo 53, 60, 77, 113, 195
airlift 72, 78, 174

225